CORWIN and PELTASON'S

Understanding the Constitution

D1531989

Fifth Edition

CORWIN and PELTASON'S

Understanding the Constitution

J. W. PELTASON
University of Illinois

HOLT, RINEHART AND WINSTON, INC.
*New York   Chicago   San Francisco   Atlanta   Dallas   Montreal
Toronto   London   Sydney*

Preface

The Constitution of the United States, the supreme law of the land, is by no means self-explanatory. In an attempt to make it understandable, this book sets forth the main features of the Constitution and the practical significance of its most important provisions as they are construed and applied today. Attention is also given to the immediate historic origins of the Constitution and its basic principles.

The central core of the Declaration of Independence and of each Article of the Constitution are discussed section by section, amplified, and interpreted in nontechnical terms. Because the constitutional system—the fundamental rules by which governmental power is organized and limited —includes, in addition to the documentary Constitution, those basic practices and customs that we have developed during the last one hundred and eighty years, these features of our government are discussed to some extent. In addition, there is a brief essay that points up the basic features of our constitutional system: federalism, separation of powers, and judicial review.

A deliberate attempt has been made to avoid legal detail and elaborate citations. The absence of extensive documentation and the attempt to simplify may give an impression of dogmatism that I should here like to disavow. The author is well aware that there is no such thing as "the interpretation" of the Constitution; the reader is warned that others would find different meaning in the words of the Constitution and in the opinions of the judges who interpret it.

If this volume succeeds in giving its readers an understanding of the document itself and an appreciation of the important role that constitutional interpretation plays in the conduct of our government, it will fulfill its purpose.

This revision covers all relevant decisions of the Supreme Court through the end of the 1968 term, that is, all decisions through June 1969. Since this term brings to a close the eventful fifteen years during which Chief Justice Earl Warren presided over the Supreme Court, I have thought it appropriate to add a few words in the text about the contributions of and conflicts about the Warren Court.

On April 29, 1963, all who revere the Constitution of the United States suffered a major loss with the death of Professor Edward S. Corwin. I think it may be said without exaggeration that "the General," as he was affectionately known by his thousands of students, knew more about the Constitution of the United States than any man who ever lived. At least those of us who had the privilege of studying under him know that Chief Justice Hughes was in error when he said that the Constitution is what the Supreme Court says it is—we know that the Constitution is what Corwin says it is.

Professor Corwin combined his mastery of knowledge about the Constitution with wisdom and powerful analytical skills so that his major works, many of which were written almost a half century ago, are still as fresh and important today as when he wrote them.

This little volume was among the least of his works. Although many of the views expressed and the words used are those of Professor Corwin retained from earlier editions, the responsibility for this revision is mine. It is more than the usual cliché, however, for me to acknowledge that whatever is its merit is attributable to the teacher; the errors to his student.

I wish to thank Prentice-Hall, Inc., for permission to quote occasional sentences from previous publications.

Professor I. Ridgway Davis of the University of Connecticut and Professor Joseph O. Payne of Palm Beach Junior College have been most generous in giving me the benefit of their helpful comments. I am also indebted to Carolyn Higgs and Janice Parrill, who have the unmatched ability to read my illegible handwriting and, without complaint, to type and retype my manuscript. I also wish to thank Miss Sabra Woolley for her skillful editing. I could not have completed this revision—or met any of my other obligations—if it were not for their help.

J. W. P.

Urbana, Illinois
January 1970

A Note on Case Citations

The number of case citations has been kept to a minimum. It is more important for the student to know what the Supreme Court has said about various phases of the Constitution and to have some feeling for the issues involved than to know the names of the cases. Nevertheless, there are some cases of such significance that knowledge of them is part of a liberal education, and still others are cited for those students who wish to inquire further. Cases that came to the Supreme Court before 1875 are cited by the name of the official court reporter. Thus *McCulloch* v. *Maryland,* 4 Wheaton 316 (1819) means that this case can be located in the fourth volume of Wheaton's *Report of Cases Argued and Adjudged in the Supreme Court of the United States* on page 316 and that the case was decided in 1819. Cases after 1875 are cited by the volume number of *United States Reports,* a publication of the Government Printing Office that records the cases adjudged in the Supreme Court. Thus the case of *Powell* v. *McCormack* is cited 395 U.S. 486 (1969) and is, therefore, found in the three hundred ninety-fifth volume of *United States Reports* on page 486 and was decided in 1969. For the special use of lawyers, two other methods of citation are employed by commercial publishers to refer to the publication of Supreme Court decisions and any explanatory and background annotation; the form of citation in this book, however, is most common. The *United States Law Week,* which is commercially published, provides the fastest service in making available complete opinions of recent Supreme Court decisions.

Contents

CORWIN and PELTASON'S

Understanding
the Constitution

Background of the Constitution

The Constitution would mean little to most English-speaking strangers because it can best be understood only within the historical situation in which it was written and has been applied. By placing the Constitution in the context of history, we learn of the conditions and conflicts that produced it and continue to give it meaning. We, therefore, begin with a brief consideration of the Declaration of Independence and the Articles of Confederation, the two most important documents affecting the background of the Constitution.

The Declaration of Independence is the first formal American state paper. It is not judicially enforceable, and it establishes no legal rights or duties. But the Declaration has had a decisive impact on the development of our governmental system. It sets forth the ideals and reflects the standards of what might be called the American Creed. This Creed, with its stress on the rights of men, equality under the law, limited government, and government by consent of the governed, infuses the structures and practices of the Constitution. The Declaration remains the American Conscience: a constant challenge to those who would subvert our democratic processes by denying persons their unalienable rights.

The Declaration of Independence

In Congress, July 4, 1776, by the Representatives of the United States of America, in General Congress assembled.

This was the first time that "the United States of America" was officially used. Previous practice was to refer to the "United Colonies." [1] *

We celebrate our independence on the anniversary of the day it was proclaimed. The actual deed, however, was approved by the Second Continental Congress two days before, when it adopted by a narrow vote Richard Henry Lee's resolution "to declare the United Colonies free and independent states." Thomas Jefferson, John Adams, Benjamin Franklin, Roger Sherman, and Robert R. Livingston were appointed to draft a declaration to accompany this resolution of independence. It was Jefferson who did most of the work.

Jefferson had the task of rallying both American and world sentiment to the cause of independence. As he later wrote, "Neither aiming at originality of principles or sentiments, nor yet copied from any particular and previous writing, it was intended to be an expression of the American Mind." [2] Jefferson drew on precedents that were known to all educated Englishmen and Americans, especially on John Locke's often-quoted *Second Treatise of Civil Government,* written in 1689. This volume was thought to be an authoritative pronouncement of established principles. Locke's ideas provided ready arguments for the American cause, and they were especially embarrassing to an English government whose own source of authority was based on them.

The Preamble

When in the Course of human events, it becomes necessary for one people to dissolve the political bands which have connected them with another,

One of the points at issue between the colonists and the English government was whether Americans and Englishmen were one people or two separate peoples. Here the Americans asserted that they formed a separate entity, previously connected with the English people but not an integral part of them. And it was the American people as a unit—not Virginians, New Yorkers, and so on—who dissolved their political bands (see page 9).

* Superior figures refer to notes found at the back of the book.

*and to assume among the powers of the earth, the separate
and equal station to which the Laws of Nature and of Nature's
God entitle them,*

Equality of sovereign nations was stated as a requirement of the law
of nature; today this would be called "international law."

*a decent respect to the opinions of mankind requires that they
should declare the causes which impel them to the separation.*

The favorable opinion of mankind was a military necessity. The demand for independence was slow in developing, and many Americans continued to hope for reconciliation with the mother country even as late as
the summer of 1776. As long as it remained a purely internal quarrel between England and her colonies, foreign governments were loath to give
military assistance; and assistance was desperately needed if the Americans were to make successful their revolutionary acts. The French were especially anxious to support any move that would weaken English power,
but they first wanted assurances that the Americans meant business. The
Declaration of Independence notified the world that the Americans were
serious, and it was both an appeal to the conscience of mankind and a call
for military help.

The American Philosophy of Government

*We hold these truths to be self-evident, that all men are cre-
ated equal, that they are endowed by their Creator with certain
unalienable Rights, that among these are Life, Liberty, and the
pursuit of Happiness.*

These ringing words introduced the American philosophy of self-government.[3] It did not necessarily follow that independence from England
would lead to free republican institutions in the United States. It is, therefore, highly significant that the Americans based their revolutionary acts
on democratic principles. The revolution was not justified so that some
Americans could govern other Americans free of English control, but so
that Americans could govern themselves. The Declaration is a declaration
of independence; it is also a defense of free government.

Many have scoffed at the assertion that all men are created equal.
They argue that such a statement flies in the face of the obvious facts—
some men have brains, talent, and virtue and others do not. John C. Calhoun and other defenders of slavery attacked the Declaration as a series of
"glittering generalities." Calhoun, who read the Declaration as meaning
"all men are born free and equal," quipped, "There is not a word of truth

in it. . . . Men are not born. Infants are born. They grow to be men. . . . They are not born free. While infants they are incapable of freedom."

The Declaration, however, does not assert that men are equal in all things. It proclaims that men are equally endowed with certain unalienable rights, among these being a right to their own lives, liberties, and pursuits of happiness. These are man's birthrights; they are not secured by an act of governmental grace or as a gift from others.

In 1776 men spoke of unalienable or natural rights; today we speak of human rights, the rights that distinguish men from the other creatures who inhabit the earth, the rights that make for the "humanness" of human beings. To some, the dignity of each individual and his inherent worth grow out of the belief that all men are the sons of God and are created in His image. To others, the equal right of all men to be treated as unique, inviolable beings is based on humanistic grounds. But for whatever reason, these truths that were self-evident to the men of 1776 underlie the culture and civilization of the free world.

How unalienable are unalienable rights? Such rights may be forfeited by wrong-doing. The government may call upon a man to sacrifice his life and liberty in defense of the nation. But that some should be called to make the sacrifice and others favored arbitrarily, or that innocent men should be made the tools of others' happiness, are actions contrary to the concept of the equal right of each man to his life and liberty.

How is the existence of slavery to be explained in a nation whose leaders proclaimed the doctrine of unalienable rights? The Declaration makes no distinction between black and white men; in 1776, most Americans believed that slavery was an evil institution that sooner or later had to be abolished. In his original draft, Jefferson blamed the Crown for the establishment of slavery in the United States and condemned the King for waging "cruel war against human nature itself, violating its most sacred rights of life & liberty." This clause offended some of the delegates from slaveholding states; in the midst of their crisis the Americans decided to fight one evil at a time, and Congress deleted this passage in order to secure united support against England. It was to be another eighty-seven years before the practices of the nation conformed in this respect to the professions of the Declaration.

> *That to secure these rights, Governments are instituted among Men, deriving their just powers from the consent of the governed,*

Men create government for the purpose of securing their preexisting natural rights. That the rights come first, that government is created to protect these rights, and that government officials are subject to the natural law were not novel ideas in 1776. These ideas were based on the concepts of a state of nature, natural law, natural rights, and the social compact. As John Locke wrote, prior to the establishment of society men lived in a *state of nature.* Thomas Hobbes, an antidemocratic philosopher, had insisted that in the state of nature where there was no government to make and enforce laws, men made war on each other and life was "solitary, poore, nasty, brutish and short." But Locke argued that even in a state of nature there was a law governing conduct—there was the *natural law,* comprising universal, unvarying principles of right and wrong, and known to men through the use of reason. For example, if an Englishman were to meet a Frenchman on an uninhabited and ungoverned island, he would not be free to deprive the Frenchman of his life, liberty, or property. Should he attempt to do so, he would violate the natural law and could rightly be punished.

Although the state of nature was not, according to Locke, a lawless condition, it was an inconvenient one. Each man had to protect his own rights, and there was no agreed-upon judge to settle disputes about the application of the natural law to particular controversies. Realizing this, men decided to make a *compact* with one another in which each would give to the community the right to create a government equipped to enforce the natural law. Thereby each man agreed to abide by the decisions made by the majority and to comply with the laws enacted by the people's representatives, provided they did not entrench upon his fundamental rights. The power of government was thus limited.

Modern social scientists and historians agree with Aristotle that men are social animals and have never lived in a presocial and pregovernmental state of nature. Government, rather than being a consciously created institution, has developed as naturally as the family. But to reject the belief that government originated through a social compact does not invalidate the belief that men are primary and governments secondary and that governments derive their coercive authority from the consent of the governed. The moral primacy of the individual remains. It is from the philosophical and ethical, rather than the historical, concept of priority of men over governments that Americans base their insistence that governments are to be evaluated by how they improve the well-being and protect the rights of individuals. Hence,

> *That whenever any Form of Government becomes destructive of these ends, it is the Right of the People to alter or to abolish it, and to institute new Government, laying its foundation on such principles, and organizing its powers in such form, as to them shall seem most likely to effect their Safety and Happiness.*

In other words, the people may abolish their government whenever it ceases to protect natural rights and becomes destructive of the ends for which it was established. In a free society where the consent of the governed is regularly expressed through open debate and free elections, it is not likely that revolutionary action will be necessary in order to alter the foundations of government. The colonists, however, had no choice. They tried first to use constitutional devices to adjust their grievances. Finally, they felt compelled to revolt and, in the eyes of English law, to become traitors.

The doctrine of revolution pronounced in the Declaration is not a legal doctrine; there is no constitutional right to engage in revolutionary conduct. Nor should the doctrine proclaimed by the Declaration be confused with Communist doctrine or with that of other groups who espouse change by use of violence. Jefferson did not defend the right of a fraction of the civic community to seize the government and use it to suppress the natural rights of the majority. The conservative nature of the revolutionary right asserted is underscored by the next sentence.

> *Prudence, indeed, will dictate that Governments long established should not be changed for light and transient causes;*

Without denying that the people have the right to change government whenever a majority of them think it destructive of their rights, the writers of the Declaration counsel caution.

> *and accordingly all experience hath shown, that mankind are more disposed to suffer, while evils are sufferable, than to right themselves by abolishing the forms to which they are accustomed. But when a long train of abuses and usurpations, pursuing invariably the same Object, evinces a design to reduce them under absolute Despotism, it is their right, it is their duty, to throw off such Government, and to provide new Guards for their future security. Such has been the patient sufferance of these Colonies; and such is now the necessity which constrains them to alter their former Systems of Government. The history of the present King of Great Britain is a history of repeated injuries and usurpations, all having in direct object the establishment of an absolute Tyranny over these States.*

Charges against the King

The specific charges leveled by the Declaration against the King are of less significance today than the other parts of the Declaration and are listed without additional comment. It is interesting to note, however, that when it came time to write the Constitution, steps were taken to guard against some of the abuses charged to the King.

To prove this, let Facts be submitted to a candid world.

He has refused his Assent to Laws, the most wholesome and necessary for the public good.

He has forbidden his Governors to pass Laws of immediate and pressing importance, unless suspended in their operation till his Assent should be obtained; and when so suspended, he has utterly neglected to attend to them.

He has refused to pass other Laws for the accommodation of large districts of people, unless those people would relinquish the right of Representation in the Legislature, a right inestimable to them and formidable to tyrants only.

He has called together legislative bodies at places unusual, uncomfortable, and distant from the depository of their Public Records, for the sole purpose of fatiguing them into compliance with his measures.

He has dissolved Representative Houses repeatedly, for opposing with manly firmness his invasions on the rights of the people.

He has refused for a long time, after such dissolutions, to cause others to be elected; whereby the Legislative Powers, incapable of Annihilation, have returned to the People at large for their exercise; the State remaining in the mean time exposed to all the dangers of invasion from without, and convulsions within.

He has endeavoured to prevent the population of these States; for that purpose obstructing the Laws for Naturalization of Foreigners; refusing to pass others to encourage their migration hither, and raising the conditions of new Appropriations of Lands.

He has obstructed the Administration of Justice, by refusing his Assent to Laws for establishing Judiciary Powers.

He has made Judges dependent on his Will alone, for the tenure of their offices, and the amount and payment of their salaries.

He has erected a multitude of New Offices, and sent hither swarms of Officers to harrass our People, and eat out their substance.

He has kept among us, in times of peace, Standing Armies without the Consent of our legislatures.

He has affected to render the Military independent of and superior to the Civil Power.

He has combined with others to subject us to a jurisdiction foreign to our constitution, and unacknowledged by our laws; giving his Assent to their acts of pretended Legislation:

For quartering large bodies of armed troops among us:

For protecting them, by a mock Trial, from Punishment for any Murders which they should commit on the Inhabitants of these States:

For cutting off our Trade with all parts of the world:

For imposing taxes on us without our Consent:

For depriving us in many cases, of the benefits of Trial by Jury:

For transporting us beyond Seas to be tried for pretended offences:

For abolishing the free System of English Laws in a neighbouring Province, establishing therein an Arbitrary government, and enlarging its Boundaries so as to render it at once an example and fit instrument for introducing the same absolute rule into these Colonies:

For taking away our Charters, abolishing our most valuable Laws, and altering fundamentally the Forms of our Governments:

For suspending our own Legislatures, and declaring themselves invested with Power to legislate for us in all case whatsoever.

He has abdicated Government here, by declaring us out of his Protection and waging War against us.

He has plundered our seas, ravaged our Coasts, burnt our towns, and destroyed the lives of our people.

He is at this time transporting large armies of foreign mercenaries to compleat the works of death, desolation and tyranny, already begun with circumstances of Cruelty & perfidy scarcely paralleled in the most barbarous ages, and totally unworthy the Head of a civilized nation.

He has constrained our fellow Citizens taken Captive on the high Seas to bear Arms against their Country, to become the executioners of their friends and Brethren, or to fall themselves by their Hands.

He has excited domestic insurrections amongst us, and has endeavoured to bring on the inhabitants of our frontiers, the merciless Indian Savages, whose known rule of warfare, is an undistinguished destruction of all ages, sexes and conditions.

In every stage of these Oppressions We have Petitioned for Redress in the most humble terms: Our repeated Petitions have been answered only by repeated injury. A Prince, whose character is thus marked by every act which may define a Tyrant, is unfit to be the ruler of a free People.

Nor have We been wanting in attention to our British brethren. We have warned them from time to time of attempts by their legislature to extend an unwarrantable jurisdiction over

*us. We have reminded them of the circumstances of our emi-
gration and settlement here. We have appealed to their native
justice and magnanimity, and we have conjured them by the
ties of our common kindred to disavow these usurpations,
which, would inevitably interrupt our connections and corre-
spondence. They too have been deaf to the voice of justice and
of consanguinity. We must, therefore, acquiesce in the necessity, which denounces our Separation, and hold them, as we
hold the rest of mankind, Enemies in War, in Peace Friends.—*

Conclusion

*We, Therefore, the Representatives of the united States of
America, in General Congress, Assembled, appealing to the
Supreme Judge of the world for the rectitude of our intentions,
do, in the Name, and by Authority of the good People of these
Colonies, solemnly publish and declare, That these United Col-
onies are, and of Right ought to be Free and Independent
States; that they are Absolved from all Allegiance to the British
Crown, and that all political connection between them and the
State of Great Britain, is and ought to be totally dissolved; and
that as Free and Independent States, they have full Power to
levy War, conclude Peace, contract Alliances, establish Commerce, and to do all other Acts and Things which Independent
States may of right do.—And for the support of this Declaration, with a firm reliance on the protection of Divine Province,
we mutually pledge to each other our Lives, our Fortunes and
our sacred Honor.*

Did the Americans declare their independence in behalf of the United
States or in behalf of each of the thirteen sovereign states? Were they
claiming for each state or for the United States sovereign rights under international law? The language is ambiguous. In later years these questions
became important as arguments arose as to the nature of the federal system, and especially as to the source of the national government's authority
in the field of external affairs.

The Supreme Court has taken the view that in 1776 all powers in the
field of foreign affairs previously vested in the English Crown passed to
the United States so that the states never did have power to make war and
peace, or deal as sovereign nations with other governments. Other Americans have insisted that it was the separate colonies that declared their independence and that all powers of the Crown passed to each state. It was
these states, so it is argued, which in turn created the central government,
first by informal acquiescence and then more formally in the Articles of
Confederation and the Constitution. Whatever the original intent, the

former view has the support of a victory at Appomattox Court House, the growth of national sentiment, and the sanction of the Supreme Court.

The men who signed the Declaration probably gave little thought to such matters; they had more immediate problems to solve. With full recognition of the gravity of their acts and their individual jeopardy, they pledged their lives, their fortunes, and their sacred honor. John Hancock of Massachusetts, president of the Continental Congress, was the first to so pledge with his famous bold signature.

The Articles of Confederation

Although the Second Continental Congress, which had assembled in May 1775, had no formal governmental authority, it raised an army, appointed a commander in chief, negotiated with foreign nations, coined money, and assumed all powers that, it claimed, belong to an independent and sovereign nation. However, it seemed desirable to legalize these practices and place Congress' operations on a more formal basis of authority. Accordingly, even before the Declaration had been proclaimed, Congress appointed a committee, headed by John Dickinson of Maryland, to draft Articles of Union. In 1777 Congress submitted these Articles to the state legislatures, but not until March 1781 did all the states approve— Maryland, acting in behalf of the six states with no land claims, held out until the seven states with claims to western lands agreed to cede them to the Union—and our second national government began to function.

The Articles of Confederation did not materially alter the structure or powers of the government that had unofficially but effectively been governing the United States since 1775. They established a league of friendship, a "perpetual Union" of states, resting expressly on state sovereignty. The state legislatures promised to treat each others' citizens without discrimination, to give full faith and credit to each others' legal acts and public proceedings, and to extradite fugitives wanted in a sister state.

The structure of the central government was quite simple. There was only a single-chamber Congress. There was no executive, although a committee consisting of one delegate from each state managed affairs when Congress was not assembled. There was no judiciary, although Congress acted as a court to resolve disputes among the states.

Each state had one vote in the Congress and each state legislature selected its own representatives to cast that vote, paid them, and could at any time recall them. The only restrictions on a state's choice were that it could send no less than two nor more than seven members and no person could be a delegate for more than three years in six or serve at the same time as an officer under the United States.

The powers of Congress were limited. The Second Article stated, "Each State retains its sovereignty, freedom and independence, and every power, jurisdiction and right, which is not by this confederation expressly delegated to the United States, in Congress assembled." In short, Congress had only those powers that were expressly delegated.

Congress could determine peace and war, send and receive ambassadors, enter into treaties—except that it could not deprive states of the right to tax imports or prohibit exports—deal with prizes taken by United States forces, coin money, fix standards of weights and measures, regulate affairs with Indians not members of any state, establish a postal system, appoint military officers in the service of the United States above the rank of colonel, and decide certain disputes that might arise among the states. Decisions on these matters required the approval of at least *nine* states and the Articles themselves could not be amended without the approval of all *thirteen* states.

Congress did not have the power to levy taxes on individuals, to regulate commerce, or to prohibit the states from coining money. To secure funds it determined how much each state should pay, but it was up to each state to collect taxes from its citizens and turn the money over to the national treasury. If a state refused to do so, there was little that Congress could do. Likewise, Congress could negotiate treaties with foreign nations, but it had no way of making states comply with the obligation thus assumed. Resembling an international organization composed of sovereign nations rather than a national government, Congress could not impose obligations directly on individuals or enforce its legislation through its own agencies. In order to enforce congressional commands, it would have been necessary to apply sanctions against the offending states as such.

Toward a More Perfect Union

In retrospect, it may appear that the Americans lacked vision when they failed to establish a more tightly knit Union and to create a strong central government. But it must be remembered that they had just fought a war against centralized authority and, with limited communications and transportation facilities, they had good reason to believe that there could be no self-government except through local government. Nor should the accomplishments of the government under the Articles of Confederation be overlooked. It successfully brought the war to a conclusion; negotiated the Treaty of Paris of 1783, which gave the United States de jure status as a nation; established an enduring system for the development of western lands; and refined the practices of interstate cooperation that gave Americans further practical experience in handling national problems.

And there were plenty of these. The English refused to withdraw their troops from western lands until the states lived up to their treaty obligations to indemnify British subjects for property confiscated during the war, and Congress was powerless to make either the British or the states comply. The Spanish threatened to close the mouth of the Mississippi to American trade; foreign commerce languished. The Americans, having ceased to enjoy the privileges of membership in the British Empire, were unable to secure treaty advantages from other nations, who had no desire to make agreements with a nation that could not enforce them.

Once the fighting stopped, pressure to cooperate was reduced, and the states started to go off in their several directions. Some printed worthless paper money, while some failed to contribute their share to support the central government. Trade barriers were established by some states in an attempt to give their own merchants special privileges, and the seaboard states levied taxes on goods going inland. Within the states, conflicts between debtors and creditors were often bitter—defaulting debtors resented the harsh laws that caused them to lose their property or go to jail; creditors resented the acts passed giving debtors longer time to pay off debts or permitting them to use inflated paper currency.

Attempts were made to amend the Articles in order to give Congress authority to collect taxes and to regulate interstate commerce. In 1781 Congress submitted an amendment to the state legislatures that would give it power to levy duties, but another flaw in the Articles was made apparent when the amendment failed because a single state, Rhode Island, refused to agree. Two years later New York vetoed a similar amendment. What could be done?

A relatively small group of important and articulate Americans had been agitating for a more vigorous national government, but general sentiment was against any drastic changes. The nationalists had to move carefully. They needed an opportunity to present their proposals to the country. Interstate conferences to discuss navigation and commercial matters gave them such a chance. After successfully negotiating an agreement with Maryland, some nationally minded Virginians proposed that all the states send delegates to Annapolis in September 1786 to discuss the establishment of a uniform system of commerce for the entire nation. But only five states sent commissioners to the Annapolis Convention.

Although disappointed by this apparent lack of interest, Hamilton of New York and Madison of Virginia persuaded the delegates who did come to try to salvage something. They adopted a report urging the states to send delegates to another convention to be held the following May in Philadelphia. It was further stated that such delegates should be authorized not only to discuss trade matters but also to examine the defects of the existing system of government and "to devise such further provisions as shall appear to them necessary to render the constitution of the Federal Government adequate to the exigencies of the Union."

Even before Congress authorized a convention, several of the state legislatures, following Virginia's lead, selected delegates. Distinguished men were chosen and the country was notified that the approaching Philadelphia Convention was to be taken seriously. After hesitation, Congress gave its consent, carefully stipulating, however, that the delegates should meet "for the sole and express purpose of revising the Articles of Confederation and reporting to Congress and the several legislatures such alterations and provisions therein as shall when agreed to in Congress and confirmed by the states render the federal constitution adequate to the exigencies of Government & the preservation of the Union." Ultimately all the states except Rhode Island selected delegates.

The Constitutional Convention

Seventy-four persons were appointed delegates to the Philadelphia Convention, but only fifty-five attended, of whom only thirty-nine took a leading part in deliberations. This distinguished group was not interested in mere political speculation but, above everything else, in establishing a government that would work; they were well equipped for the task. Seven of the delegates had served as governors of their respective states, thirty-nine had served in Congress, eight had had previous experience in constitution-making within their own states. Despite this wealth of experience, the Convention was composed mainly of comparatively young men. The youngest was only twenty-six, six were under thirty-one, and only twelve were over fifty-four. They were all men of consequence—merchants, manufacturers, planters, bankers, lawyers. The small farmers and city mechanics were not represented; the back-country rural areas were greatly underrepresented, although this was not the case in several of the state ratifying conventions.

Conspicuous by reason of their absence from the Convention were Patrick Henry, Samuel Adams, John Adams, John Hancock, Tom Paine, and Thomas Jefferson—the fiery democratic leaders of the Revolution. Henry had been appointed but refused to attend; he was not in favor of revising the Articles of Confederation. "I smelt a rat," he is reported to have remarked. Jefferson and John Adams were abroad, representing the United States in a diplomatic capacity, Paine had returned to England, and Hancock and Samuel Adams had not been chosen delegates.

Six men stand out as leaders of the Convention: General Washington, James Madison, Edmund Randolph, Benjamin Franklin, James Wilson, and Gouverneur Morris—three from Virginia, three from Pennsylvania.

Washington, first citizen of Virginia and of the United States, was unanimously selected to preside over the convention. He had been extremely reluctant to attend and had accepted only when persuaded that his prestige was needed to assure the success of the Convention. Although he seldom spoke, his influence was vitally felt both in informal gatherings and in the Convention sessions. The universal assumption that he would become the first President under the new government inspired confidence in it.

Madison, only thirty-six at the time, was one of the most learned and informed of the delegates. He had been a member both of the Congress and of the Virginia Assembly. Foreseeing the future significance of the Convention, Madison always sat in the front of the room, where he could hear all that was said; he kept a detailed record of the proceedings. Even today, Madison's notes remain our major source of information concerning the Convention.

Edmund Randolph, thirty-four, was governor of Virginia, and a member of one of Virginia's first families. Although he declined to sign the Constitution, he later advocated its ratification.

Benjamin Franklin, at eighty-one, was the Convention's oldest member. Second only to Washington in the esteem of his countrymen, Franklin had a firm faith in the people. Despite his great age, Franklin played an active role. At critical moments, his sagacious and humorous remarks broke the tension and prevented bitterness.

Most of Franklin's speeches were read by his fellow delegate James Wilson. This Scottish-born and Scottish-trained lawyer had signed the Declaration of Independence and represented his state in Congress. He was a strong supporter of Madison; his work on the Convention's Committee on Detail, although inconspicuous, was very important.

In sharp contrast to Franklin, the third Pennsylvania delegate, Gouverneur Morris, was strongly aristocratic in his sympathies. He was an eloquent and interesting speaker and addressed the Convention more often than any other member, and his facility with the pen is shown by the fact that he was chosen to write the final draft of the Constitution. Years later he began a letter, "The hand that writes this letter wrote the Constitution."

Besides these six, there were others of outstanding prominence at the Convention: George Mason, Charles Pinckney, Roger Sherman, Alexander Hamilton, Luther Martin, to mention a few. Hamilton, representing New York, did not play as important a role as one might expect; his influence was nullified to a great extent by his associates from New York who opposed the Constitution. Hamilton lost influence, also, through his advocacy of a strong and completely centralized national government. At the opposite extreme was Luther Martin from Maryland, who was an ardent and fearfully boring champion of the small states. As soon as it was apparent that his views were in the minority, Martin went back to Maryland.

Convention Debates and Procedures

The Virginia delegates, who were anxious to establish a strong central government, took advantage of an eleven-day delay in the opening of the Convention—a delay due to the failure of a sufficient number of delegations to appear at the time the Convention was scheduled to open—to prepare a series of proposals. This gave the nationalists time to prepare a plan that imparted to the debates a general direction that the less nationalistically inclined delegates were never able to reverse. Eventually the Virginia Plan, with modifications, became the Constitution.

Immediately after Washington was chosen to preside and rules of procedures were adopted—of which the rule of secrecy was perhaps the most significant—Randolph introduced Virginia's fifteen resolutions. The Virginia Plan contained some startling proposals. The Convention's mandate from Congress and most of the delegates' instructions from their state legislatures restricted them to the consideration of amendments to the Articles of Confederation. The Virginians, however, proposed a completely new instrument of government differing fundamentally from the Articles. They proposed that a central government be established with power to pass laws and with authority to enforce these laws through its own executive and judicial branches. They proposed that Congress be a bicameral (two-house) legislature in which states should be represented on the basis of wealth or population; that this Congress be given all powers vested in the existing Congress plus the authority "to legislate in all cases to which the separate states are incompetent, or in which the harmony of the United States may be interrupted by the exercise of individual legislation."

For the first two weeks, the Convention discussed the Virginia Plan. Delegates from the less populous states were afraid that their interests would be overlooked by a national legislature dominated by representatives from the large states. They favored a less powerful national government with more independence of action by the states. They counterattacked on June 14 when Paterson of New Jersey introduced nine resolutions, the New Jersey Plan, as an alternative to Virginia's scheme. Although proposing that Congress be given the power to regulate commerce and levy taxes, Paterson's proposals would not have significantly altered the Articles of Confederation. All states were to have the same weight in a single-chambered national Congress, a plural executive was to administer the law, and a single national Supreme Court was to supervise the interpretation of national laws by the state courts. Although some of its provisions were incorporated in the Constitution, the New Jersey Plan was ultimately rejected and the delegates resumed discussion of the Virginia Plan.

Small-state delegates grew increasingly discontented with the deliberations, and there were threats of withdrawal. Presently the Convention became deadlocked over the crucial issue of representation in the upper house of the proposed Congress. Finally, a committee of eleven, one delegate from each state, was appointed to work out a compromise. Three days later, on July 5, the committee presented its report, known to history as the Connecticut Compromise. The nationalists conceded that in the upper house each state should have equal representation, but on condition that money bills originate in the lower chamber. Furthermore, slaves were to be counted as three fifths of the free population both in determining representation in the lower house and in apportioning direct taxes among the states according to population. Delegates from the less populous states, being thus mollified, were then ready to support the establishment of a strong central government.

There remained, however, many other differences still to be reconciled: questions about the suffrage, the structure and authority of federal courts, the procedures for selecting the President, and so on. But on many basic issues, the delegates were in general agreement. All supported the idea of a republican form of government; all agreed that the powers of the national government should be distributed among a legislative, an executive, and a judicial branch. Without extended debate, it was decided to impose limitations on the power of the states to coin money or to interfere with the rights of creditors. By the end of the summer, the delegates had a document to present to the nation.

Final Day

On September 17, 1787, after four months of debate, the delegates took their seats. General Washington called the meeting to order. The secretary began to read the final copy of the Constitution. When he finished, Dr. Franklin rose; too feeble to speak for himself, the good doctor turned to his fellow delegate James Wilson and asked him to read a speech that he had prepared for the occasion. The delegates stirred in their seats. "Mr. President," said Wilson, his strong voice giving emphasis to the wisdom of one of America's sages:

> I confess that there are several parts of this constitution that I do not at present approve, but I am not sure I shall never approve of them. . . .
> The older I grow, the more apt I am to doubt my own judgment, and to pay more respect to the judgment of others. . . .
> On the whole, Sir, I cannot help expressing a wish that every member of the Convention who may still have objections to it, would with me, on this occasion doubt a little of his own infallibility—and to make manifest our unanimity, put his name to this instrument.

At the conclusion of his speech, Franklin shrewdly moved that the Constitution be signed by the members in the "following convenient form, viz., 'Done in Convention by the unanimous consent of the States present the 17th of Spr. &c—In Witness whereof we have hereunto subscribed our names.' " This ambiguous form had been drawn up by Gouverneur Morris in order to gain the support of those members who had qualms about giving their approval to the Constitution. It was introduced by Franklin so that it might have a better chance of success.

The roll was called on Franklin's motion. The results: ten ayes, no nays, and one delegation divided—the motion was approved!

The delegates then moved forward to sign. Only three persons present at this historic meeting refused to place their names on the Constitution —others who had opposed the general drift of the Convention had already left Philadelphia.[4] As the last member came forward to sign, Franklin, Madison's notes tell us,

> . . . looking towards the president's chair, at the back of which a rising sun happened to be painted, observed to a few members near him, that painters had found it difficult to distinguish, in their art, a rising from a setting sun. "I have," said he, "often and often in the course of the session, and the vicissitudes of my hopes and fears as to its issue, looked at that behind the president, without being able to tell whether it was rising or setting; but now, at length, I have the happiness to know that it is a rising, and not a setting sun."

Their work over, the delegates adjourned to the City Tavern to relax and celebrate a job well done.

Ratification Debate

The Constitution was not ratified until after a bitter struggle within the states, especially in Virginia, Massachusetts, and New York. Both in the campaign for the election of delegates to the ratifying conventions and in the conventions themselves, the Constitution was subjected to minute and searching debate.

By the end of June 1788, ten states had ratified, one more than was needed. But New York still had not acted, and because of its central geographic location, ratification by New York was essential for the success of the new government. All during the previous winter and spring the debate had been intense. Hamilton, fearful of the outcome, had secured the assistance of James Madison and John Jay to write a series of articles to win over the people of New York. The influence of these articles, since known as *The Federalist Papers,* on the outcome of the ratification struggle is sometimes exaggerated; that they did help bring about the final favorable verdict is undoubted. Written under pressure and for "partisan purposes," nevertheless they quickly became the most important contemporary comment on the Constitution; because of their penetrating discussion of the basic problems of government and their profound analysis of our constitutional system, they remain today one of America's outstanding contributions to the literature of political science.

Basic Features
of the Constitution

The provisions of the Constitution are best understood within the context of certain basic features that underpin the entire document and establish the character of the American system of government: federalism, separation of powers, and judicial review.

Federalism

A federal government is one in which a *constitution* divides governmental power between a central and subdivisional governments, giving to each substantial functions. In contrast, the unitary systems are ones in which a constitution vests all governmental power in a central government. In a unitary system, the central government may delegate authority to local units; what it gives, however, it has the constitutional authority to take away. In a federal system, the constitution is the source of both central and subdivisional authority; each unit has a core of power independent of the wishes of those who control the other level of government. Examples of governments that are federal in form and practice are those of Switzerland, Australia, Canada, and India.

Constitutional Basis of American Federalism

1. The Constitution grants certain legislative, executive, and judicial powers to the national government.
2. It reserves to the states powers not granted to the national government.

19

3. It makes the national government supreme. The Constitution, all laws passed in pursuance thereof, and treaties of the United States are the supreme law of the land. American citizens, most of whom are also state citizens (see pages 148–151), owe their primary allegiance to the national government; officers of the state governments, of course, owe the same allegiance.

4. The Constitution denies some powers to both national and state governments, some only to the national government, and still others only to the state governments.

Conflicting Interpretations of American Federalism

Throughout our history, political conflicts have generated debates about the nature of nation-state relationships. Can the national government embargo exports? Can slavery be outlawed in the territories? Does the national government have the power to regulate railroad rates, forbid racial discrimination, and so on? Which government owns the oil under the marginal seas? Can a state require racial segregation in public schools? Frequently the groups supporting particular interpretations of the national-state relationship have switched positions, depending upon the immediate issue. As issues and times have changed, so also have the details of the arguments. It is, however, a useful oversimplification to classify the arguments into two broad schools—the states' rights and the nationalist positions.

The states' rights interpretation rests on the basic premise that the Constitution is a compact among the states. The states, it is argued, created the national government and gave it certain limited powers. In case of doubt as to whether a particular function has been given to the national government or reserved to the states, the doubt should be resolved in favor of the principal parties to the constitutional contract—the states—and against their agent—the national government. Hence, the national government's powers should be construed narrowly and should not be expanded by interpretation. The clause conferring upon Congress the power to legislate when "necessary and proper" to carry into execution the powers assigned to the national government (see page 63), confers only the authority to legislate if it is *absolutely* necessary to effect one of the national government's express powers.

According to the states' rights interpretation, the existence of the national government does not in any way curtail the full use by the states of their reserved powers. However, the existence of the reserved powers of the states does restrict the scope of the national government's granted powers. For example, since the power to regulate agriculture is one of the powers reserved to the states, the national government may not use its enumerated powers in such a way as to regulate agriculture. And suffusing the states' rights orientation toward our federal system is the assumption that state governments are closer to the people and so more accurately reflect their wishes than does the national government. The national government has to be watched carefully to make sure that it does not deprive the people of their liberties.

Nationalists, on the other hand, reject the whole idea of the Constitution as a compact among the states and deny that the national government is an agent of the states. Rather, they argue, the Constitution is a supreme law coming from "We the people of the United States." It was the people, not the state governments, who created the national government and they gave it sufficient power to accomplish the great objectives listed in the Preamble. The national government is not a subordinate of the states. In order not to frustrate the people's intentions, the powers of the national government should be construed liberally. In addition to construing broadly each of the powers expressly given to the national government, a liberal construction of the "necessary and proper" clause gives Congress the right to adopt any means that are convenient and useful in order to carry into effect expressly delegated powers. The national government should not be denied power unless its actions clearly conflict with express constitutional limits or clearly have no constitutional basis.

The nationalists also deny that the reserved powers of the states set limits to the national government's use of its delegated authority. The national government, for example, may use to the fullest its power to regulate commerce among the states, and the fact that such regulation may touch upon matters otherwise subject to the reserved powers of the state is without constitutional significance. Furthermore, the states may not use their reserved powers—for example, the power to tax—in such a way as to interfere with the programs of the national government. The national government represents all the people, each state only a part of the people. When acting within its sphere, the national government is supreme (see Supremacy Article, pages 100–101).

In 1819, the Supreme Court had its first of many occasions to choose between these two interpretations of our federal system when the great case of *McCulloch* v. *Maryland* came before it.[1] Maryland had levied a tax against the Baltimore branch of the Bank of the United States, which McCulloch, the cashier, refused to pay on the ground that a state could not tax an instrumentality of the national government. Maryland's attorneys argued that the national government did not have the power in the first place to incorporate a bank, but even if it did, the states had the power to tax it.

John Marshall, speaking for the Supreme Court, gave his full support to the nationalist position. Although the power to incorporate a bank is not among the powers expressly delegated, it is a necessary and proper —that is to say, convenient and useful—means of carrying into effect such delegated powers as caring for the property of the United States, regulating currency, and promoting interstate commerce.

"Let the end be legitimate, let it be within the scope of the Constitution, and all means which are appropriate, which are plainly adapted to the end, which are not prohibited, but consist with the letter and spirit of the Constitution, are constitutional." [2] Moreover, admitting that the states have the power to tax, they may not tax instruments created by the national government, inasmuch as "the power to tax involves the power to destroy."

McCulloch v. *Maryland* to the contrary notwithstanding, many continued to champion the states' rights interpretation. Among the spokesmen for this view, albeit with varying emphases, have been Thomas Jefferson, Chief Justice Roger B. Taney (Marshall's immediate successor) John C. Calhoun, the Supreme Court majority of the 1920s, and today such men as Senator Eastland and others who argue that the states have the power to operate racially segregated public schools despite Supreme Court decisions to the contrary. In addition to John Marshall, the nationalist interpretation has been supported, again with varying emphases, by Abraham Lincoln, Theodore Roosevelt, Franklin Roosevelt, and throughout most of our history by the Supreme Court. That the nationalist interpretation has been dominant most of the time can be seen from the following description of national and state powers.

Classification of National Powers

Classification by Function   Powers may be classified by *function* as legislative, executive, or judicial. The problems growing out of this classification will be discussed in the section on separation of powers (page 25).

Classification by Constitutional Source   1. *Enumerated powers* are those that the Constitution expressly grants—for example, the power to raise and support armies and navies.

2. *Implied powers* are those that may be inferred from power expressly granted—for example, the power to draft men from the express power to raise armies and navies.

3. *Resulting powers* are those that result when several enumerated powers are added together—for example, the authority to make paper money legal tender for the payment of debts results from adding together the enumerated powers to coin money, to regulate interstate commerce, and to borrow money.

4. *Inherent powers* are those powers in the field of external affairs that the Supreme Court has declared do not depend upon constitutional grants but grow out of the very existence of the national government (see page 35).

Classification by Relation to State Powers 1. *Exclusive powers* are those that only the national government may exercise—for example, the power to conduct foreign relations and to establish uniform rules of naturalization. In some cases the Constitution explicitly gives the national government exclusive power or expressly denies the states the right to act; in others the nature of the national power involved is found by the Supreme Court to rule out state actions.

2. *Concurrent powers* are those that the national government shares with the states—for example, the power to tax. Whenever action by the national government conflicts with state action, it is the former that prevails.

3. *Expressly limited powers* are those that the Constitution denies to the national government—for example, the power to tax exports. (Here we are describing limitations on national power in relation to state governments, not limits in behalf of civil liberties; see pages 65–68 and 104–108.)

4. *Implied limitations on national power* are those limitations that grow out of the nature of the federal system. Thus, although the national government is supreme, the Constitution creates a federal system in which states are basic units. The national government may not, for example, use its taxing powers to destroy the states or to make it impossible for them to govern.

Reserved Powers of the States

The reserved powers of the states may be classified according to the *nature and subject* of the power.

1. Power to tax and to spend. This power, like all powers reserved to the states, may not be used to place a burden on the national government or to frustrate its activities or to conflict with national regulations.

2. To take private property, the power of eminent domain. Under the Constitution (see pages 130–131) the states (as well as the national government) may take property only for public purposes and must compensate the owners.

3. To regulate local commerce and those aspects of interstate commerce that in the opinion of Congress or, in case of Congress' silence, in the judgment of the Supreme Court are appropriate for state regulation (see pages 57–58).

4. To regulate persons and property in order to promote the public welfare, known as the police power. This power, like all state powers, must be exercised in a manner consistent with constitutional limitations. It is the Supreme Court—an agency of the national government—that makes the final determination in case of an alleged conflict between a state's exercise of its powers and a national constitutional limitation.

5. To establish a republican form of state government. The Constitution leaves each state free to establish its own form of state and local government subject to the limitation that it must be republican in form (see page 95). In their respective state constitutions, the people of each state may impose additional limitations upon state officials and deny them powers beyond the restrictions of the Constitution. They cannot, of course, deprive state officials of responsibilities that the Constitution imposes upon them—for example, the power to ratify or reject constitutional amendments, which is vested by the Constitution under certain circumstances in the state legislatures (see page 96).

Federalism Today

Speaking precisely and technically, Congress has no general grant of authority to do whatever it thinks necessary and proper in order to promote the general welfare or to preserve domestic tranquility (see pages 52, 64). But as a result of the emergence of a national economy, the growth of national allegiances, and a world in which total war could destroy us in a matter of minutes, our constitutional system has evolved to the point where the national government has ample constitutional authority to deal with any national or international problem.

As recently as the Great Depression of the 1930s, constitutional scholars and Supreme Court justices seriously debated whether Congress could enact legislation dealing with agriculture, labor, commerce, education, housing, social security, welfare. Only a decade or so ago, there were constitutional questions about the authority of Congress to legislate against racial discrimination. And while there are still a few subjects—for example, regulation of marriage and divorce—about which the Supreme Court might interpose objections to national legislation because of the principles of federalism, in fact it is now a more accurate generalization to make a technical error and talk about Congress' power to do whatever it believes is necessary and proper to promote the general welfare than not to do so.

Federalism no longer imposes serious constitutional restraint on the power of Congress, or the President, or the federal courts. Today constitutional restraints on national power stem from provisions designed to protect the liberties of the people rather than from those provisions designed to preserve the powers of the individual state governments.

Separation of Powers
and Checks and Balances

Another basic feature of the Constitution is the distribution of national powers among three departments that are given *constitutional* and *political* independence of each other. The President's power, for example, comes not from Congress but from the Constitution. And most importantly, the personnel of each of the three branches are chosen by different procedures and hold office independently of the other branches. It is this independence of the three branches, not just the distribution of functions, which is the central feature of our system of separation of powers. England also has executive, legislative, and judicial branches, but the English government is not established according to the principle of separation of powers inasmuch as the legislature chooses the executive and the executive depends upon the legislature both for retention of office and for authority.

In addition to separate functions and considerable political and constitutional independence, each branch has weapons with which to check the others. The President has a qualified veto over Congress, the courts interpret the laws, but the President and the Senate select the judges; the President is commander in chief of the armed forces, but Congress provides them, and so on.

The framers of the Constitution feared concentration of powers in a single branch. To them, separation of powers and checks and balances were desirable to prevent official tyranny and, even more importantly, to prevent a single segment of the population—majority or minority—from gaining complete control of the government. It was hoped that by making each branch accountable to different groups, a variety of interests would be reflected. Hence compromises and a balancing of interests would result.

The doctrine of separation of powers is more accurately described as a "sharing of powers by separated institutions." Each department is given a voice in the business of the others, and each is made dependent upon the cooperation of the others in order to accomplish its own business. It is through this blending of powers by politically independent branches that the doctrine of checks and balances is made effective.

The blending of duties beyond that specifically authorized by the Constitution is often necessary to accomplish the business of government. This fact has resulted in a considerable straining of the constitutional doctrine that what the Constitution gives to each department, it should not give away; that each department should stick to its own last. For example, the Constitution vests the legislative authority in Congress; what the Constitution gives to it, Congress is not supposed to delegate to others. The

Supreme Court has recognized, however, that in view of the complexity of the conditions that Congress is called upon to regulate, it is impossible for that body to make all policy decisions. As a result, the Court has approved considerable delegation of discretion. Nowadays it is sufficient if Congress sets down a general policy. Once it has done this, it may authorize administrative officials to make rules to carry the general policy into effect. By so doing, Congress retains its "essential" legislative duties and delegates merely what the Courts have labeled "quasi-legislative" power. Thus the Supreme Court has sustained congressional delegation of authority to the Interstate Commerce Commission to establish "fair and reasonable" interstate railroad rates, to the Federal Trade Commission to prevent "unfair methods of competition" in interstate commerce, to the Federal Communications Commission to regulate radio and television in "the public interest, convenience, and necessity." [3] Congress, however, always retains the power to rescind its delegation or to alter the policies enacted by those to whom it has given quasi-legislative discretion. Congressional delegation of legislative authority to private associations or individuals is unconstitutional.[4]

The constitutional separation of powers has been altered by two other developments: the growth of national political parties and the increased legislative influence of the President. National parties, however, are such loosely organized political instruments that even when the President and a majority of the Congress belong to the same party, they are often ineffective devices for coordinating governmental action. More significant has been the President's expanding role as chief legislator. Today, the President is expected to have a legislative program of his own and to use his powers and prestige to secure its adoption by Congress. The growth of presidential leadership has brought the legislative and executive branches into closer relationship than perhaps many of the Founding Fathers anticipated, and undoubtedly many of them would be surprised to discover that the President has been able to take over so many and such important legislative responsibilities. At the same time, the traditional independence of Congress has remained intact; the President is frequently compelled to deal with legislators whose own political security is greater than his own.

Separation of powers is of especial importance in the case of the federal judiciary's independence. Both the mores of our politics and the design of the Constitution give judges a large measure of independence. Although, as we shall presently note, this independence is relative, the Founding Fathers took special precautions to isolate the judiciary from executive and legislative influence. They did not wish the judges to be subject to executive dominance because they remembered how certain English kings had used judges to punish enemies and reward friends. They were also afraid that there might be times when Congress and the President might respond to political and social convulsions and act hastily and oppressively. The judges, it was hoped, with their independence and political security would be more likely to withstand transitory gusts of popular passion and to take a more detached and long-range view. The relative independence of the judges from political influences takes on additional significance because they have the important power of judicial review.

Judicial Review

Judicial review is the power of judges, ultimately those of the Supreme Court, to interpret the Constitution and to refuse to enforce those measures that in their opinion are in conflict with the Constitution. It is because the judges are the official interpreters of the Constitution that a study of the American Constitution is in such large measure a study of judicial decisions and opinions.

The Constitution does not specifically grant the courts the power to interpret the Constitution, but it furnishes sufficient verbal basis for this power. The first assertion of the power against an act of Congress was made in Chief Justice John Marshall's famous decision, in 1803, in the great case of *Marbury* v. *Madison*.[5] The case, which was preceded by several similar holdings by some state courts under their respective state constitutions, arose out of the following situation.

The Federalists had lost the election of 1800, but before leaving office they succeeded in creating several new judicial posts. Among these were forty-two justice-of-peaceships for the District of Columbia, to which the retiring Federalist President, John Adams, appointed forty-two Federalists. The Senate confirmed these appointments and the commissions were signed and sealed, but Adams' Secretary of State, John Marshall, failed to deliver certain of them. When the new President, Thomas Jefferson, assumed office, he instructed his Secretary of State, James Madison, not to deliver seventeen of these commissions, including one for William Marbury. Marbury decided to take action, and consulting the law he found that Section 13 of the Judiciary Act of 1789 declared: "The Supreme Court . . . shall have the power to issue . . . writs of mandamus, in cases warranted by the principles and usages of law, to . . . persons holding office, under the authority of the United States." (A writ of mandamus is a court order directed to an officer requiring him to perform a certain "ministerial" duty as required by law.) Without further ado, Marbury, through his attorneys, went before the Supreme Court and asked the justices to issue a writ of mandamus to Secretary Madison ordering him to deliver the commission. The Court, speaking through Marshall, who had now become Chief Justice, held that Section 13 of the Judiciary Act of 1789 was repugnant to Article III, Section 2 of the Constitution (see pages 88–89) inasmuch as the Constitution itself limited the Supreme Court's original jurisdiction to cases "affecting ambassadors, other public ministers and consuls, and those to which a state is party." Since Marbury fell in none of these categories, the Court declined to take jurisdiction of his case, Section 13 to the contrary notwithstanding.

Where did the Supreme Court derive the authority thus to gainsay Congress? Marshall reasoned that the Constitution is law, that it is the duty of courts to interpret the law in order to decide cases in accordance with it, and that therefore the Supreme Court had the authority and indeed was duty-bound to interpret the Constitution, and of course to prefer it to any other law. He also pointed out that the Constitution enjoins the courts to enforce as the supreme law of the land only those acts of Congress that are "in pursuance of the Constitution" (Article VI, Section 2). Therefore, the Court must first determine whether a law *is* in pursuance of the Constitution before it is entitled to enforce it as "law of the land."

Although this argument is logically a very cogent one, there continues to be heated debate to this day concerning the soundness of the result. Critics, including several Presidents, have argued that the Constitution is "supreme law" because it emanates from the people. Therefore, the most politically responsible agencies, Congress and the President, ought to have as much right to interpret it as the least politically responsible agency— the Supreme Court.

Also questioned has been Marshall's assumption that the Constitution is law in the ordinary sense; and suited to judicial interpretation. The Constitution, it is argued, is a *political* document, not susceptible to interpretation by the ordinary judicial processes. Nor have critics of judicial review accepted the argument that it is a necessary check on Congress and the President. They argue that Congress and the President are checked by the voters, whereas the only regular check on the judges is their own self-restraint, which seems at times to be lacking.

Most of the criticism of judicial review is directed, it should be noted, against review of acts of Congress, although it is today rarely exercised adversely to such acts. That there must be a central review of state action by the Supreme Court is generally conceded. As Justice Holmes once put the matter: "I do not think the United States would come to an end if we lost our power to declare an Act of Congress void. I do think the Union would be imperiled if we could not make that declaration as to the laws of the several states." [6]

Restrictions on Judicial Review

The Doctrine of Political Questions   John Marshall asserted in *Marbury* v. *Madison* that constitutional questions are justiciable, but his successor, Chief Justice Roger B. Taney, established the doctrine that some constitutional questions are political and are not to be answered by the courts.[7] Political questions as those that the Constitution clearly directs to the Congress or the President, that lack judicially discoverable standards for resolving, that are impossible of deciding without an initial policy determination of a kind clearly for nonjudicial discretion, that would be impossible for a court to handle without expressing lack of the respect due to the Congress or the President, that involve an unusual need for unquestioning adherence to a political decision already made, or that could create embarrassment by leading to conflicting pronouncements by Congress, President, and the Courts.[8] For example, the Supreme Court has ruled that it is for the President to determine which foreign government is to be recognized by the United States, for Congress to determine if a sufficient number of states have ratified a constitutional amendment within a reasonable time to make the ratification effective (see page 97), for Congress and the President to determine in case of conflicting claimants which government of a state is the legitimate one, for Congress to determine whether states have the republican form of government as is required by the Constitution.[9] Since the Supreme Court decides which are justiciable and which are political questions, this limitation on the authority of the courts is a self-imposed one.

Prior to 1962, the Supreme Court had refused to allow federal judges to get involved in the "political thicket" of determining which legislative districting schemes were constitutional. State courts followed suit. The only redress available was from the legislature. Since the legislatures were the products of the allegedly discriminatory district arrangements, and since the rural groups who benefited from the status quo and dominated the state legislatures had no desire to alter the existing pattern of representation, appeals by city voters for more equitable representation were ineffective.

A hint that the Supreme Court might alter its stand came when it refused to allow the doctrine of political questions to keep it from declaring unconstitutional an Alabama law that had redefined the city boundaries of Tuskegee in such a way as to remove from the city all but four or five of its Negro voters.[10] If the judges would consider whether manipulation of an election unit discriminated against Negro voters, perhaps they would consider if such manipulations violated the constitutional rights of city voters.

Finally, in *Baker* v. *Carr,* the Supreme Court ruled that schemes for determining the boundaries and for apportioning representatives to the state legislature do raise justiciable questions under the equal protection clause of the Fourteenth Amendment (see page 151). Since then, the Supreme Court has expanded the doctrines of *Baker* v. *Carr* to cover the drawing by state legislature of congressional district boundaries (*Wesberry* v. *Sanders*),[11] unit-voting schemes for choosing state officers,[12] and local governmental units that exercise legislative functions, such as county commissioners (*Avery* v. *Midland County*).[13] The Supreme Court has ruled that any voting scheme that gives one group of persons more influence in the outcome of an election [14] or more representation in a legislature than another group violates the equal protection clause, and that in a two-chamber legislature both chambers must be based on representation by population (*Reynolds* v. *Sims*).[15] The Court has insisted upon as absolute a mathematical equality among legislative districts as is possible.[16]

The Nature of Judicial Power

Judges can decide a constitutional (or any other) issue only when a bona fide case is brought before them over which their court has jurisdiction. On some issues—for example, the constitutionality of a congressional appropriation (see page 53)—it is difficult to arrange a case in which the issue could be raised. Other issues—for example, the nature of the President's responsibility to formulate legislative programs or the constitutional authority of the President to send munitions to our allies without congressional authorization—are not of the kind that can readily be raised in a lawsuit. Therefore, many important constitutional developments take place outside the judicial forum. Even those questions that can be raised in a law are often not brought before the courts for many years, if at all. There was no judicial interpretation until 1926, for example, of the President's authority to remove executive officers or until 1969 of each congressional chamber's authority to determine the qualifications of its members.[17]

Since congressmen, presidents, governors, legislators, school boards, and many others have a duty to act constitutionally, often they have to measure their actions against their own reading of the Constitution; there is no Supreme Court decision that is relevant. Judges are the authoritative, but not the only, interpreters of the Constitution.

Canons of Judicial Interpretation Throughout its history, the Supreme Court has developed certain rules of interpretation to guide federal judges. Among the rules—sometimes ignored but generally followed —are these:

1. Do not decide a constitutional issue unless it is absolutely necessary in order to dispose of the case.
2. Whenever there is a choice, interpret a law in such a way as to render it constitutional.
3. If necessary to make a constitutional ruling, restrict it as narrowly as possible and do not anticipate or decide issues not immediately before the court.[18]

The Political Process   Courts are deliberately isolated from political battles and partisan conflicts; in a free society, however, they can never, at least over a period of time, interpret the Constitution in a manner at variance with the desires of most of the people. Judges have neither the power of the sword nor of the purse, and in order to make their decisions meaningful they have to have the support of most of the people most of the time. Whenever they hand down rulings that arouse the hostility of significant numbers, it is not at all certain that the rulings can be made to stick; often they do not.

Judges, unlike congressmen and even the President, are not immediately accountable to the electorate. But in time, as judges resign, retire, or die, the President, who is elected by a national majority, nominates and the Senate confirms new judges to fill vacancies. The views of these new judges will more likely reflect the demands of contemporary majorities. At times, congressional majorities and the President, and the groups they represent, have been so strongly opposed to certain Supreme Court decisions that they have changed the laws to alter the structure or size of courts in order to secure decisions more consistent with their wishes. Time after time, new judges—sometimes even the old ones—have found it necessary to reinterpret the Constitution to adjust it to changing demands. Judges interpret the Constitution, but they, like all other public officials, are servants, not masters, of the electorate.

Failure to recognize that the judges' power is limited may lead people to believe that the Supreme Court can guarantee, for example, freedom of speech, or insure the preservation of our constitutional system. Judges both lead and respond to the values of the nation. But only insofar as they reflect the views of most of the people can they guarantee free speech or preserve republican government. If most of the people are strongly opposed to freedom of speech the chances are we shall not have it. If most desire it, the chances are that the Supreme Court will hand down decisions protecting it. In short, the Constitution ultimately is not "what the judges say it is," but what the people want it to be.[19]

The Warren Court—The End of an Era

The 1968 presidential election well illustrates the impact of our political system on constitutional interpretation. As a result of that election —and perhaps its most important consequence—Richard M. Nixon rather than Hubert H. Humphrey will appoint the men to serve on the Supreme Court, and because of a somewhat unusual combination of circumstances, he is likely to appoint a sufficient number of men to change the character of the Court and the course of constitutional interpretation.

Even before the election it was clear that the winner would have the opportunity to nominate a Chief Justice, for at the close of the 1967 term (June 1968) Chief Justice Earl Warren had announced that he wished to retire from the Court as soon as his successor could be appointed. Although a Republican, Warren's constitutional philosphy was more consistent with that of President Johnson or Hubert Humphrey rather than with that of President Nixon. By announcing his retirement before the election Warren gave President Johnson an opportunity to appoint his successor. President Johnson proposed to promote Justice Abe Fortas to serve as Chief Justice and to appoint Judge Homer Thornberry, a federal circuit judge from Texas, to fill Justice Fortas' seat. The Senate, however, refused to confirm Justice Fortas' promotion, in part because of hostility to President Johnson, in part because of displeasure with the Warren Court's constitutional interpretations, in part because of the belief that it would be more proper for the newly elected President to make the nomination, in part because of allegations that Justice Fortas had engaged in financial transactions thought to be improper for a member of the Supreme Court. (In 1969 Justice Fortas resigned from the Supreme Court after further charges.) As a result, it was left to President Nixon to appoint Chief Justice Warren's successor.

President Nixon appointed, and the Senate quickly confirmed, Warren Earl Burger, a judge of the Court of Appeals for the District of Columbia, whose constitutional orientation, as reflected in his comments on and off the bench, is less liberal than that of Chief Justice Warren, especially in the area of the administration of criminal justice.

To replace Justice Fortas, President Nixon nominated Judge Clement Haynsworth, Jr., Chief Judge of the Court of Appeals for the Fourth Circuit, but in the face of objections by labor and civil rights leaders, and after allegations about his financial transactions, the Senate refused to confirm the appointment. Nevertheless, because of the advanced age of several of the sitting justices, it is probable that before the end of his first term President Nixon will be called on to make additional appointments to the Supreme Court. The Warren Court has come to an end.

It is difficult to summarize briefly all the significant constitutional developments of the last fifteen years during which Chief Justice Warren presided over the Supreme Court. But among other things the Supreme Court declared racial segregation in all its forms unconstitutional, enlarged the authority of Congress to legislate against racial discrimination, insisted upon the equal administration of justice, expanded the provisions of the Bill of Rights to apply to the actions of state and local officials, enlarged the scope for political speech and for the frank discussion of manners and morals, raised higher the wall between church and state, and insisted that legislative bodies be reapportioned to reflect equality among voters regardless of where they live.

The Warren Court's involvement in our political life is not unique. The Supreme Court has always been in the center of our major domestic political battles. And since interpretation of the Constitution is in the highest sense a political matter, that is, choosing among conflicting political values, the justices have frequently been under attack by those who differ with their decisions. But until the Warren Court the more usual pattern was for the Supreme Court to reflect conservative views and values, and thus the criticism came from those of liberal persuasion. Not so the Warren Court, for it has led the way in the battles against racial discrimination and in the extension of the areas of personal liberty. Its critics are those who believe that it has moved too quickly, opened too widely the opportunities for expression of political and social views, imposed too many restraints on police and prosecutors, and forced on the nation too vigorously its own ideas of how best to establish representative legislative bodies.

The never-ending process of developing our constitutional system continues. With what consequences remains to be seen. Prophecy with respect to the course of Supreme Court decision-making is always risky, but it seems unlikely that the general direction of the Warren Court will be reversed. More likely, the pace will be slower.

The Constitution
of the United States

The Preamble

We the People of the United States, in Order to form a more perfect Union, establish Justice, insure domestic Tranquility, provide for the common defence, promote the general Welfare, and secure the Blessings of Liberty to ourselves and our Posterity, do ordain and establish this Constitution for the United States of America.

The Preamble is the prologue of the Constitution. It proclaims the source of the Constitution's authority and the great ends to be accomplished under it.

From the Preamble we learn that the Constitution claims obedience, not simply because of its intrinsic excellence or the merit of its principles, but also because it is ordained and established by the people. "The government of the Union," said Chief Justice Marshall, ". . . is emphatically and truly, a government of the people. In form, and in substance, it emanates from them. Its powers are granted by them, and are to be exercised directly on them, and for their benefit." [1] The people are the masters of the Constitution—not the reverse.

Article I

The Legislative Article

Section 1

All legislative Powers herein granted shall be vested in a Congress of the United States,

It is significant that of the three branches of the national government the legislative branch is mentioned first. The framers of the Constitution desired "a government of laws and not of men," [2] and expected Congress, except in time of war or emergency, to be the central and directing organ of the government.

With one very important exception, Congress has no legislative powers except those "herein granted" by the Constitution. Powers not granted or powers that cannot reasonably be implied from the granted powers are denied to Congress and reserved to the states (see the Tenth Amendment). By way of contrast, the British Parliament has complete legislative powers over all matters.

The field of foreign relations provides the principal exception to the general rule. As "necessary concomitants of nationality," the Supreme Court has said that the national government would have full power with respect to the external relations of the United States, even if the subject were not mentioned in the Constitution. The power to acquire territory by discovery and occupation, the power to make international agreements that are not treaties in a constitutional sense, the power to expel undesirable aliens are not among the powers that are specifically granted by the Constitution to the national government; they are *powers inherent in its national character.* For the source and scope of such powers, one must turn to international law and practice, not to the Constitution. As a member of the society of nations, the United States has the same powers as any other nation in the field of external relations. [3]

Section 1

[continued] which shall consist of a Senate and House of Representatives.

By granting legislative powers to two distinct branches of Congress, a bicameral legislature was created, as contrasted with a single-chamber or unicameral legislature. Of the framers, only Benjamin Franklin favored a single-chamber legislature. The others felt that two chambers were needed in order that representation in one might be based on population, whereas in the other the states would be represented as states and hence equally. Also, it was thought, the two chambers would serve as a check upon each other and prevent the passage of ill-considered legislation. Bicameralism also conformed to the framers' general belief in balanced government, a government that would represent the interests of all parts of society. The House, it was thought, would reflect the attitudes of the popular or democratic elements, and the Senate would reflect the views of the aristocratic elements.

Section 2

1. The House of Representatives shall be composed of Members chosen every second Year

Some of the framers favored annual terms, believing that "where annual terms end, tyranny begins"; Madison and others favored a three-year term. They compromised on a two-year term. The House has several times proposed an amendment to extend the terms of its members to four years; the Senate has refused to concur, in part because of the senators' fears that their brethren in the House would be able, during the off-year elections, to run for the Senate without having to resign their House seats. In January 1964, President Johnson urged Congress to consider a four-year term amendment but with the stipulation that no member of the House could run for any other elective office while retaining his House seat. Nothing came from this effort, partly because of the belief that it is desirable to have a mid-term election as a check on the popularity of the presidential party, partly because of the fear that if the terms of House members always coincided with a presidential election, representatives would be too subject to presidential influence. Their elections would, therefore, become too submerged in presidential politics.

Section 2

1. [continued] by the People of the several States,

In the Great Compromise, the framers agreed that while senators were to be chosen by the state legislatures (see pages 15–16), representatives were to be elected by the people. In 1963, the Supreme Court, in *Wesberry* v. *Sanders,* gave this tenet additional significance by holding that a state legislature is also required to establish congressional districts consisting as nearly as practicable of an equal number of people. Said the Court, "One man's vote in congressional election is to be worth as much as another's." [4] Since then the Court has laid down very stringent standards to insure the application of the principle of one man, one vote: a state legislature in drawing congressional districts must justify any variance from precise mathematical equality among congressional districts by showing that it made a good-faith effort to come as close as possible to this mathematical equality. The desire to maintain specific interest orientations of particular districts, for example, urban or rural, is no justification for the lack of this mathematical equality.[5]

Section 2

1. [continued] and the Electors in each State shall have the qualifications requisite for Electors of the most numerous Branch of the State Legislature.

The word "electors" in this paragraph means voters. In the original Constitution, representatives were the only members of the national government to be chosen directly by the voters. In 1787, the qualifications for voting varied widely from state to state. In the Constitutional Convention, a majority of the delegates believed that the suffrage should be limited to those who possessed some kind of property; since they could not agree as to the amount or kind of property that should be required, they finally left it to the individual states to determine the qualifications of voters for representatives.

Subject to the Fourteenth, Fifteenth, Nineteenth, and Twenty-fourth Amendments, the individual states fix the suffrage qualifications. The right to vote in an election, including a primary, in which congressmen or presidential electors are chosen, is, nevertheless, a right conferred by the Constitution—in the above provision and in the Seventeenth Amendment—and the national government accordingly has power to protect the voter in the exercise of this right against private fraud or violence and against state discrimination (see page 43).[6]

Section 2

2. No Person shall be a Representative who shall not have attained to the Age of twenty five Years, and been seven Years a Citizen of the United States, and who shall not, when elected, be an Inhabitant of that State in which he shall be chosen.

In other words persons who are twenty-five years old or older, who have been citizens of the United States for seven years, and who are citizens of the state that they represent are constitutionally eligible for membership in the House of Representatives. Neither the House of Representatives nor the Congress nor any state legislature may add to these constitutional qualifications (see page 43). Persons who lack the qualifications at the time of election may nevertheless be admitted to the House (or to the Senate) as soon as they become qualified.

Although the Constitution does not require a member of Congress to reside in the district he represents, politically it is almost essential that he be a resident, since the voters normally refuse to elect a nonresident. By way of contrast, under British practice, members of Parliament are often elected to represent districts other than those in which they live. Our insistence upon local residence reflects and supports the prevalent belief that a representative's primary obligation is to his own district rather than to the country as a whole.

Section 2

3. Representatives and direct Taxes shall be apportioned among the several States which may be included within the Union, according to their respective Numbers,

After each decennial census (see below), Congress apportions representatives among the several states according to population. The requirement that direct taxes be apportioned among the states by population is of little significance, due to the Sixteenth Amendment (see page 161). Other than income taxes, Congress does not levy direct taxes.

Section 2

3. [continued] **which be determined by adding to the whole Number of free Persons, including those bound to Service for a Term of Years,** *and excluding Indians not taxed,* **three fifths of all other Persons.** *[emphasis added]*

The term "other persons" meant slaves. Because of the Thirteenth and Fourteenth Amendments, the emphasized words are obsolete.

Section 2

3. [continued] The actual Enumeration shall be made within three Years after the first Meeting of the Congress of the United States, and within every subsequent Term of ten Years, in such Manner as they shall by Law direct. The Number of Representatives shall not exceed one for every thirty Thousand.

This restriction on the size of the House of Representatives is now meaningless. With the 1970 census, our resident population (excluding the District of Columbia) is expected to be two hundred and three million. The constitutional limit would allow for 6,766 members (203 million divided by 30,000). Obviously, a chamber this size would be of little value; Congress, by law, has limited the number of representatives to 435, approximately one representative for every 471,000 persons.

Congress, after determining the number of representatives to which a state is entitled, has left it primarily up to the state legislatures to divide their respective states into congressional districts, each of which elects one representative. Prior to *Wesberry* v. *Sanders,* the state legislatures were under no constitutional restraints in drawing these districts. The party in control carved up the state in such a way that the voters of the opposing party were concentrated in as few districts as possible, a practice known as "gerrymandering." The *Wesberry* requirement that congressional districts be composed, as nearly as is praticable, of an equal number of people will make gerrymandering more difficult but not impossible.

Section 2

3. [continued] but each State shall have at Least one Representative

In the 1970 census, three states, Wyoming, Vermont, and Alaska, are likely to have fewer than 471,000 inhabitants; each, however, will be given its constitutional minimum.

Section 2

3. [continued] and until such enumeration shall be made, the State of New Hampshire shall be entitled to chuse three, Massachusetts eight, Rhode-Island and Providence Plantations one, Connecticut five, New-York six, New Jersey four, Pennsylvania eight, Delaware one, Maryland six, Virginia ten, North Carolina five, South Carolina five, and Georgia three.

This was a temporary provision until a census could be taken to determine the basis of representation. It has no significance today.

Section 2

4. When vacancies happen in the Representative from any State, the Executive Authority shall issue Writs of Election to fill such Vacancies.

The chief significance of this clause is the insurance that vacancies in the House of Representatives are not filled by gubernatorial appointment as is the case with vacancies in the Senate (see page 162). In many instances, when the next election is less than a year away, governors do not call special elections.

Section 2

5. The House of Representatives shall chuse their speaker and other Officers; and shall have the sole Power of Impeachment.

In form, the Speaker of the House is chosen by the House of Representatives; in fact, he is chosen by the majority party, or more precisely, by a majority of the majority party (see pages 49–51). The duties and powers of the Speaker and of the other officers are determined by the rules and practices of the House. Curiously enough, the Constitution does not specify that the Speaker must be a member of the House. The framers simply assumed that the examples of the British House of Commons and of the state assemblies would be followed.

"Power of impeachment" means the power to accuse and to bring formal charges against a person. It is a common error to think that the power to impeach means the power to remove a person from office; in fact, it is only the first step in that direction (see pages 41–42).

Section 3

1. The Senate of the United States shall be composed of two Senators from each State, chosen by the Legislature thereof, for six Years; and each Senator shall have one Vote. [emphasis added]

The emphasized portion of this paragraph has been superseded by the Seventeenth Amendment (see pages 161–162).

The framers adopted equal representation of all states in the Senate at the insistence of the smaller states, who made it their price for accepting the Constitution. As a result of this victory, the 243,000 inhabitants of Alaska and the 331,000 inhabitants of Wyoming have the same number of representatives in the Senate as the 19 million inhabitants of New York and the 21 million of California. It means that, on the one hand, the New England States, with 6 percent of the total population, have 12 percent of the Senate seats; the Mountain States, with only 4 per cent of the total population, have 16 percent. On the other hand, the Middle Atlantic States, with 19 percent of the total population have only 6 percent of the Senate seats; the East North Central States with 19 percent of the total population, have only 10 percent. These figures account for the disproportionate influence that the mining and agricultural interests, and especially the former, have sometimes exerted through the Senate upon legislation.

Section 3

2. Immediately after they shall be assembled in Consequence of the first Election, they shall be divided as equally as may be into three Classes. The Seats of the Senators of the first Class shall be vacated at the Expiration of the second Year, of the second Class at the Expiration of the fourth Year, and of the third Class at the Expiration of the sixth Year, so that one third may be chosen every second Year;

As a result of this original division of senators into three classes, the Senate has been a continuous body. Only one third of the senators' terms expire at the same time; hence at least two thirds of its members at any time have been members of the preceding Congress.

*2. [continued] and if Vacancies happen by Resignation, or oth-
erwise, during the Recess of the Legislature of any State, Executive thereof may make temporary Appointments until the
next Meeting of the Legislature, which shall then fill such Vacancies.*

This clause was modified by the Seventeenth Amendment, which provides for the direct election of senators (see pages 161–162).

*3. No Person shall be a Senator who shall not have attained to
the Age of thirty years, and been nine Years a Citizen of the
United States, and who shall not, when elected, be an Inhabitant of that State for which he shall be chosen.*

(See page 44).

*4. The Vice President of the United States shall be President
of the Senate, but shall have no Vote, unless they be equally
divided.*

The Vice President has much less control over the Senate than the
Speaker has over the House. For example, he must recognize senators in
the order in which they rise and ask for recognition, while the Speaker has
discretionary powers in recognizing members from the floor. These and
other differences grow out of congressional customs and usages; they do
not stem from the Constitution.

The first Vice President, John Adams, exercised his "casting vote"
some twenty times, a record that still stands.

*5. The Senate shall chuse their other Officers, and also a Pres-
ident pro tempore, in the Absence of the Vice President, or
when he shall exercise the Office of President of the United
States.*

The President pro tempore of the Senate is chosen by the majority
party. He is normally the member of the majority party with the longest
continuous service in the Senate. Unlike the Vice President, he can, being
a senator, vote on any matter before the Senate.

*6. The Senate shall have the sole Power to try all Impeach-
ments.*

When the House of Representatives impeaches a federal officer, he is tried before the Senate.

Section 3

6. [continued] When sitting for that Purpose, they shall be on Oath or Affirmation. When the President of the United States is tried, the Chief Justice shall preside: And no Person shall be convicted without the Concurrence of two thirds of the Members present.

The House has impeached twelve civil officers of the United States, of whom the Senate has convicted only four. Although Supreme Court Justice Samuel Chase and President Andrew Johnson were impeached (1802 and 1868), the Senate failed to sustain the charges against them; all those convicted by the Senate were judges of inferior federal courts.

Section 3

7. Judgment in Cases of Impeachment shall not extend further than to removal from Office, and disqualification to hold and enjoy any Office of honor, Trust or Profit under the United States: but the Party convicted shall nevertheless be liable and subject to Indictment, Trial, Judgment and Punishment, according to law.

(See page 83).

Section 4

1. The Times, Places and Manner of holding Elections for Senators and Representatives, shall be prescribed in each State by the Legislature thereof; but the Congress may at any time by Law make or alter such Regulations, except as to the Places of chusing Senators.

Congress has established the first Tuesday after the first Monday in November in the even-numbered years as the date for the election of senators and representatives, except when other times are prescribed by state constitutions. Now that Maine has amended its constitution to abandon its September election, all states hold these elections on the same day.

Congress requires that the district system be used for the election of representatives and that elections be by secret ballot. Also, Congress has placed a limit on the expenditures of candidates seeking election to Congress and has taken steps to prevent corrupt and fraudulent practices in connection with these elections. The Supreme Court has interpreted the word *elections* to include primaries and preprimaries in which candidates for the Senate and House are nominated, if such primaries effectively control the choice or are state regulated.[7] Congressional power as to times, places, and manner consequently extends to such primaries.

Until the Voting Rights Act of 1965, Congress used this paragraph of Section 4, Section 2 of this Article, and the Seventeenth Amendment as the basis for legislation designed to protect the right to vote, rather than resorting to the broader authority granted by the Fourteenth and Fifteenth Amendments. Federal judges were authorized to hear civil suits brought by persons deprived illegally of the right to vote in elections in which *federal* officers are chosen or against state officials who deprived persons of the right to vote in any election because of race.[8] Until the Civil Rights Act of 1957, the Department of Justice could only bring criminal prosecutions, a difficult and ineffective way to protect the right to vote. In 1957 it was permitted to initiate civil suits, since aggrieved individuals often lack the means to do so. Finally, with the Voting Rights Act of 1965, Congress elected a more comprehensive program to protect the rights of voters and based this legislation primarily on the authority given to it by the Fifteenth Amendment (see pages 159–161).

Section 4

2. The Congress shall assemble at least once in every Year, and such Meeting shall be on the first Monday in December, unless they shall by Law appoint a different Day.

The Twentieth Amendment has superseded this paragraph. (See page 164).

Section 5

1. Each House shall be the Judge of the Elections, Returns and Qualifications of its own Members,

Does this section authorize each chamber to add to the stipulated constitutional qualifications or does it merely authorize each house to determine if a particular member has these qualifications? Prior to 1969 both the House and the Senate had adopted the former construction, and on occasion each chamber had denied duly elected persons their seats because they were morally or politically objectionable to a majority of the respective chambers. For example, in 1900 the House refused to admit Brigham H. Roberts from Utah because he was a polygamist. These precedents, which spring in the first instance from the practice of the British Parliament and the early state legislatures, were relied on by the House of Representatives in 1967 when it excluded Adam Clayton Powell, Jr., because of his alleged financial misconduct. The Speaker ruled that since the question was whether Powell should be excluded rather than expelled (see below), only a majority was necessary, although in fact the vote on exclusion was passed by more than two thirds.

Powell and thirteen voters from his district asked the District Court of the District of Columbia for a declaratory judgment that the House had acted unconstitutionally and for an order requiring House officers to pay Powell his salary. Both the District Court and the Court of Appeals (Chief Justice Burger, then a sitting judge on the Court of Appeals) dismissed Powell's complaint, arguing that the question was not justiciable and that for the judges to rule would violate the doctrine of separation of powers.

By the time the case was before the Supreme Court, Powell had been reelected and admitted to Congress. Many observers felt that the Court would avoid handling such a politically ticklish issue by holding the issue to be moot, or that if it did accept the case, it would either rule that the issue was a "political question" (see page 29) or that the long historical practice of the Congress had settled the construction in favor of allowing each chamber to add to constitutional qualifications. But Chief Justice Warren, with only Justice Stewart dissenting, held that Section 5 merely authorizes the House to determine if its members meet the standing qualifications prescribed in the Constitution.[9] Since Congressman Powell met these qualifications, the House had been without power to exclude him from its membership. The Supreme Court, however, returned to the lower courts the determination of whether the Sergeant at Arms of the House might properly be ordered to release to Powell his back pay. If the lower court so decides (and it is sanctioned by the Supreme Court), and the House refuses to comply, a head-on clash between the Court and the Congress may still result.

Section 5
1. [continued] and a Majority of each [house] shall constitute a Quorum to do Business; but a smaller Number may adjourn from day to day, and may be authorized to compel the Attendance of absent Members, in such Manner, and under such Penalties as each House may provide.
2. Each House may determine the Rules of its Proceedings, punish its Members for disorderly Behaviour, and, with the Concurrence of two thirds, expel a Member.

Although it takes only a majority—that is, the majority of a quorum—to prevent a member-elect from being seated, it takes two thirds of a quorum to expel a member once he has been admitted to membership or "seated." Since congressmen are not liable to impeachment, expulsion by their respective chambers is the only way they may be unseated—except, of course, by defeat at the polls.

Section 5

3. Each House shall keep a Journal of its Proceedings, and from time to time publish the same, excepting such Parts as may in their Judgment require Secrecy; and the Yeas and Nays of the Members of either House on any question shall, at the Desire of one fifth of those Present, be entered on the Journal.

This is consistent with the belief that in a republic the proceedings of the legislature should be published except in unusual circumstances.

The *Journal* should not be confused with the *Congressional Record*. The *Journal* is the official record of congressional acts, resolutions, and votes, whereas the *Record* purports to be a report of what is *said* in each house. In fact, because of the practice of freely allowing members to "revise and extend their remarks," as well as to print articles, speeches, poems, and so on by nonmembers, much appears in the *Congressional Record* that was never said on the floors of Congress.

By the parliamentary device of resolving itself into a Committee of the Whole, the House of Representatives can avoid the constitutional necessity of a roll-call vote on the demand of one fifth of those present. On the other hand, when the House of Representatives is in session, a minority, by demanding a roll call, which takes between thirty and forty-five minutes, has a weapon to defend itself against a "steam-rolling" majority. But if Congress wished to use the mechanical devices that are available today, the roll could be taken in a fraction of this time.

Section 5

4. Neither House, during the Session of Congress, shall, without the Consent of the other, adjourn for more than three days, nor to any other Place than that in which the two Houses shall be sitting.

Section 6

1. The Senators and Representatives shall receive a Compensation for their Services, to be ascertained by Law, and paid out of the Treasury of the United States.

Although elected by the people of the states from congressional districts, congressmen must look to the national treasury for their compensation. During the struggle for ratification of the Constitution, many persons had objected to this provision because it permits congressmen to determine their own salaries. In practice, congressmen have been somewhat reluctant to increase their salaries or even to set them at a figure high enough to allow persons of moderate means to serve in Congress without financial embarrassment. The financial demands on a congressman are great; ordinarily he must maintain two residences and meet many political and social obligations. As of 1970, congressmen receive a yearly salary of $42,500 plus allowances for operation of their offices.

Section 6

1. [continued] They shall in all Cases, except Treason, Felony and Breach of the Peace, be privileged from Arrest during their Attendance at the Session of their respective Houses, and in going to and returning from the same;

Congressmen are granted this privilege to protect them from interference in the pursuit of their duties. They are not exempt from the obligations of the laws, from the jurisdiction of the courts, or from summons in civil cases. The exemption extends only to *arrest* for minor offenses while engaged in congressional business.

Section 6

1. [continued] and for any Speech or Debate in either House, they shall not be questioned in any other Place.

On the few occasions that the Supreme Court has construed this section, it has done so broadly. Congressmen are exempt from arrest, prosecution, or suit for anything they say on the floors of Congress or in committee, or in committee reports, regardless of how libelous, slanderous, or seditious it may be. What a defendant said or wrote as a congressman may not be introduced as evidence in any criminal prosecution nor may there be a judicial inquiry into his motives for making a speech on the floor of Congress.[10] And because of this clause, the Supreme Court in the Powell case, although permitting the suit to be entertained against congressional employees such as the Sergeant at Arms, ruled that it would be improper to join as parties to the suit the Speaker of the House and other congressional officials. It is the responsibility of each chamber to discipline its own members who abuse the privilege of unlimited right of speech, a responsibility that understandably the chambers have been loath to exercise.

Section 6

2. No Senator or Representative shall, during the Time for which he was elected, be appointed to any civil Office under the Authority of the United States, which shall have been created, or the Emoluments whereof shall have been increased during such time; and no Person holding any Office under the United States, shall be a Member of either House during his Continuance in Office.

A member of Congress may not serve in the executive branch of the government and retain his membership in Congress. This rule, which stems from the doctrine of separation of powers, contrasts sharply with the British system in which most high executive ministers are members of Parliament. But the rule does not prevent the appointment of congressmen as temporary representatives of the United States at international conferences. Senators frequently serve temporarily as a member of the United States delegation to the United Nations General Assembly. There is no constitutional prohibition against a congressman serving as a state officer, but many state constitutions prohibit such dual officeholding; in any case, the situation rarely arises since there seldom are enough offices to go around.

Section 7

1. All Bills for raising Revenue shall originate in the House of Representatives; but the Senate may propose or concur with Amendments as on other Bills.

This provision, which is based on the theory that the House is more directly responsive to the will of the people than the Senate, was inserted in the Constitution at the insistence of the more populous states in order to relate taxation to representation. It has not, however, kept the Senate from originating revenue measures in the guise of amending House bills, by striking out an entire measure except the title and the enacting clause. This paragraph, moreover, does not have the same significance that it had in 1787, when senators were chosen by state legislatures.

Section 7

2. Every Bill which shall have passed the House of Representatives and the Senate, shall, before it become a Law, be presented to the President of the United States; if he approve he shall sign it, but if not he shall return it, with his Objections to that House in which it shall have originated, who shall enter the Objections at large on their Journal and proceed to reconsider it. If after such Reconsideration two thirds of that House shall agree to pass the Bill, it shall be sent, together with the Objections, to the other House, by which it shall likewise be reconsidered, and if approved by two thirds of that House, it shall become a Law. But in all such Cases the Votes of both Houses shall be determined by yeas and Nays, and the Names of the Persons voting for and against the Bill shall be entered on the Journal of each House respectively. If any Bill shall not be returned by the President within ten Days (Sundays excepted) after it shall have been presented to him, the Same shall be a

Law, in like Manner as if he had signed it, unless the Congress
by their Adjournment prevent its Return, in which Case it shall
not be a Law.

Although the framers expected Congress to be the dominant branch
of the government, they did not wish it to be in a position to arrogate to
itself all powers. So they gave the President a qualified veto both to prevent Congress from overstepping its boundaries and to enable him to influence the actual course of legislation.

After a bill has been passed in *identical* form by both houses of Congress it is presented to the President, who can do one of three things:

First, he can sign the bill and it becomes the law of the land.

Second, he can return it to the house in which it originated, stating
the reasons for his disapproval. If the bill is then repassed by a two-thirds
vote of *both* houses, which means two thirds of a quorum of the members
thereof, it becomes law despite the President's veto. On the other hand, if
the bill does not secure the approval of two thirds of a quorum of the
members of *both* houses, the veto is sustained and the bill does not become
law.

Third, the President can refuse to sign the bill but can retain possession of it. It then becomes law at the end of ten days (excluding Sundays)
after its presentation to him *if Congress is still in session*. But if Congress
adjourns before the lapse of the ten days (excluding Sundays), the bill does
not become law, in which case it is a victim of what is known as a "pocket
veto." Congresses have occasionally remained in session until ten days
have elapsed in order to prevent the President from defeating their measures in this manner.

Unlike many state governors, the President cannot approve parts of a
bill and veto other parts; he must give his approval or disapproval to the
bill as a unit. Because the President does not have an "item veto," Congress has been able to get measures past the President by using "riders," a
term for provisions that are not germane to the main purpose of a bill. Riders are most effective when tacked on to appropriation bills, thus forcing
the President to accept them in order to secure funds for the operations of
the government.

Section 7

3. Every Order, Resolution, or Vote to which the Concurrence
of the Senate and House of Representatives may be necessary
(except on a question of Adjournment) shall be presented to
the President of the United States; and before the Same shall
take Effect, shall be approved by him, or being disapproved by
him, shall be repassed by two thirds of the Senate and House

*of Representatives, according to the Rules and Limitations pre-
scribed in the Case of a Bill.*

Despite the inclusive language of this section there are, in addition to questions of adjournment, certain orders, resolutions, and votes that require the concurrence of both houses but are not presented to the President.

When a constitutional amendment is proposed by a two-thirds vote in both houses of Congress—that is, by a vote of two thirds of a quorum thereof—it is submitted immediately for ratification without being sent to the President for his approval or disapproval. Congress does not exercise ordinary legislative powers when it proposes constitutional amendments, but it operates under the powers given it in Article V. This is a self-contained, complete statement of methods for amending the Constitution, and it omits the President from the amending procedure.

The second exception is the "concurrent resolution." This formerly was not legislation but, for the most part, merely gave expression to congressional sentiments or opinions. Recently, a more important use has been found for it in connection with laws delegating powers to the President. By stipulating in the original law that the powers delegated may be rescinded by "concurrent resolution," the President is denied the opportunity to use his veto and thus to require a two-thirds vote to withdraw powers that were granted him by a majority.

This use of the concurrent resolution has sometimes been criticized as an evasion of Article I, Section 7. At any rate, Congress will probably continue to use it in this fashion. The development of this practice is an excellent example of congressional constitutional interpretation.

Congressional Organization and Procedure: The Unwritten Constitution

The Constitution provides the barest outline of congressional organization and gives a partial description of how Congress operates. Other basic practices have developed over the last one hundred and seventy years. Of special importance are the role of political parties, the selection of committee leaders, and the rules governing debate.

Political Parties in Congress   The nature of the party system is as significant as the formal Constitution in determining how a governmental institution operates. The Soviet one-party system, for example, makes meaningless the formal constitutional discretion of the Soviet legislature. The constitutional structure of the English and French parliaments is much the same, yet the French multiparty system leads to a kind of legislature very different from the highly cohesive English two-party system.

If political parties are so important, why is our Constitution silent about their organization and operation? The Founding Fathers considered parties divisive and baleful influences. Although they knew that "factions," as they called parties, might develop, they hoped that the constitutional arrangements would curtail party influences and make it difficult for them to operate. To a considerable extent, they were successful. Parties have not been decisive organizations in determining the outcome of legislative struggles nor have they served as important agencies to coordinate the executive and legislative branches. They have, however, always played a role of some significance in the operation of Congress. Congressional candidates are nominated by parties, they run in elections as representatives of a party, and the majority party in each house "organizes" that chamber.

Prior to the opening of a Congress,* each party in each chamber holds an organizing meeting. (The Republicans call their meetings a conference, the term also used by Senate Democrats; House Democrats still keep the older name "caucus.") At these meetings, the parties nominate their candidates for the various congressional and party offices, the most important in the case of the representatives being the Speaker of the House and in the case of the senators, the Majority Leader. These party conferences also confirm the assignments of their own party members to the standing committees of the Congress (the formal appointment is made subsequently by the chamber); elect the floor leaders and their assistants, known as "whips"; and select policy committees to mold strategy during the coming sessions.

Each party may also hold conferences during the course of the sessions, but only the recommendations of the organizing conferences receive the united support of party members. All Democratic House members, for example, support their party's candidate for Speaker; all Republicans support their conference's candidate. Thus the party with the most members selects the Speaker and other House officers. The Vice President, who presides over the Senate, may belong to the minority party in the Senate, but the President pro tempore who presides in his absence is always a member of the majority party.

Despite attempts to build the parties into organizations to coordinate legislative actions within Congress (and between Congress and the President), the parties do not necessarily dominate or determine legislative policy. Senators from Wisconsin, to cite one example, are likely to support

---

* We have a new Congress every two years that inaugurates its first session in January of odd-numbered years. The second session meets the following January; unless the party line-up in the chamber has changed because of deaths, resignations, or special elections, the organization does not change.

legislation favorable to the dairy industry irrespective of party affiliation or of the desires of party leaders. On most votes, members of both parties can be found on both sides. Nevertheless, on many key issues, party affiliation is important. Parties also provide the primary organization in Congress for the development of legislative programs.

Selection of Committee Chairmen   The standing committees process bills, hold investigations, and recommend legislative action. They are composed of members of both parties, each party being represented in approximately the same ratio as its strength in the entire chamber. If the Republicans, for example, make up 60 percent of the membership of the Senate, then they hold 60 percent of the positions on most Senate committees. The majority party always controls the chairmanships.

The chairmen of the standing committees are influential leaders. By the rule of seniority, the member of the majority party who has had the longest continuous service on the committee becomes chairman. The senior member of the minority party is known as the "ranking" minority member. No matter how brilliant, experienced, or famous a freshman congressman is, his name is placed at the bottom of the committee list. He cannot become chairman until his party has a majority in the chamber and he has acquired more service on the committee than any other member of his party on the committee.

What is the effect of the rule of seniority? Areas where there is lively competition between two strong parties have less influence in Congress than the one-party (primarily rural) regions, where political interest is slight and there is a tendency to send the same man back to Congress election after election. When the Democrats control a chamber, Southerners hold many of the important committee chairmanships in that chamber. When the Republicans control, it is Republicans from the safe Republican regions who hold most of these important positions. Conflicts between congressional leaders and the White House often reflect this basic difference in constituencies. The congressional leaders tend to represent the values of people living in rural and small town regions—the one-party areas— but the President is more likely to reflect the values of the urban-based groups who were important in his election (see the Electoral College, pages 141–145).

Rules of Debate   With so many members and so many issues, the time of the House is carefully controlled. The House Rules Committee, except for certain privileged matters, normally stipulates the amount of time and the conditions under which the House may debate legislation (the Rules Committee recommends, but its recommendations are almost always accepted by the House). Representatives may be ruled out of order if their remarks are not pertinent to the topic at hand, and they speak subject to rigorously enforced time limits.

In the Senate, however, debate is practically unlimited. Once a senator gains the privilege of the floor, he can talk on any subject for as long as he can stay on his feet. This rule of unlimited debate permits a few determined senators to tie up the business of the Senate by filibustering— talking to delay or to prevent the Senate from voting. Senators who strongly object to a measure seldom have to engage in a filibuster. Merely by threatening to do so, they are normally able to deter the Senate leaders from attempting to bring the objectionable measure before the Senate for consideration.

Once a filibuster is begun, it is extremely difficult to stop. Under Senate Rule 22, it takes a two-thirds vote of the senators present and voting to bring debate to a close—to apply cloture or closure as it is called. Since 1917 when Rule 22 was adopted, the Senate has invoked cloture only eight times. However, southern senators, who used to be able to block civil rights bills by filibustering them to death, are now finding it more difficult to do so. Three times in recent years the Senate has used Rule 22 to choke off an anticivil rights filibuster. Nonetheless, the power to talk and talk and talk remains a significant weapon of senate minorities in forcing compromises and forestalling legislation.

Section 8

Enumeration of Congressional Powers

Section 8 enumerates the legislative powers granted to Congress. In interpreting these powers, we should never, as Chief Justice Marshall put it, forget that it is a *Constitution* we are reading, a Constitution that was "intended to endure for ages to come, and consequently to be adapted to the various *crises* of human affairs.[11] Furthermore, each separately enumerated grant should be read as if paragraph 18 of this section (see page 63) were a part of it.

Section 8
1. The Congress shall have Power to lay and collect Taxes, Duties, Imposts and Excises, to pay the Debts and provide for the common Defence and general Welfare of the United States;

This paragraph grants to Congress the important power of the purse. A word of caution—"the general welfare" clause is tied to the power to tax and to spend: There is no general power granted to Congress to legislate for the general welfare. But as we have noted in discussing federalism, as a result of the liberal construction of congressional powers and the demands of our times, there are no longer serious constitutional limits on the ability of Congress to do what it considers necessary and proper to promote the general welfare.

James Madison argued in vain that Congress could tax and spend only in order to carry out one of its other granted powers—that is, Congress could tax and spend to establish post offices and post roads [Section 8(7)], to regulate commerce with foreign nations [Section 8(3)], and so on. From the first, nevertheless, the power of Congress under this clause has been interpreted as being *in addition* to its other powers and, hence, as exercisable in its own right without reference to them. Today, Congress taxes and spends hundreds of millions of dollars every year to aid agriculture, education, and business; to alleviate conditions of unemployment; and to promote low-cost housing, despite the fact that none of these things is specifically within its other delegated powers.

Approximately seventeen percent of the money the states and local governments spend comes nowadays from the federal government. Congress normally places conditions on its grants: states are required to match some of the federal funds, create agencies that meet federal specifications to administer the programs, submit plans to federal officials, and allow federal inspection in order to insure compliance with federal standards. Through these conditional "grants-in-aid," Congress has been able to induce states to expand their welfare programs, to adopt merit systems in certain parts of their civil service, to secure uniform marking of nationally supported highways, to improve the training of the national guard, to operate programs on a nonsegregated basis, and so on.

It is difficult, and until recently impossible, to secure a judicial hearing on the constitutionality of a federal grant-in-aid. In 1923 the Supreme Court told Massachusetts that it lacked standing to challenge the constitutionality of a federal grant program because a state may not stand between the national government and the national government's own citizens.[12] At the same time the Supreme Court told a private taxpayer, Miss Frothingham, that her interest in avoiding an increase in tax liability did not give her sufficient standing to challenge the Maternity Act of 1921 on the grounds that Congress had invaded the legislative province of the states.[13] For twenty-five years these decisions were construed as an absolute bar to taxpayer suits challenging the constitutionality of federal expenditures. But in 1968 the Supreme Court in *Flast* v. *Cohen* modified the *Frothingham* decision by permitting federal taxpayers to challenge the constitutionality of those provisions of the Elementary and Secondary Act of 1965 that channel federal funds for instructional materials to religious and sectarian schools. The Establishment Clause (see page 108), Chief Justice Warren explained, operates as a specific constitutional limitation upon the exercise by Congress of the taxing and spending power. Unlike Miss Frothingham who had merely argued that Congress had exceeded its general authority, in

Flast v. *Cohen* the taxpayers contended that Congress had breached a specific limitation upon its taxing and spending authority. Here they had standing to raise the issue.[14]

Whether *Flast* v. *Cohen* will eventually lead to an overruling of *Frothingham* or be limited to taxpayer challenges under the Establishment Clause remains to be seen. The difference between the two cases is difficult to discern, and the line between permissible and impermissible taxpayer suits hard to explain. What the Court majority in *Flast* was apparently trying to establish was the right of taxpayers to challenge federal expenditures that arguably conflict with specific constitutional limitations, but not to allow taxpayers to challenge a federal expenditure merely because of a contention that the federal government is invading fields reserved to the states.

If Congress can spend for regulatory purposes, can it also tax for such purposes? Although the Supreme Court in the past has struck down ostensible tax laws because they regulated subjects reserved to the states,[15] today, if the measure is a tax on its face, judges are not likely to inquire into congressional motives or to set aside the tax because it is actually an attempt to regulate subjects reserved to the states. However, in recent years, the Supreme Court has carefully scrutinized congressional tax measures that conflict with specific rights secured by the Constitution. For example, Congress has attempted to regulate narcotics, gamblers, and dangerous weapons under the guise of elaborate tax laws. But, in order to comply with the federal tax laws, gamblers, narcotics peddlers, and sellers of dangerous weapons had to, in effect, produce evidence that they were engaging in illegal activity. Under these circumstances, the Court has ruled that the tax measures violated the guarantees against compelling persons to testify against themselves (see pages 125–128) and cannot be applied against persons who plead the Fifth Amendment.[16] Of course Congress can heavily tax activities—for example dangerous white phosphorus matches; the fact that the impact of the tax might make the activity uneconomic raises no constitutional problem.

Thus the power to tax and to spend has become one of the two major sources—the other is the power to regulate commerce (see pages 55–58)—of the so-called national police power. What is meant by "police power" is the power to regulate persons and property for the safety, health, and welfare of society. Congress has no general grant of police power, but it may use its delegated powers for police-power purposes.

Section 8

1. [continued] but all Duties, Imposts and Excises shall be uniform throughout the United States;

Despite the rule of constitutional interpretation that the Constitution never uses two words when one would do, the words *duty, impost,* and *excise* all overlap more or less. Technically, a "duty" is any monetary obligation to government; an "impost" is a tax on imports or exports; an "excise" is a tax imposed on the performance of an act, the engaging in an occupation, or the enjoyment of a privilege and also on the sale, use, or consumption of things—for example, liquor taxes, tobacco taxes, and taxes on the privilege of using the corporate form for doing business.

The uniformity requirement prevents, for example, the levying of a tax of three cents a pound on tobacco in New York and of four cents a pound in California.

Section 8

2. [In all subsequent paragraphs of Section 8 the words "The Congress shall have the power" are understood.] To borrow Money on the Credit of the United States;

Congress borrows money by authorizing the sale of government securities to banks, businesses, and private individuals. The most important forms of government securities are bonds, treasury certificates, and treasury notes.

Section 8

3. To regulate Commerce with foreign Nations, and among the several States, and with the Indian Tribes;

The "commerce" clause is another important peg upon which Congress has developed a national police power. It is also an excellent demonstration of the fact that the vague words and phrases of certain sections of the Constitution have enabled a document written in 1787 in the days of the oxcart to be adapted to the needs of modern industrial society.

"Commerce," in the sense of this clause, includes not only buying and selling (traffic), but all forms of commercial intercourse, of transportation, and of communication—even radio and television broadcasting. Congress' power extends to the commerce if it is carried on with foreign nations, with the Indian tribes, or *"affects* more states than one." The power of Congress over such commerce is the power to "regulate" it, that is, to *govern* it. In the words of Chief Justice Marshall in *Gibbons v. Ogden,* this power "is complete in itself, may be exercised to its utmost extent, and acknowledges no limitations other than are prescribed in the Constitution." [17]

Congress, therefore, is not obliged when regulating "commerce among the states" to consider the effect of its measures on matters that have been generally regulated by the states. Indeed, it may regulate intrastate activities (those within a state) when these substantially affect interstate or foreign commerce. And, although its measures are usually intended to benefit commerce, they are not required to do so. Congress may even prohibit or greatly restrict commerce in order to promote the national health, safety, and welfare, and for humanitarian purposes. From 1808, it proscribed the African slave trade. Many years later, it prohibited the transportation of lottery tickets between the states and, still later, the transportation of liquor into states having "dry laws." Since 1920, it has made it a federal crime to use the channels of interstate commerce for the shipment of stolen automobiles or impure foods or use these channels in the traffic of white slavery. Congress has also closed the channels of interstate commerce to goods of enterprises engaged in commerce or production for commerce that do not pay all employees minimum wages and overtime pay as prescribed by federal law.[18] To make this law effective, Congress has not only banned the interstate transportation of goods so produced but has also made it a federal offense to produce goods under such conditions when the goods are "intended" for sale in interstate commerce (Fair Labor Standards Act). To safeguard interstate commerce from interruption by strikes, Congress may regulate employer-employee relations in business and industries that "affect" such commerce and has done so (the Wagner and Taft-Hartley Acts).[19]

The 1964 Civil Rights Act forbidding discrimination because of race, religion, or national origin in places of public accommodation and employment is based on Congress' authority to regulate commerce among the states. As the Supreme Court said (*Heart of Atlanta Motel* v. *United States*), "Congress' action in removing the disruptive effect which it found racial discrimination has on interstate travel is not invalidated because Congress was also legislating against what it considers to be moral wrongs." [20] Congress may also extend its laws to a local place of public accommodation, since its power over interstate commerce extends to the regulation of local incidents that might have a substantial and harmful effect upon that commerce. Congress has authority to enact such laws because discrimination restricts the flow of interstate commerce, and because interstate commerce is being used to support the discrimination.

In 1969 the Supreme Court sustained the application of the Civil Rights Act to what Justice Black in dissent characterized as "this country people's recreation center, lying in what may be, so far as we know, a little 'sleepy hollow' between Arkansas hills miles away from any interstate highway" because the park leased its paddle boats from an Oklahoma company, its juke box was made outside of Arkansas and it played records manufactured outside the state; ingredients served in the snack bar were obtained from out-of-state sources, and as the Court majority speaking through Justice Brennan wrote, "it would be unrealistic to assume that none of the 100,000 patrons actually served by the Club each season was an interstate traveler." Justice Black did not question that Congress could bar racial discrimination under its powers stemming from the Fourteenth Amendment (see pages 157–159), but he felt the commerce clause should not be stretched "so as to give the Federal Government complete control over every little remote country place of recreation in every nook and cranny of every precinct and county in every one of the 50 states." But he dissented alone.[21] It is a measure of the scope of national authority under the commerce clause, and the present acceptance of its broad and liberal construction, that even opponents of federal civil rights legislation have concentrated their attack on the merits rather than on the constitutionality of such enactments.

From the commerce clause, Congress also derives its full powers over the "navigable waters of the United States," including the waters that may be made navigable by "reasonable improvements." These waters, the Supreme Court has said, "are subject to national planning and control"; the authority of Congress over them "is as broad as the needs of commerce." "Flood protection, watershed development, recovery of the cost of improvements through utilization of power are . . . parts of commerce control." [22]

The commerce clause is important, moreover, not only as a grant of power to Congress but also as a *restriction* on state power. In giving this power to the national government, the Constitution took it away from the states, at least in large part. Therefore, whenever a state, in professed exercise of its taxing power or police power, passes a law that materially affects interstate or foreign commerce, the question necessarily arises whether this is not really an unconstitutional regulation of foreign or interstate commerce. Of course, if the state law conflicts with a federal regulation, the federal regulation supersedes. Congress may specifically allow states to regulate certain aspects of interstate or foreign commerce, but in the silence of Congress, the Supreme Court determines whether the state regulation is permissible.

In the exercise of this great power, the Court has handed down hundreds of decisions (some of which involved vast commercial or financial interests); it has laid down scores of rules about which voluminous treatises have been written. There is, naturally, no space for such matters in a small book like this. The general nature of the Court's task can, however, be briefly stated: It is to weigh the *local* interest against the *general* commercial interest and then to give the right of way to the interest that the Court deems, all things considered, to be the more important one.

Out of the scores of hundreds of examples that might be given, here are a few: Arizona was not allowed to impose a fourteen passenger or sev-

enty freight car limit on interstate trains.[23] Arkansas could require interstate trains to carry a "full-crew" as defined by the state legislature.[24] Illinois could not require interstate trucks to be equipped with specific kinds
of contour mudguards.[25] Illinois could not require a mail order house that
owned no tangible property in Illinois, did not advertise in the state or
have salesmen located there, to collect a use tax from Illinois consumers
who purchased goods via the catalogues they received,[26] (but where firms
maintain local agents in the taxing state or have outlets, use taxes may be
collected). Alabama could collect a tax on traveling photographers.[27] On
the other hand, states may not levy taxes on "salesmen" from out of a state
who come into a state merely for the purpose of soliciting interstate orders.

There is certainly no field in which the Court's reviewing power has
been more valuable than this one. Although we have fifty state legislatures,
we have one national economic and industrial system—one prosperity.
Nor is there any field in which the Court has, on the whole, done better
work in maintaining the national authority "in full scope without unnecessary loss of local efficiency." [28] In interpreting the due process clause of
the Fourteenth Amendment, the Court has frequently been lured into
questionable positions by that will-o'-the-wisp word *liberty,* but commerce-clause cases are generally down-to-earth cases, well seasoned with
facts and figures.[29]

Section 8

*4. To establish an uniform Rule of Naturalization, and uniform
Laws on the subject of Bankruptcies throughout the United
States;*

"Naturalization" is the legal process by which a foreigner is admitted
to citizenship.[30] In view of the inherent power of any sovereign nation to
determine its own membership, the naturalization clause must today be
reckoned superfluous. By virtue of this same inherent power, moreover,
Congress has the right to say which foreigners may enter the United States
or its possessions, for what purposes, and on what conditions; it can provide for the removal, by administrative action, of aliens who are in the
country contrary to the laws.[31]

The main purpose of laws on the subject of "bankruptcies" is to enable debtors to obtain release from their obligations upon the surrender of
their property to their creditors. Thus are "the wholly broke made whole
again." Congress has passed several such laws, each successive one marking a wider application of the idea.

Section 8

*5. To coin Money, regulate the Value thereof, and of foreign
Coin, and fix the Standard of Weights and Measures;*

This power, in conjunction with the power to borrow money on the credit of the United States, gives Congress the authority to issue paper money and to make it legal tender for the payment of all debts.

Section 8

6. To provide for the Punishment of counterfeiting the Securities and current Coin of the United States;

It would seem that Congress has this power even without this clause (see paragraph 18, page 63).

Section 8

7. To establish Post Offices and post Roads;

This clause, combined with the power to regulate interstate commerce and to spend for the general welfare, permits Congress to subsidize airlines, railroads, and shipping companies and to grant money to the states for road building and maintenance. But the fact is that through its powers to tax and to spend for the general welfare, Congress could perform these same functions even in the absence of this grant. This too, then, is a superfluous clause.

Section 8

8. To promote the Progress of Science and useful Arts, by securing for limited Times to Authors and Inventors the exclusive Right to their respective Writings and Discoveries;

Congress has secured to authors, musicians, and artists the protection of copyrights and to inventors the protection of patents. Anyone who creates by his own skill, labor, and judgment an original book, periodical, lecture, play, musical composition, map, print, photograph, motion picture, or work of art may secure a copyright by sending two complete copies of the work together with the application and the fee—in most cases, six dollars—to the Copyright Office in the Library of Congress. The copyright gives to the author an exclusive right to his work for twenty-eight years, and it may be renewed for another twenty-eight years. It may also, like any other property right, be sold, assigned, licensed, or willed.

Persons who invent or discover any *new* and *useful* art, machine, manufacture, composition of matter, certain types of plants, and so on, may secure a patent from the Patent Office located in the Department of Commerce. A patent gives the patent holder the exclusive right to his invention or discovery for seventeen years and, like a copyright, may be sold, assigned, or willed. Litigation growing out of conflicting patents may be appealed to a special court—the Court of Customs and Patent Appeals in Washington, D.C.

Under this clause, Congress does not have power to protect trademarks, which are words, letters, or symbols used in connection with merchandise to point out the ownership and origin of the product; it does, however, have power under the commerce clause to protect trademarks used in interstate commerce. Trademarks that are registered with the Patent Office need not be original, but they must be distinctive. Registration of a trademark grants the right to its exclusive use in interstate commerce for twenty years with unlimited rights of renewal.

Section 8

9. To constitute Tribunals inferior to the supreme Court;

All federal courts, except the Supreme Court, rest exclusively on acts of Congress. Any court, except the Supreme Court, can be abolished by act of Congress.

Section 8

10. To define and punish Piracies and Felonies committed on the high Seas, and Offences against the Law of Nations;

Congress can make any crime under international law a crime under national law. In the past, this has not been important because international law has dealt chiefly with governments rather than individuals. Recent developments in the direction of placing *individuals* under the obligations of international law may give this paragraph unexpected importance.

Section 8

11. To declare War, grant Letters of Marque and Reprisal, and make Rules concerning Captures on Land and Water;

The purpose of this clause was to transfer to Congress a power that in Great Britain belonged to the King, or the executive branch. This purpose has not been realized. Especially because of his initiative in the direction of our foreign relations, the President has been primarily responsible for our participation in all our great wars; the part of Congress has been largely that of a rubber stamp (see page 77).

Letters of marque and reprisal formerly authorized private individuals to prey upon the shipping and property of enemy nations without being considered pirates. The Pact of Paris of 1856 bans this practice.

Section 8

12. To raise and support Armies,

Under conditions of total war this and the ensuing clause, plus the inherent powers of the national government in the field of foreign relations (see page 35), confer greater powers than the entire remainder of the Constitution. These include the power to draft men and materials for the armed forces; to establish price ceilings; to requisition property; to allocate and ration materials, to direct the production, marketing, and consumption of all products; and to do whatever is "necessary and proper" to further the successful prosecution of a war. In the words of the late Chief Justice Hughes, "The power to wage war is the power to wage war successfully." [32] One must have a wide-ranging imagination to comprehend the full scope of these powers. It was under these powers that Congress, in 1946, passed a law establishing the Atomic Energy Commission and giving it control of materials, plants, and information dealing with atomic energy—a statute that has been termed "the most remarkable exercise of governmental power" in the entire history of the country.

Section 8

12. [continued] but no Appropriation of Money to that Use [raise and support armies] shall be for a longer Term than two Years;

This limitation is to insure the dependence of the Army on Congress and is a reflection of the framers' belief in civilian supremacy and their fear of standing armies. Even this provision (and that discussed on page 77) did not assuage the fears of many who, like Thomas Jefferson, felt that standing armies were incompatible with free government. The framers, however, wisely avoided prohibiting the national government from maintaining an army. The democratic principle of civilian supremacy still retains its validity. It is illustrated, for example, by the fact that the President, a civilian elective official, is commander in chief of the Army, Navy, and Air Force.

Section 8

13. To provide and maintain a Navy;

The Navy was not thought to be a threat to liberty, and no limitations were placed on appropriations for it. Moreover, a two-year limitation would not be feasible, as the construction of naval vessels often takes longer than two years and appropriations have to be pledged in advance.

Inasmuch as the framers did not foresee the development of air power, the 1947 act of Congress creating the Air Force as an independent element of national military power rests on the general *inherent* power of the national government in the fields of foreign relations and national defense (see page 35).

14. To make Rules for the Government and Regulation of the land and naval Forces;

The power here conferred is, in wartime, shared by the President in his capacity as commander in chief. Congress' power under this section, like all its powers, is subject to specific constitutional limitations. Persons in the land and naval forces do not have precisely the same constitutional freedoms as do those not subject to military jurisdiction, but recently the Supreme Court has narrowed the definition of who is subject to the rules for the government and regulation of the land and naval forces (see page 124). So far, however, it has not severely restricted Congress' authority to make whatever rules it sees fit for those who are subject to military jurisdiction.

15. To provide for calling forth the Militia to execute the Laws of the Union, suppress Insurrections and repel Invasions;

From an early date, the President has been authorized by Congress to employ not only the state militias but also the armed forces of the United States against "combinations of persons too powerful to be dealt with" by the ordinary judicial processes.[33] Although in 1957 Congress repealed an 1866 statute specifically authorizing the President to use armed forces to enforce civil rights legislation, it left in effect older statutes that empower the President to use troops to enforce all federal laws and federal court orders when ordinary processes are inadequate. In recent years, both Presidents Eisenhower and Kennedy used their authority under these statutes to dispatch troops to break up combinations of persons who were interfering or threatening to interfere with the execution of federal court orders (see pages 83, 86). When the President calls the militia, now known as the National Guard, into federal service, he exercises the same control over it as he does over any unit of the armed forces of the United States.

In the exercise of these powers, the President may, in case of "necessity," declare "martial law." Of this, there are various degrees and kinds, the most extreme being that in which military courts temporarily take over the government of a region.[34]

16. To provide for organizing, arming, and disciplining, the Militia, and for governing such Part of them as may be employed in the Service of the United States, reserving to the States respectively, the Appointment of the Officers, and the Authority of training the Militia according to the discipline prescribed by Congress;

Congress and the states cooperate in the maintenance of the National Guard. Normally, it operates under the direction of the states, subject to provisions made by Congress. When called into the service of the United States, the National Guard becomes a part of the United States Military Forces and is subject to government by Congress and the President. When the National Guard is not in federal service, Congress can still exercise a considerable degree of control through conditions attached to grants of money to the states for the National Guard.

Section 8
17. To exercise exclusive Legislation in all Cases whatsoever, over such District (not exceeding ten Miles square) as may, by Cession of particular States, and the Acceptance of Congress, become the Seat of the Government of the United States, and to exercise like Authority over all Places purchased by the Consent of the Legislature of the State in which the Same shall be for the Erection of Forts, Magazines, Arsenals, dock-Yards, and other needful Buildings;—And

Although the Twenty-third Amendment grants citizens of the District of Columbia the right to vote in presidential elections, at the present time, Congress, which has complete governmental power over the District, has assumed to itself the responsibility for serving as the city council of the District. It spends a day every fortnight it is in session passing city ordinances. The laws are administered by a Commissioner who is known as the Mayor, an Assistant to the Commissioner, and a nine-member council, all of whom are appointed by the President with the consent of the Senate. The Commissioner prepares the budget for the District, which is submitted to Congress through the Bureau of the Budget. There is no constitutional reason why Congress could not allow the citizens of the District to elect their own officials, and it would make good sense both to improve congressional efficiency and to secure justice for the citizens of the District. The demands for a larger measure of home rule are becoming ever more insistent. Not too far below the surface and complicating the question of "home rule" is the fear of some southern congressmen that, because of the large number of Negroes now resident in the District, home rule would lead to a more drastic attack on the pattern of racial discrimination that still persists in the capital city of the United States.

Section 8
18. To make all Laws which shall be necessary and proper for carrying into Execution the foregoing Powers, and all other Powers vested by this Constitution in the Government of the United States, or in any Department or Officer thereof.

As is the case with the general welfare clause, this clause (variously known as the "necessary and proper clause," "elastic clause," and "coefficient clause") is subject to misunderstanding. Congress is not here granted the power to make all laws that shall be necessary and proper for any purpose whatsoever but only to make laws that shall be necessary and proper *in order to execute its enumerated powers or to execute powers vested by the Constitution in the President, the Senate, or the courts.*

As we have noted, in the famous case of *McCulloch* v. *Maryland,* Chief Justice Marshall construed the word *necessary* to mean convenient or useful and rejected the narrow interpretation, "indispensable." As an example: the authority to establish a Federal Reserve Banking System is not among the enumerated powers of Congress, but Congress can do so because it is a "necessary and proper" (that is, *convenient*) way of executing its powers to lay and collect taxes, to borrow money on the credit of the United States, and to regulate interstate commerce.

"Inherited" Powers: The Power to Investigate

In addition to specifically vested powers, each house of Congress enjoys important powers by inheritance, as it were, from the English Parliament and the early state legislatures. One important inherited power is that of conducting investigations in order to gather information needed to legislate, to propose constitutional amendments, or to perform other constitutional functions.[35] As a necessary adjunct to its investigating power, each house may subpoena witnesses and punish those who refuse to produce documents or answer questions. Each chamber may itself determine a witness' guilt and have that witness held in custody for as long as it is in session. In addition, Congress has made it a crime to refuse to answer pertinent questions or produce pertinent testimony, and the present practice is for the chamber to turn the recalcitrant witness over to the United States district attorney for prosecution before the courts.[36]

What, then, are the constitutional limits to Congress' investigating authority? Or to be more precise, what are the limits on the authority of Congress to compel persons to furnish materials or answer questions? Congress cannot use its investigatory power, any more than it can use its legislative power, to abridge the freedoms protected by the First Amendment. Yet the First Amendment does not restrict the authority to investigate to the same extent as it does restrict the authority to legislate. If Congress is not allowed to investigate, how can it determine if legislation is warranted? Despite the fact that the Supreme Court has warned Congress that the First Amendment does set boundaries to its investigatory authority, as yet a majority of the justices has never been mustered to sustain an actual claim that compelled testimony, even about political beliefs and activities, did in fact abridge rights secured by the First Amendment.

The doctrine of separation of powers also limits Congress' investigatory power. As the Supreme Court stated it, "The power to investigate must not be confused with any of the powers of law enforcement; those powers are assigned under our Constitution to the Executive and Judiciary." Congress "has no power to expose for the sake of exposure." [37] It may compel answers only if the information sought is needed by Congress in the pursuit of its legitimate business.

Since witnesses before congressional committees are not on trial in a formal sense, the committees are not required to give witnesses the same rights they would have in a court of law. But committees must comply with whatever procedural rules they chose to adopt.[38] In addition, witnesses have the right under the Fifth Amendment to refuse to answer questions if the answers would expose them to the risk of criminal prosecution. (See pages 125–128 for more extended comment on the protections against self-incrimination.)

By far the most important restraint on congressional investigations has been the Supreme Court's insistence on a strict construction of the federal law defining the offense of contempt of Congress. Contempt of Congress, as defined by the law, is the refusal to answer *pertinent* questions. Before the Supreme Court is willing to permit convictions it insists: (1) that the parent chamber has clearly authorized the committee to make the particular investigation. (In the case of investigations by committees of the House of Representatives, since neither the House nor its committees are continuing bodies, the authorization must occur during the term of Congress in which the investigation takes place); (2) that the committee has authorized the investigation; (3) that the committee has made clear to the witness the subject under investigation, the pertinency of the question to the subject, and why the committee has insisted that he answer it; (4) that the grand jury indictment has specified what subject was under committee investigation and which pertinent questions the defendant has been charged with refusing to answer.[39]

In short, despite the Supreme Court's warning to the Congress that it must exercise its investigatory authority within the confines of the Constitution, so far the Court has not placed any substantive restriction on the scope of congressional investigations; it has, however, insisted on scrupulous procedural compliance.

Section 9

Limitations on Congressional Powers

Whereas Section 8 enumerates the legislative powers of the national government, Section 9 limits them. Section 9 and Section 10 that restricts the powers of the state governments, were originally looked on as a kind of Bill of Rights.

Section 9
1. The Migration or Importation of such Persons as any of the States now existing shall think proper to admit, shall not be prohibited by the Congress prior to the Year one thousand eight hundred and eight, but a Tax or duty may be imposed on such Importation, not exceeding ten dollars for each Person.

This paragraph refers to the importation of slaves into the United States and is today of historical interest only.

Section 9
2. The Privilege of the Writ of Habeas Corpus shall not be suspended, unless when in Cases of Rebellion or Invasion the public Safety may require it.

One example of the writ of habeas corpus is an order issued by a court to an arresting officer requiring him to bring a specified person before the court and state why that person is being held in custody. If the arresting officer cannot justify the holding of the prisoner, the judge will order his release.

Although there is some doubt, it is now generally held that Congress is ordinarily the proper authority to order the suspension of the privilege of the writ in times of rebellion or invasion, subject to review by the courts. Nevertheless, in situations in which the President can validly declare martial law, he can also suspend the writ. The greater power includes the lesser (see page 62).

State courts may not inquire into the reasons persons are held under the authority of the United States; federal courts do have jurisdiction to determine if persons are being improperly held by federal or state authorities. The Supreme Court has instructed federal district judges to scrutinize with care the contentions of those who claim they are being imprisoned as the result of unconstitutional trials and federal court business has expanded tremendously under the habeas corpus jurisdiction.

Section 9
3. No Bill of Attainder or ex post facto Law shall be passed.

A bill of attainder is a legislative punishment. Congress determines what conduct shall be considered a crime, but no one may be punished until after a judicial trial. Two recent congressional enactments have run afoul of this constitutional limitation: a provision in an appropriation bill that three named federal employees should not receive any compensation from the federal treasury other than for military or jury services, unless reappointed to office by the President with the advice and consent of the Senate (*United States* v. *Lovett*);[40] a provision that no person who is or has been during the preceding five years a member of the Communist party should serve as an officer of a labor union (*United States* v. *Brown*).[41] In both cases, the Supreme Court held that to deprive people of employment is punishment; Congress lacks constitutional power to inflict such punishment upon named individuals or upon members of a particular political group.

An ex post facto law is a retroactive *criminal* law that works to the detriment of any individual—for example, a law making a particular act a crime when committed, or a law increasing the punishment for a crime after it was committed. The prohibition of ex post facto laws does not prevent the application of civil laws retroactively nor does it prevent the retroactive application of penal laws that work to the benefit of an accused, for example, a law decreasing a punishment.

Section 9

4. No Capitation, or other direct, Tax shall be laid, unless in Proportion to the Census or Enumeration herein before directed to be taken.

A capitation tax is a poll or head tax. The precise meaning of the term *direct* tax is today uncertain (see page 61).

Section 9

5. No Tax or Duty shall be laid on Articles exported from any State.

Although Congress cannot tax articles exported from states, it can, under its power to regulate commerce with foreign nations, prohibit these exports by such means as embargoes.

Section 9

6. No Preference shall be given by any Regulation of Commerce or Revenue to the Ports of one State over those of another: nor shall Vessels bound to, or from, one State, be obliged to enter, clear, or pay Duties in another.

By giving to Congress the power to regulate interstate and foreign commerce, the states were prevented from discriminating against the commerce of sister states (see pages 56–57). This section prevents Congress, in regulating such commerce, from discriminating against the trade of a single state or of a group of states.

Section 9

7. No Money shall be drawn from the Treasury, but in Consequence of Appropriations made by Law; and a regular State-

*ment and Account of the Receipts and Expenditures of all pub-
lic Money shall be published from time to time.*

It is this clause that, more than any other, gives Congress control over the acts of the other branches of government, the President, the courts, the military, and so on, since all depend on Congress for money to carry out their functions.

Section 9

*8. No Title of Nobility shall be granted by the United States:
And no Person holding any Office or Profit or Trust under them,
shall, without the Consent of the Congress, accept of any present, Emolument, Office, or Title, of any kind whatever, from
any King, Prince, or foreign State.*

Acquainted with the history of previous republican governments, and aware of the ability of foreign sovereigns to bribe and corrupt republican officials, the framers of the Constitution took precautions to prevent any foreign state from securing undue influence within the executive agencies of the national government.

Section 10

Limitations on States

*1. No State shall enter into any Treaty, Alliance, or Confedera-
tion; grant Letters of Marque and Reprisal;*

When the government of the United States was formed, the individual states lost their international personalities, if, in fact, they ever possessed them. Constitutionally the states can neither negotiate with foreign states nor have any direct relations with them. In short, the national government possesses a monopoly over the foreign affairs of the United States. The way in which states exercise their reserved powers, however, may affect our relations with other countries—for example, nations may be antagonized by state laws denying aliens certain rights. But states may not exercise their reserved powers in such a way as to intrude on the national government's exclusive right to deal with international affairs. For example, states traditionally regulate the distribution of estates, but these regulations must give way if they impair the effective exercise of the nation's foreign policy. As a result, the Supreme Court struck down a provision of an Oregon law that required a nonresident alien, before he would be allowed to inherent personal property, to prove that he would receive the benefit of the money without confiscation in whole or in part by his government. The Supreme Court held that, in order to apply this law, Oregon probate courts would be inquiring too deeply into questions of foreign policy and their decisions would adversely affect the exclusive power of the central government to deal with these foreign nations.[42]

Section 10

1. [continued] [No state shall] coin Money; emit Bills of Credit; make any Thing but gold and silver Coin a Tender in Payment of Debts; pass any Bill of Attainder, ex post facto Law, or Law impairing the Obligation of Contracts, or grant any Title of Nobility.

After the Revolution, the thirteen states, operating under the weak and ineffective Articles of Confederation, passed through a difficult period of readjustment as a result of the economic and political dislocations of the war's aftermath. Many citizens were in debt; the farmers who had speculated freely in land while prices were rising, were especially burdened. Property and debtor laws were extremely harsh. Defaulting debtors were thrown into jail and deprived of all their holdings. In many states, the legislatures, responsive to the pressure of the farmers, passed laws to alleviate the lot of debtors. Paper money was made legal tender for the payment of debts, bankruptcy laws were passed, and sometimes the courts were closed to creditors. These laws, in turn, aroused the creditor classes, who, feeling that their rights had been infringed, demanded action to put a stop to such "abuses" of power by the state legislatures. Creditors, in fact, were foremost among the groups that brought the Constitutional Convention about; the prevention of such interferences with private rights by the state legislatures was one of the major purposes of the Convention. As James Madison put the matter in a speech to his fellow delegates, meddlings with private rights by the state legislatures "were evils which had, more perhaps than anything else, produced this Convention." The paragraph above was the principal result of this concern.

The framers, when they spoke of "contracts" whose obligations could not be impaired by state law, had in mind the ordinary contracts between individuals, especially contracts of debt. However, the meaning of the word was early expanded by judicial interpretation to include contracts made by the states themselves, including franchises granted to corporations. As a result, the "obligation of contracts" clause became prior to the Civil War the most important defense of the rights of property in the Constitution. States were prevented from passing any law, whether in the interest of the public welfare or not, that might materially disturb rights secured by contract.[43] In the late 1830s, however, the Supreme Court began to restrict the application of the obligation of contracts clause; by the 1890s,[44] it had been established that all franchises should be narrowly construed in favor of the states and that all contracts implicitly recognized the general police power of the states to regulate property (including contract rights) for the public welfare. Today, the due process clauses of the Fifth and Fourteenth Amendments have largely replaced the contract clause as safeguards of the property right.

2. No State shall, without the Consent of the Congress, lay any Imposts or Duties on Imports or Exports, except what may be absolutely necessary for executing its inspection Laws: and the net Produce of all Duties and Imposts, laid by any State on Imports or Exports, shall be for the Use of the Treasury of the United States; and all such Laws shall be subject to the Revision and Controul of the Congress.

Without the express consent of Congress, but subject to congressional revision, states may levy an inspection tax on imports and exports. (Inspection laws are concerned with quantity and quality.) Congress, not the courts, decides whether or not the inspection tax is more than "what may be absolutely necessary for executing . . . inspection laws." With this minor exception, states may not tax imports or exports without the consent of Congress. Imports, goods brought into the country, may not be taxed by a state until they are sold, removed from the original package, or put to the use for which they were imported. Although goods transported from one state to another are not imports, they are protected against arbitrary state taxation by the interstate commerce clause (see pages 56–57).

3. No State shall, without the Consent of Congress, lay any Duty of Tonnage, keep Troops, or Ships of War in time of Peace, enter into any Agreement or Compact with another State, or with a foreign Power, or engage in War, unless actually invaded, or in such imminent Danger as will not admit of delay.

A duty of tonnage is a charge upon a vessel according to its tonnage for entering or leaving a port or navigating in public waters.

A state has the constitutional right, without the consent of Congress, to provide for and maintain a militia; it may not keep a standing army.

"Reciprocity statutes" are not compacts. Thus a Kentucky law granting certain privileges to out-of-state drivers of motor vehicles whose states grant Kentucky drivers the same privileges would not require the consent of Congress, nor would an agreement between neighboring states with respect to weight limitations on the public highways. On the other hand, the agreement between New York and New Jersey establishing the New York Port Authority for the governance of the New York harbor rests on congressional approval. It should be added that Congress may give its consent in advance, as it has done many times—for example, when it authorized states to make civil defense compacts which are to become effective sixty days after each agreement has been transmitted to Congress, unless Congress disapproves by concurrent resolution.

Article II

The Executive Article

Section 1
1. The executive Power shall be vested in a President of the United States of America.

What is the significance of the fact that the words *herein granted* that appear in the Legislative Article are omitted in the Executive Article? Does Section 1 confer "the executive power" on the President or does it merely designate the title of the man who is given certain specified duties by the rest of the Article?

Despite the decision of the Steel Seizure Case (see below), the more general view, and the one that conforms to presidential practices, is that this section does give the President a power that has never been defined or enumerated and, in fact, cannot be defined since its scope depends largely upon circumstances. Although not so broad, this executive power is akin to the prerogative formerly claimed by the English Crown to act for the public good "without the prescription of the law" and "sometimes even against it. . . ." [45] The President can issue proclamations of neutrality, remove executive officals from office, make executive agreements with foreign nations, and take emergency action to preserve the nation, although such powers are not specifically granted him by the Constitution.

During the Korean War, President Truman ordered the Secretary of Commerce to take temporary possession of the steel mills in order to avoid a strike that would disrupt production of steel desperately needed to produce the weapons of war. No law authorized this action. The Taft-Hartley Act gave the President the authority to seek an eighty-day court injunction against strikes that jeopardized the national safety, but the President refused to do so because the union had previously agreed to postpone the strike for a much longer period.

Where did the President secure his authority to order this seizure? From his power as chief executive and commander in chief, argued the attorneys for the government. But the steel companies challenged this contention and the Supreme Court held that the President had acted unconstitutionally.[46] Only Justice Black, however, clearly denied that the President had any general executive powers. Four other justices joined with him to reject the President's claim to act in this particular instance but did so because Congress had indicated by the Taft-Hartley Act that the President should not seize property to avert strikes. In the absence of this legislation, a different question would have been presented. Moreover, it is possible that if the justices had been convinced that the emergency action was absolutely necessary, they would not have interfered even in face of the Taft-Hartley Act. These conjectures are not susceptible of proof or documentation. When it is remembered that three justices agreed with the President and four limited their rulings to the particulars of the immediate case, the Steel Seizure Decision does not appear to undermine the general position that the President has the authority to act without prescription of law and, perhaps in desperate situations even against the law, to preserve the national safety, subject, however, to the peril of subsequent judicial reversal, of impeachment, or of political defeat.

Section 1
1. [continued] He shall hold his Office during the Term of four Years, and, together with the Vice President, chosen for the same term, be elected, as follows:

See also the Twenty-second Amendment (pages 167–168) and the Twenty-fifth Amendment (pages 170–172).

Section 1
2. Each state shall appoint, in such Manner as the Legislature thereof may direct, a Number of Electors, equal to the whole Number of Senators and Representatives to which the State may be entitled in the Congress: but no Senator or Representative, or Person holding an Office of Trust or Profit under the United States, shall be appointed an Elector.

At various times some state legislatures have directed the selection of electors by the legislature itself, by the voters in districts, by the voters of the entire state, and by a combination of these methods. At the present time except for Maine (see page 145) all electors in all states and in the District of Columbia are elected by the voters on a state-wide ticket.

In exercising this power, state legislatures are subject to all of the express constitutional commands: a legislature could not deny the right to vote for electors because of race or sex or devise a scheme that would give the voters in one part of the state more electoral votes than those in another district. A state may not adopt procedures for nominating electors that would make it impossible for minor parties to get their presidential electoral candidates on the ballot (see page 152),[47] or which would impose greater demands on those who live in populous areas than are placed on those who live in rural areas in order to secure a place on the ballot (see page 154).[48]

Section 1

3. [This paragraph has been superseded in its entirety by the Twelfth Amendment.] The Electors shall meet in their respective States, and vote by Ballot for two Persons, of whom one at least shall not be an Inhabitant of the same State with themselves. And they shall make a List of all the Persons voted for, and of the Number of Votes for each; which List they shall sign and certify, and transmit sealed to the Seat of the Government of the United States, directed to the President of the Senate. The President of the Senate shall, in the Presence of the Senate and House of Representatives, open all the Certificates, and the Votes shall then be counted. The Person having the greatest Number of Votes shall be the President, if such Number be a Majority of the whole Number of Electors appointed; and if there be more than one who have such Majority, and have an equal Number of Votes, then the House of Representatives shall immediately chuse by Ballot one of them for President; and if no Person have a Majority, then from the five highest on the List the said House shall in like Manner chuse the President. But in chusing the President, the Votes shall be taken by States, the Representation from each State having one Vote; A quorum for this Purpose shall consist of a Member or Members from two thirds of the States, and a Majority of all the States shall be necessary to a Choice. In every Case, after the Choice of the President, the Person having the greatest Number of Votes of the Electors shall be the Vice President. But if there should remain two or more who have equal Votes, the Senate shall chuse from them by Ballot the Vice President.

The framers of the Constitution had a great deal of difficulty in working out the procedures for selecting the President and the Vice President. Selection by Congress was rejected on the theory that it would make the President dependent on Congress and would violate the doctrine of separation of powers. Election by the state legislatures was rejected because of lack of confidence in the state bodies which "had betrayed a strong propensity to a variety of pernicious measures." [49] Direct popular election was rejected because the less populous states felt that the more populous states would always elect the President, and because most of the delegates were of the opinion that the extent of the country rendered "it impossible that the people can have the requisite capacity to judge of the respective pretensions of the Candidates." [50] So, for lack of something better, the framers devised the system set forth in Section 1 (3), which they expected would work in somewhat the following fashion: The several state legislatures would prescribe procedures to select the most eminent persons in the states—electors—who would then cast their electoral ballots for the two men they considered the most qualified to serve as President. When the votes of the electors of the various states were collected, the person with the most votes, provided they were a majority of those cast by the whole number of electors, was to be declared President; the person with the second highest vote was to be Vice President. It was expected that almost every elector would cast one vote for a candidate from his own state, and the votes would be so dispersed that often no person would have a majority. In this case, the House of Representatives, voting by states, would make the final selection from among the five candidates receiving the highest electoral vote.

But the framers reckoned without political parties, which by completely changing the operation of the electoral system, made the original provision for it unworkable. The failure became apparent in the election of 1800, when Jefferson and Burr tied in "the Electoral College" for first place. It was the first major breakdown of the constitutional system, and the Twelfth Amendment was needed to repair the breach (see page 141).

Section 1
4. The Congress may determine the Time of chusing the Electors, and the Day on which they shall give their Votes; which Day shall be the same throughout the United States.

Congress early designated the first Tuesday after the first Monday in November in presidential election years as the day for the selection of electors. Since electors are now pledged to cast their ballots for the candidates of their party (see pages 141–145), the November election in effect determines who will be the next President and Vice President. The electors do not give their votes, however, until the first Monday after the second Wednesday in December. On that date, the electors assemble at such place as their respective state legislatures direct (normally the state capitol), give their votes, and certify six lists, which are distributed as follows: one is sent by registered mail to the President of the Senate, two are delivered to the Secretary of State of their respective states, two are sent by registered mail to the Administrator of General Services, and one is delivered to the federal district judge of the district in which the electors have assembled. No chances are taken of losing these precious documents, which usually record a foregone certainty. Then in January (see the Twentieth Amendment, page 164) the President of the Senate, in the presence of the Senate and the House of Representatives (see the Twelfth Amendment, page 141), opens the certificates and the electoral vote is "counted"; the winners are formally proclaimed "elected." [51]

Section 1

5. No Person except a natural born Citizen, or a Citizen of the United States, at the time of the Adoption of this Constitution, shall be eligible to the Office of President;

This clause contains the only constitutional distinction between naturalized and natural-born citizens. When combined with the Fourteenth Amendment (see page 148), which confers equal constitutional protection on citizenship whether acquired by birth or naturalization, this clause supports the Supreme Court's decision in *Schneider* v. *Rusk* that Congress lacks power to make extended residence abroad ground for expatriation of naturalized but not of natural-born citizens (see page 149).[52]

Whether a person born abroad of American parents is a natural-born citizen within the meaning of this section has not yet been decided.

Section 1

5. [continued] neither shall any Person be eligible to that Office who shall not have attained to the Age of thirty five Years, and been fourteen Years a Resident within the United States.

The Twelfth Amendment states explicitly that the same qualifications are required for eligibility to the Vice Presidency.

Before the election of President Hoover, there was some question whether the fourteen-year residence requirement meant any fourteen years or fourteen consecutive years immediately prior to election. Although a legal resident, Hoover had been abroad a good part of the fourteen years immediately preceding his nomination. His election settled any doubts; the interpretation of this requirement came from the most authentic source —the same source that created the Constitution—the people.

Section 1

6. In Case of the Removal of the President from Office, or of his Death, Resignation, or Inability to discharge the Powers and Duties of the said Office, the Same shall devolve on the Vice President, and the Congress may by Law provide for the Case of Removal, Death, Resignation or Inability, both of the President and Vice President, declaring what Officer shall then act as President, and such Officer shall act accordingly, until the Disability be removed, or a President shall be elected.

This clause is supplemented by the Twenty-fifth Amendment (see pages 170–172). The Twenty-fifth Amendment confirms the precedent established by John Tyler when he succeeded to the Presidency on Harrison's death. He signed all state papers, "John Tyler, President of the United States": and established that upon the death or resignation of the President, the Vice President becomes President. In the event of the President's disability, the "powers and duties" of the Presidency devolve upon the Vice President; he serves only as Acting President.

If there is no Vice President, a contingency less likely to occur with the adoption of the Twenty-fifth Amendment, by act of Congress, the line of succession is the Speaker of the House, the President pro tempore of the Senate, the Secretary of State and on through the list of cabinet officers in the order in which their departments were created. No one, however, may act as President unless he possesses the constitutional qualifications of a President; cabinet members serve only until either a Speaker or a President pro tempore becomes qualified.

The Twenty-fifth Amendment provides procedures to determine who shall judge whether the President is unable to discharge his duties (see pages 170–172).

Section 1

7. The President shall, at stated Times, receive for his Services, a Compensation, which shall neither be encreased nor diminished during the Period for which he shall have been elected,

To preserve the President's independence, Congress is prohibited from increasing or diminishing his salary during the period for which he is elected.

Section 1

7. [continued] and he shall not receive within that Period any other Emolument from the United States, or any of them.

This provision was inserted to prevent the President's own state from compensating him and to ensure his independence of any state. He is totally dependent upon the federal government for his salary, which is now $200,000 per year. He also receives the use of the White House, free secretarial and executive assistance, and $90,000 annually for travel and official allowances.

Section 1

8. Before he enter on the Execution of his Office, he shall take the following Oath or Affirmation:—"I do solemnly swear (or affirm) that I will faithfully execute the Office of President of the United States, and will to the best of my Ability, preserve, protect and defend the Constitution of the United States."

The Chief Justice of the United States normally administers this oath of affirmation, but any judicial officer may do so. Calvin Coolidge's father, a justice of the peace, administered the oath to his son.

Section 2

1. The President shall be Commander in Chief of the Army and Navy of the United States, and of the Militia of the several States, when called into the actual Service of the United States;

A civilian, the President, is commander in chief of our armed forces. (Although the Air Force is, of course, not mentioned in the Constitution, the President's status as commander in chief of that branch of the armed forces is not in question.) This is another provision to insure civilian supremacy over the military.

Congress shares with the President his authority over the armed forces. It supplies the money and makes regulation for their governance. While it has the power to "declare war," the President is able to give orders to the Army, Navy, and Air Force that may lead to hostilities, as well as to direct our foreign relations to that end. President Polk, by sending troops into disputed territory, deliberately precipitated the Mexican War. President Truman ordered American forces to resist communist aggression in Korea; President Johnson used military power to intervene in Santo Domingo; Presidents Eisenhower, Kennedy, and Johnson ordered American forces into Vietnam, although before the major escalation of our military effort in Vietnam, President Johnson secured from the Congress a resolution supporting his action. An example of the President's power over the armed forces that had amusing rather than serious consequences occurred when President Theodore Roosevelt sent the Navy halfway around the world after Congress had threatened to withhold appropriations for a global tour. Congress was then presented with the choice of appropriating money to bring the fleet home or leaving it where it was.

Throughout our history, Congress has resisted the President's predominant role in controlling our military forces. The most recent illustration is the adoption by the Senate in June of 1969 of a resolution that a commitment to use armed forces to assist a foreign government should result only from affirmative action taken by the legislative and executive branches of the United States Government by means of a treaty, statute, or concurrent resolution of both Houses of Congress specifically providing for such commitment. This "sense of the Senate" resolution has little, if any, constitutional significance: it is an admonition to the President to consult with Congress, but he is under no constitutional obligation to do so. However, it reflects more important political restraints. As recent history well illustrates, the President runs a serious risk of defeat for himself and his party at the next election if he uses the armed forces, with or without congressional approval, as an instrument of foreign policy, and the result is a substantial number of American casualties over an extended period of time.

The President appoints all military officers with the consent of the Senate. He governs hostile territories subjugated by our armed forces until their disposition is determined by Congress or by treaty. As commander in chief, he has within his hands the ultimate decision on all matters of strategy.

His "war powers" are, however, vastly more than purely military ones. During the Civil War President Lincoln, as "a war measure" and without congressional authorization, declared all slaves in areas in rebellion to be "free" (Proclamation of Emancipation). Moreover, the President's powers as commander in chief are augmented by his "executive powers" and by such powers as Congress may delegate to him. Under the conditions of total war, when the distinction between soldier and civilian may be blurred and the entire nation in arms, the resulting "aggregate of powers" may be very great, although not unlimited. Outside the theater of war, the courts will review his acts. During the Second World War, President Roosevelt authorized the Army to create "defense zones" on the West Coast; under his order (supported by an act of Congress) 112,000 Japanese, two thirds of whom were citizens of the United States, were forced out of their homes and put in concentration camps. These measures were reviewed and sustained by the Supreme Court on the general ground of military necessity.[53] But the President's order establishing martial law in Hawaii after the attack on Pearl Harbor was held by the Court to have lacked such justification and, therefore, to have been illegal.[54]

Section 2

1. [continued] he [the President] may require the Opinion, in writing, of the principal Officer in each of the executive Departments, upon any Subject relating to the Duties of their respective Offices,

Although there is no mention of the Cabinet in the original Constitution, that body came into existence as early as 1793; from the beginning, the President's power over the heads of the major executive departments has extended beyond merely requiring written reports upon subjects relating to the duties of their respective offices. Cabinet members serve at the President's pleasure, and his control over their official acts is complete. The executive departments, and usually their duties, however, are created by law, and the money needed for their operation comes from Congress.

Section 2

1. [continued] and he shall have Power to grant Reprieves and Pardons for Offences against the United States, except in Cases of Impeachment.

A reprieve postpones punishment. A full pardon restores a man to his full civil rights and revives his legal status in other respects. The President can pardon before or after conviction or during the trial, but he cannot exempt anyone from the law. The President's pardoning power extends only to offenses against the United States, not those against the laws of the states.

Section 2

2. He shall have Power, by and with the Advice and Consent of the Senate, to make Treaties, provided two thirds of the Senators present concur;

The President, through the Secretary of State, is free to seek the advice of senatorial leaders, especially members of the Senate Committee on Foreign Relations. Nevertheless, the Senate has usually done very little advising. The President negotiates a treaty, and then presents it to the Senate for its approval. Prior to 1919, Senate consideration of treaties took place in "executive session," behind closed doors, unless the Senate specially ordered otherwise. The final step in the making of a treaty is its ratification, which is the President's act.

There are several explanations for the two-thirds vote requirement. The southern states were afraid that their northern sisters—who were in a majority—would negotiate trade conventions that would be disadvantageous to the South. They remembered that John Jay of New York, Secretary of Foreign Affairs under the Confederation, had proposed a treaty with Spain conceding the right to close the mouth of the Mississippi at New Orleans in return for concessions to northern merchants. The two-thirds rule gives sectional groups a veto upon such treaties. In addition to being international compacts, treaties are "supreme law of the land," so that their self-executing provisions are enforced by courts like any other law (see pages 100–102); this fact, too, is sometimes urged in favor of the two-thirds requirement.

Now that the United States takes a continuous part in international negotiations, the process of treaty-making has achieved considerable significance. At the same time, the two-thirds rule makes it possible for a few senators representing perhaps a minority of the electorate to block treaties desired by the majority, and many have suggested that ratification be by a simple majority of *both* houses of Congress. There are, however, some senators, who think that the treaty-making procedures should be made more difficult. Adherents to this view have proposed that in addition to the two-thirds requirement, the approval of both houses be required before a treaty shall operate as law. In point of fact, since the House of Representatives must approve any appropriations or any legislation necessary to carry out the terms of the treaty, it already enjoys considerable power in this area.

Securing a two-thirds vote of the Senate for treaty ratification has imposed obstacles to the adoption of programs, and it is not surprising that various ways have been devised to get around these obstacles. One is the joint resolution of Congress—an ordinary legislative procedure. Texas was annexed in this fashion after the Senate refused to do so by treaty. Another device is the executive agreement, of which there are two types: (1) Inasmuch as Congress and the President have cognate powers in the field of foreign affairs, it is constitutionally permissible for Congress to delegate to the President larger powers than would be allowable in domestic affairs. Thus, the President is often empowered by Congress to make executive agreements—for example, reciprocal tariff agreements. (2) As part of his undefined executive powers, growing out of his authority to appoint and receive diplomatic officials, and as the nation's official spokesman, the President has the power to negotiate agreements with foreign nations that do not require the consent of Congress. As long as these agreements are not countermanded by Congress they, like treaties, become "law of the land." It was once thought that executive agreements differed from treaties in that they were concerned with affairs of less importance; in fact, executive agreements have sometimes dealt with highly important matters —for example, in September 1940, President Roosevelt handed over to Great Britain fifty naval vessels in exchange for certain leases of military bases. Apparently the only certain distinction between a treaty and an executive agreement today is that a treaty requires confirmation by "two-thirds of the Senators present," while an executive agreement is not submitted to the Senate. Again we perceive how the Constitution has been developed by action taken under its provisions.[55]

Section 2
2. *[continued] and he [the President] shall nominate, and by*

and with the Advice and Consent of the Senate, shall appoint Ambassadors, other public Ministers and Consuls, Judges of the supreme Court, and all other Officers of the United States, whose Appointments are not herein otherwise provided for, and which shall be established by Law: but the Congress may by Law vest the Appointment of such inferior Officers, as they think proper, in the President alone, in the Courts of Law, or in the Heads of Departments.

Officers who are appointed by the President by and with the advice and consent of the Senate (only a majority vote is required) are known as "superior" or senatorial officers. Officers who can, if Congress permits, be appointed by the President alone, by the courts, or by heads of departments are known as "inferior" officers.

The Senate has normally refused to approve local federal appointments over the objection of the senator from the state in which the office is located, provided the senator is of the same party as the President. This practice, known as "senatorial courtesy," permits the senators to veto presidential appointments and gives them extensive control over federal patronage in their several states. Because of this custom, senators from the state in which the appointment is to be made are usually consulted by the President before he sends the appointments to the Senate for confirmation.

Section 2
3. The President shall have Power to fill up all Vacancies that may happen during the Recess of the Senate, by granting Commissions which shall expire at the End of their next Session.

The word "happen" here has come to mean "happen to exist." The clause, in this sense, allows the President to fill temporarily *any* vacancies while the Senate is recessed, no matter how or when they occurred.

Section 3
He shall from time to time give to the Congress Information of the State of the Union, and recommend to their Consideration such Measures as he shall judge necessary and expedient;

The opening address of the President at each annual session of Congress is known as the State of the Union Message. Washington and John Adams gave their addresses in person, but Jefferson sent his in writing. President Wilson revived the practice of personally delivering the speech.

At the beginning of each session, the President is now also required by law to send to Congress a budget message and an economic report. From time to time, he sends messages, addresses Congress on specific subjects, and makes recommendations for legislation. In this manner, he is able to focus national attention on national problems. As an extension of this practice, a great many bills, although formally intorduced by congressmen, actually originate in the executive departments.

Section 3

[continued] he may, on extraordinary Occasions, convene both Houses, or either of them,

Whenever the President thinks it necessary, he can call special sessions of Congress. Once in session, Congress has full powers. In contrast, more than half of the state legislatures, when called into special session, are limited to discussion and action on the particular matters laid before them by the governor.

The Senate has been called into special session by itself, while the House has never been. The reason for the difference is that the Senate has been summoned to ratify treaties and appointments, which it does without the concurrence of the House.

Section 3

[continued] and in Case of Disagreement between them, with Respect to the Time of Adjournment, he may adjourn them to such Time as he shall think proper;

The President has never been called upon to exercise this duty.

Section 3

[continued] he shall receive Ambassadors and other public Ministers;

The President is the only officer who can speak officially for the United States to foreign governments. Conversely, foreign governments may speak to the United States only through the President, usually via his agent, the Secretary of State. The President's power to receive ambassadors includes the power to recognize new states or governments.

The nature of the problems of foreign policy requires that the initiative and general direction be in the President's hands. The increasing importance of foreign relations during the last several decades accounts in no small part for the increasing power of the President in all fields.

Section 3

[continued] he shall take Care that the Laws be faithfully exe-
cuted, and shall Commission all the Officers of the United
States.

This clause, plus the undefined executive power clause, gives the President unrestricted power to remove all *executive* officers. He is charged with the duty of faithfully executing the laws and therefore must have control over those through whom he operates. This unlimitable removal power, however, does not extend to officers who have quasi-legislative or quasi-judicial functions conferred upon them by act of Congress, such as members of the Federal Trade Commission, the Interstate Commerce Commission, or the Atomic Energy Commission. The President has no authority to remove these officers except as given to him by Congress.[56]

As we have pointed out (see page 62), Congress very early authorized the President to use the armed forces when necessary to overcome combinations too powerful to be dealt with by the courts in the enforcement of the laws. Thus the President's duty to see that the laws are enforced is supported by his powers as commander in chief.

Section 4

The President, Vice President and all civil Officers of the
United States, shall be removed from Office on Impeachment
for, and Conviction of, Treason, Bribery, or other High Crimes
and Misdemeanors.

All civilian officers of the United States are liable to impeachment. Congressmen are not officers of the United States within the meaning of this section and can be removed from office only by a two-thirds vote of their respective houses.

The punishment for impeachment extends only to removal from office and disqualification from holding any office of profit or trust under the United States, but the impeached officer may be subjected to subsequent criminal proceedings (see page 42).

Jefferson attempted to turn the impeachment procedure into a device for political control. He felt that incompetent or politically objectionable officers, especially judicial officers, who had not committed a legal wrong should, nevertheless, be liable to impeachment and removal from office. He failed to get this interpretation accepted; unfitness and incompetence are not grounds for impeachment—the officer must be guilty of a legal wrong or something akin to one.

Article III

The Judicial Article

Section 1
The judicial Power of the United States, shall be vested in one supreme Court, and in such inferior Courts as the Congress may from time to time ordain and establish.

The Supreme Court is the only federal court that is definitely required by the Constitution. The Founding Fathers were purposely vague about the nature of the court system because they were unable to agree on the need for inferior federal courts. But the First Congress created such courts and they have always been part of our federal court system. Under present legislation, there are eighty-nine district courts, eleven courts of appeals, one Court of Claims, and one Court of Customs and Patent Appeals. All are inferior to the Supreme Court, all exercise the judicial power of the United States.

Congress has also established other courts—a Court of Military Justice, a district court in Puerto Rico, for example—as necessary and proper ways of carrying into execution certain of its legislative powers. Judges of these so-called legislative or "Article I" courts may be given nonjudicial duties and may be selected by other procedures and serve for other terms than those prescribed by the Constitution for judges of "Article III" courts who exercise the judicial power of the United States. Congress has stipulated fixed terms for judges of some legislative courts, giving them some nonjudicial duties; for other legislative courts, it has provided for life terms for their judges. It is often difficult to know whether a court has been created to exercise the judicial power of the United States under Article III or a legislative power of Congress under Article I. For example, prior to 1956, it was assumed that the United States Customs Court was an Article I court; in that year Congress declared it to be a court created under Article III. The Supreme Court has not ruled on the matter. It has, however, upheld a similar congressional declaration with respect to the Court of Claims and the Court of Customs and Patent Appeals.[57]

The Constitution merely prescribes the boundaries to the judicial power of the United States. Except for the original jurisdiction of the Supreme Court, no federal court has any power to hear any case unless Congress has conferred it.

Judicial power, the only kind of power that the constitutional courts may exercise, is the power to pronounce a judgment and carry it into effect between the parties to a "case," that is, a real and substantial controversy involving legal questions between persons having an actual or possible adverse interest. Before a person may invoke judicial power, he must have standing, that is, he must be able to show past or immediate threat to a legal right or show that he is in real jeopardy. A merely speculative or abstract interest is not sufficient to set the judicial power in motion. Unlike the International Court of Justice and some state courts, federal courts refuse to give advisory opinions. They may, nevertheless, render "declaratory judgments" on the respective legal rights of parties in order to head off litigation between them or to free one or both of them from uncertainty regarding their rights as, say, under an ambiguous contract; such judgments are binding on both parties.

Section 1

[continued] The Judges, both of the supreme and inferior Courts, shall hold their Offices during good Behavior, and shall, at stated Times, receive for their Services, a Compensation, which shall not be diminished during their Continuance in Office.

The Constitution provides for the appointment of judges by the President with the consent of the Senate, but it is silent about the size of the courts and the qualification of the judges. Today there are nine members of the Supreme Court; at various times the number has been six, seven, and ten. The number of judges serving on a district court or a court of appeals varies with the number and nature of the cases to be handled. Usually one judge hears a case in a district court, and three circuit judges hear cases in a court of appeals.

Although the Constitution here refers to members of both the Supreme Court and the inferior courts as judges, in Article I, Section 3, paragraph 6, it refers to the "Chief Justice." Since the Judiciary Act of 1789, members of the Supreme Court have always been referred to as "Justice" and more formally as "Mr. Justice." The Chief Justice is properly designated as the Chief Justice of the United States, not of the Supreme Court.

The term "good behavior" means virtually for life, since a federal judge can be removed from office only through the regular impeachment process. Interesting constitutional issues are presented by the action of the Judicial Council of the Tenth Circuit (the judges of the court of appeals). It ruled that a district judge was "unable or unwilling to discharge efficiently the duties of his office," and it issued an order directing him to take no action in any case or proceeding. In all probability the matter will be presented to the Supreme Court to determine if these proceedings conform to the constitutional mandate that judges are to hold office during good behavior and can be removed from office only through impeachment proceedings. The judge in question is still "in office," but he cannot act as a judge.

In order to insure the independence of the judiciary, Congress is prohibited from decreasing a judge's salary during his term in office, although (unlike the President's) it may be increased. The Supreme Court formerly held that income taxes could not be levied against the salaries of federal judges, but this decision was reversed in 1937. Judges now are protected only from decreases that are specifically directed at their compensation.

Section 2
1. The judicial Power shall extend to all Cases, in Law and Equity, arising under this Constitution, the Laws of the United States, and Treaties made, or which shall be made, under their Authority;—

This means that the judicial power of the federal courts may be extended by Congress to all cases in which it is necessary to interpret the Constitution, or some law or treaty of the United States, in order to dispose of the case. For example, if X is tried and convicted of murder under state law in a state court, he could still ask the United States Supreme Court to pass on his contention that his trial was not a fair one under the due process clause of the Fourteenth Amendment.

The distinction between cases in law and cases in equity is inherited from England. In the former, the party bringing the case usually asks for damages; in the latter, he usually asks for an injunction. The common law is supposed to compensate for injury already done, while equity tries to prevent the injury from occurring.

Section 2
1. [continued] to all Cases affecting Ambassadors, other public Ministers and Consuls;—

Since the national government is responsible for good relations between the United States and foreign governments, it was reasoned that cases affecting *foreign* public ministers should be within the judicial power of the United States. For the federal courts to assume jurisdiction, these officials must be materially affected by the case without necessarily being parties to it.

Section 2
1. [continued] to all Cases of admiralty and maritime Jurisdiction;—

This jurisdiction is concerned with ships and shipping. Under the English rule, it extended only to the high seas and those rivers in which the tide ebbed and flowed. Under the Constitution, however, such jurisdiction reaches all "navigable waters of the United States," whether or not subject to the ebb and flow of the tide.

Section 2

1. [continued] to Controversies to which the United States shall be a Party;—to Controversies between two or more States;—between a State and Citizens of another State;— [emphasis added]

The Eleventh Amendment modified the emphasized portion of this section.

Section 2

1. [continued] between Citizens of different States;—

The Supreme Court has held that Article III poses no obstacle to the legislative extension of federal jurisdiction, founded on diversity, so long as any two adverse parties are not co-citizens.[58] Corporations are considered citizens of the state of their incorporation. Congress has legislated that diversity of citizenship cases involving amounts of less than $10,000 shall not be entertained by the federal courts (although they may be brought there for other reasons—for example, under the antitrust or patent laws).

Section 2

1. [continued] between Citizens of the same State claiming Lands under Grants of different States, and

At the time of the adoption of the Constitution, many states had conflicting claims to western lands. Today this clause is unimportant.

Section 2

1. [continued] between a State, or the Citizens thereof, and foreign States, Citizens or Subjects.

This clause also was modified by the Eleventh Amendment.

In summary, the judicial power of the United States extends to the following cases in law and equity:

1. To those cases because of the *nature of the dispute:*
   a. Cases arising under the Constitution, under a federal law, or under a federal treaty.
   b. Cases arising under admiralty and maritime jurisdiction.
   c. Cases involving title to land that is claimed because of grants of two or more states.

2. To those cases because of the *parties to the dispute:*
   a. Cases in which the United States is a party.
   b. Cases in which a state is a party.
   c. Cases in which the parties are citizens of different states.
   d. Cases that affect foreign ambassadors, ministers, and consuls.

The mere fact that the Constitution grants power to the federal courts over certain types of cases does not, of itself, exclude state courts from exercising concurrent jurisdiction. But Congress is free to make the federal jurisdiction exclusive and has done so, for example, in the following cases: crimes against the United States; suits for penalties and forfeiture authorized by the laws of the United States; civil cases of admiralty and maritime jurisdiction; prize cases (cases arising out of the capture of enemy or abandoned property on the high seas); cases involving patent and copyright laws of the United States; cases arising under bankruptcy laws of the United States; cases to which a state is party (except between a state and its citizens or a state and citizens of another state or foreign country); and cases involving foreign ambassadors and other public ministers.

Within any state, there are two court systems—the state court system and the federal court system—neither of which is superior or inferior to the other. Over some matters both systems have jurisdiction, over others only the state courts, and over still others only the federal courts have jurisdiction. A dispute between two citizens of New York over the terms of a contract signed in New York would be within the exclusive jurisdiction of the New York courts. A suit involving more than $10,000 between citizens of different states would be within the jurisdiction of either the federal courts or the courts of the state in which the defendant is located. A suit arising under the Sherman Antitrust Act would be within the exclusive jurisdiction of the federal courts.

Section 2
2. In all Cases affecting Ambassadors, other public Ministers and Consuls, and those in which a State shall be Party, the supreme Court shall have original Jurisdiction. In all the other Cases before mentioned, the supreme Court shall have appellate Jurisdiction, both as to Law and Fact, with such Exceptions, and under such Regulations as the Congress shall make.

Original jurisdiction is the power to hear and decide cases in the first instance. Appellate jurisdiction is the power to hear and decide appeals from the decisions of lower courts. In all cases, except those mentioned above, the Supreme Court has only appellate jurisdiction and, furthermore, only such appellate jurisdiction as is specifically granted it by Congress. The completeness of the control by Congress of the Supreme Court's appellate jurisdiction is illustrated by the following case. In 1868, the Supreme Court announced that it would hear the appeal of a certain newspaper editor who had challenged the constitutionality of one of the Reconstruction acts. After the Court had heard the case argued and was still considering its decision, Congress passed a law that prevented the appeal of that type of case to the Supreme Court, which thereupon held that it had no power to decide the case. The result was that the Court was deprived of an opportunity to pass upon the constitutionality of the Reconstruction acts.[59]

Despite the great and increasing volume of federal litigation, the Supreme Court has been able to keep up with its work ("to clear its docket"), because Congress has given it the authority to select for review only the most important cases. There are certain types of cases, however, that the Supreme Court is under obligation to review when asked to do so by the proper party. For example:

1. Final judgments rendered by the highest state court to which the case could be carried in which a decision was made where there is drawn in question the validity of a treaty or statute of the United States, and the decision is against validity.

2. Final judgments rendered by the highest state court to which the case could be carried in which a decision was made where there is drawn in question the validity of a state statute on the ground of its being repugnant to the Constitution, treaties, or laws of the United States, and the decision is in favor of its validity.

3. Decisions of a United States court of appeals in which a state statute is held to be invalid as repugnant to the Constitution, treaties, or laws of the United States.

4. Decisions of federal district courts holding an act of Congress unconstitutional in any civil action to which the United States or one of its agencies or officers is a party.

5. Certain other decisions of district courts that require a three-judge district court—for example, injunctions restraining enforcement of state or federal law on the grounds of unconstitutionality, injunctions restraining the enforcement of an order of the Interstate Commerce Commission.

With the exception of these kinds of cases, which are said to go to the Supreme Court "on appeal," the Supreme Court has discretion whether or not it will review a case. It accepts, "on writ of certiorari," only those cases that it considers to be of sufficient public importance to merit its attention. The formal distinction between the discretionary "certiorari" and the mandatory "on appeal" procedures should not be given too much weight. The Supreme Court also dismisses many appeals "for want of a substantial federal question." In short, the Supreme Court has wide discretion in determining which cases it will review, whether the cases are presented to it by certiorari or by appeal.

Section 2
3. The Trial of all Crimes, except in Cases of Impeachment, shall be by Jury; and such Trial shall be held in the State where the said Crimes shall have been committed; but when not committed within any State, the Trial shall be at such Place or Places as the Congress may by Law have directed.

This section guarantees the right to a trial by jury to persons accused by the national government of a crime. (See also the Sixth Amendment.)

Section 3
1. Treason against the United States, shall consist only in levying War against them, or in adhering to their Enemies, giving them Aid and Comfort. No Person shall be convicted of Treason unless on the Testimony of two Witnesses to the same overt Act, or on Confession in open Court.

This section does not prevent Congress from making a capital crime of sedition—using force and violence short of war in opposition to the laws or conspiring to do so. It may be possible for an alien to commit treason against the United States because while within the boundaries of the United States he owes our government temporary allegiance.

No person may be convicted of treason on the basis of circumstantial evidence alone. The accused must make a confession in open court, or there must be two witnesses to the overt act, which act, either by itself or along with other evidence, convinces the jury of the defendant's guilt.[60]

Section 3
2. The Congress shall have Power to declare the Punishment of Treason, but no Attainder of Treason shall work Corruption of Blood, or Forfeiture except during the Life of the Person attainted.

In sixteenth- and seventeenth-century England "attainders of treason" worked "corruption of blood," thereby making it impossible for the traitor's family to inherit from him. Having been traitors themselves in rebelling against King George, the framers may have felt a certain tenderness for such unfortunates.

Article IV
Interstate Relations

Section 1
Full Faith and Credit shall be given in each State to the public Acts, Records, and judicial Proceedings of every other State. And the Congress may by general Laws prescribe the Manner in which such Acts, Records and Proceedings shall be proved, and the Effect thereof.

This clause applies especially to judicial decisions. Suppose that a Pennsylvania court awards X a $5000 judgment against Y, also a Pennsylvanian; after moving to New York, Y refuses to pay up. Thanks to the full faith and credit clause, X does not have to prove his case all over again and secure a new judgment against Y from the New York courts. The New York courts will give full faith and credit to the Pennsylvania judgment and in appropriate proceedings will enforce the judgment even if it is not one that the New York courts would have granted originally.

Or suppose that X, a New Yorker, while driving his car in New Jersey, injures Y or his property, and then returns to New York without doing anything about it. Following a certain procedure, Y may sue X in the New Jersey courts; if they decide in his favor, the New York courts will be obliged to aid Y in collecting the judgment in his favor— whether X appeared in the case or not.

How much faith and credit must a state give to a divorce decree granted by another state? Seldom have the judges been presented with a more vexatious question. The material question raised is that of "domicile." Each state has the power to regulate the marriage and divorce of its own residents. Clearly, a divorce granted by a state to two bona fide residents must be given full faith and credit by all the other states, although they might not themselves have granted the divorce for the grounds alleged. However, if a North Carolinian, for example, should go to Nevada and obtain a divorce after the six weeks necessary under Nevada law, his divorce, although valid in Nevada, is not necessarily one that the Constitution requires the North Carolina courts to recognize. The Supreme Court has ruled that under such circumstances the North Carolina courts refuse to recognize the Nevada decree on the ground that Nevada courts "lacked jurisdiction" to grant the divorce because the plaintiff in the eyes of North

Carolina had not acquired a bona fide "domicile" in Nevada.[61] If both parties to the divorce, however, make their appearance in the divorce-granting state and the issue of domicile is raised and decided, neither they nor their heirs can in any other court challenge the validity of the divorce on the ground that the state lacked jurisdiction. It is a rule of American jurisprudence, *res judicata,* that a person is entitled to his "day in court" and may not raise the issue again in an independent proceeding ("a collateral proceeding," as the lawyers call it).[62]

Section 2

1. The Citizens of each State shall be entitled to all Privileges and Immunities of Citizens in the several States.

A state must accord out-of-state citizens the same treatment as its own, but it is not required to give them special privileges. It therefore may not deny citizens of other states access to its courts or deny them the equal protection of its laws or tax them at discriminatory rates. Political rights, however, may be made to depend on residence, as also may the right to attend state-supported institutions. In a recent decision (see page 151) the Supreme Court held that a state could not distinguish between those who have resided in the state for less than a year and other residents for the purpose of establishing eligibility for welfare payments; it made a point of stating: "We imply no view of the validity of waiting period or residence requirements determining eligibility to vote, eligibility for tuition-free education, to obtain a license to practice a profession, to hunt or fish, and so forth. Such requirements may promote compelling state interests on the one hand, or, on the other, may not be penalties upon the exercise of the constitutional right to travel." [63] Now that the Court has opened these questions, the invitation to raise them in appropriately drawn lawsuits is likely to be accepted.

Section 2

2. A Person charged in any State with Treason, Felony, or other Crime, who shall flee from Justice, and be found in another State, shall on Demand of the executive Authority of the State from which he fled, be delivered up, to be removed to the State having Jurisdiction of the Crime.

This paragraph provides for what is known as "interstate rendition" or, more commonly, "extradition." Despite its positive language, there is no judicial method of compelling a state to extradite fugitives from justice. In a celebrated case of this kind several years ago, the governor of New Jersey refused to extradite a fugitive from a Georgia chain gang; Georgia was helpless. In most cases, however, escaped prisoners are returned, under an old act of Congress, to the states from which they fled by the governor of the state to which they fled. Furthermore Congress has made it a federal crime to travel in interstate or foreign commerce with the intent to avoid prosecution or confinement by a state for certain felonies.[64] Those who violate this law are to be brought back to the federal judicial district in which the original crime was alleged to have been committed, making it possible for federal officers to turn the fleeing felon over to state officials for prosecution or confinement.

Section 2

3. No Person held to Service or Labour in one State, under the Laws thereof, escaping into another, shall, in Consequence of any Law or Regulation therein, be discharged from such Service or Labour, but shall be delivered up on Claim of the Party to whom such Service or Labour may be due.

The Thirteenth Amendment, abolishing slavery, nullified this "Fugitive Slave" clause.

Section 3

1. New States may be admitted by the Congress into this Union;

The normal procedure is as follows: (1) a petition is filed by the inhabitants of a territory for admission to the Union; (2) a congressional resolution is approved by the President authorizing the inhabitants of the territory to draw up a constitution; (3) the proposed constitution is approved by a majority of both houses of Congress and by the President; and (4) the territory is admitted into the Union.

Although Congress and the President may withhold their approval of admission until the "state" complies with or agrees to certain conditions, once a state is admitted, it possesses the same political powers as the other states. For example, in 1910, President Taft vetoed legislation admitting Arizona to the Union because its proposed constitution permitted the voters to recall state judges. After deleting this clause, Arizona was admitted (in 1912) and promptly proceeded to restore the objectionable provision. Since the right to determine the method of selection, tenure, and removal of its own judges is a political power enjoyed by all states, Arizona's power in this respect could not be less than that of other states; the condition was unenforceable.

In other cases, such as the conditions relating to the public lands in the state, they may be enforced as contracts that do not detract from a state's political power. When admitted to the Union, Minnesota agreed, in return for certain public lands she received from the national government, not to tax land still owned in the state by the national government. This agreement the Court enforced.[65]

The Civil War conclusively settled the question of whether or not a state can constitutionally withdraw from the Union. In the words of the Supreme Court, ours is "an indestructible Union composed of indestructible States." [66]

Section 3
1. [continued] but no new State shall be formed or erected within the Jurisdiction of any other State; nor any State be formed by the Junction of two or more States, or Parts of States, without the Consent of the Legislatures of the States concerned as well as of the Congress.

Five states have been formed within the jurisdiction of other states with the consent of the legislatures concerned and of Congress: Vermont from New York in 1791, Kentucky from Virginia in 1792, Tennessee from North Carolina in 1796, Maine from Massachusetts in 1820, and West Virginia from Virginia in 1863. At the time Texas was admitted to the Union, Congress consented to the division of the state into five states if the Texas legislature should ever so wish.

Section 3
2. The Congress shall have Power to dispose of and make all needful Rules and Regulations respecting the Territory or other Property belonging to the United States; and nothing in this Constitution shall be so construed as to Prejudice any Claims of the United States, or of any particular State.

When Puerto Rico, the Philippines, and Hawaii were annexed, the question arose whether or not "the Constitution followed the flag." The chief difficulty sprang from the fact that the new territories had not been molded in the political and legal traditions of the Constitution. To apply all the provisions of the Constitution, for example, it would have necessitated in some areas, the trial of offenses by juries composed of illiterates. Yet, if the Constitution did not apply, would not the inhabitants be without any safeguards against arbitrary rule?

The Constitution did not offer a clear solution, but the Supreme Court met the problem by distinguishing between "fundamental" and "formal" parts of the Constitution and by holding that in "unincorporated territories," those that Congress has neither explicitly nor by implication made an integral part of the Union (presently all territories are unincorporated), only the fundamental provisions of the Constitution, those that guarantee fair trials, freedom of speech, and so on, applied, unless and until Congress provided otherwise.[67]

Section 4
The United States shall guarantee to every State in this Union a Republican Form of Government,

Although the Constitution does not define "a republican form of government," the framers undoubtedly meant a form that, as distinguished from aristocracy, monarchy, or direct democracy, rests on the consent of the people and operates through *representative* institutions. Since the Supreme Court has ruled that the determination of what is a republican form is a political question, interpretation of the clause belongs to Congress. So if Congress permits the senators and representatives of a particular state to take their seats in Congress, that state must be deemed to have "a republican form of government" within the meaning of the Constitution. For example, in 1902 Oregon adopted the "initiative" whereby its citizens are enabled to legislate directly without the intervention of the legislature. Simply stated, the initiative procedure calls for two steps: (1) securing signatures of a required number of voters to a petition calling for submission of a proposed law to the electorate; (2) submission of proposal to the voters in a general election. If approved by the voters, the proposal becomes law. A company that had been taxed under a law passed by the initiative procedure argued that it transgressed this constitutional provision; but the Court refused to intervene, holding that "violation of the . . . guaranty of a republican form of government . . . cannot be challenged in the courts.[68]

Section 4
[continued] and shall protect each of them against Invasion;

Invasion of a state by a foreign power would also be an invasion of the United States.

Section 4
[continued] and on Application of the Legislature, or of the Executive (when the Legislature cannot be convened) against domestic Violence.

Congress has delegated to the President the authority to send troops into a state to protect it from "domestic violence," on the request of the appropriate state authority. In 1842, there were two governments in Rhode Island, each of which claimed to be the legitimate one. When President Tyler indicated that he was prepared to send troops to defend one of these against the "domestic violence" of the other, he was at the same time determining which government was the legitimate one. The Supreme Court, in refusing to intervene, identified the question as "political" in nature.[69]

When the President finds it necessary, in order to enforce federal laws or federal judicial decrees or to preserve the property or "the peace of the United States," he may send federal law-enforcement agents or even troops to the scene of resistance. Under such circumstances, the President neither acts at the request of state officials nor by their leave. He does not need their consent and may act even against their wishes. Under such circumstances, he is not "ordering troops into a state" but enforcing the laws of the United States that cover the length and breadth of the land [70] (see pages 62–63 and 83).

Article V

The Amending Power

> *The Congress, whenever two thirds of both Houses shall deem it necessary, shall propose Amendments to this Constitution, or, on the Application of the Legislatures of two thirds of the several States, shall call a Convention for proposing Amendments, which, in either Case, shall be valid to all Intents and Purposes, as Part of this Constitution, when ratified by the Legislatures of three fourths of the several States, or by Conventions in three fourths thereof, as the one or the other Mode of Ratification may be proposed by the Congress;*

An amendment may be proposed by a two-thirds vote of *both* houses of Congress or by a national convention called by Congress on the application of the legislatures of two thirds of the states. All twenty-five of the amendments added to the Constitution so far were proposed by Congress.

We have not had a constitutional convention since 1787 and there are many unanswered questions about how such a convention might operate. How would delegates be chosen? Would each state have one vote within such a convention or as many votes as it has senators and representatives? What would be the power of the convention once assembled? If a convention is called into being, what is to keep it from acting as did the Constitutional Convention of 1787, which ignored the limitations imposed on it and assumed authority to determine how its own work would be ratified? Within what kind of time period must legislative petitions be collected in order for there to be the necessary two thirds? These and a host of other questions have lost their "academic quality" as the result of petitions to Congress by the legislatures of thirty-three states—one short of the necessary two thirds—to call a convention to consider amendments relating to the apportionment of state legislatures, or more precisely to propose amendments to reverse Supreme Court decisions requiring legislative bodies to be apportioned according to population. If the additional legislature should add its petition, Congress will be faced with deciding what to do. Not the least important of the questions to be answered is whether the petitions from all the states are valid: some of them are more than six years old and were put forward by legislatures that have since been reapportioned.

Several state legislatures have also adopted resolutions calling on Congress to propose an amendment that would permit the legislatures of two thirds of the states to propose amendments directly, without congressional approval, to the state legislatures. The adoption of such an amendment permitting an alteration in our Constitution without any action by an agency of the national government would fundamentally change the nature of federal-state relations. It would change what has become a union of people into a union of states. It would be a retreat in the direction of the Articles of Confederation. It is unlikely that Congress will propose or call a convention to propose such an amendment.

Proposed amendments must be ratified by the legislatures of three fourths of the states (all amendments except the Twenty-first were ratified by this method) or by special state conventions of three fourths of the states. Congress decides which method of ratification shall be used. When Congress proposed the Twenty-first Amendment repealing prohibition, it left each state to determine for itself the manner in which delegates to its ratifying convention should be chosen.

Although a state legislature, after voting against ratification, may change its mind and ratify, it may not withdraw a ratification once given. When three fourths of the states have ratified a proposed amendment, the Administrator of General Services, subject to the direction of Congress, promulgates the amendment as part of the Constitution.

To be effective, ratifications must happen within a reasonable time. Congress may determine in advance of state action what constitutes a "reasonable time." It has done so in the case of the last five amendments it proposed by stipulating when each was submitted that unless it were ratified within seven years it would not become part of the Constitution. In the absence of a congressionally established time limit, the courts will not determine what constitutes a "reasonable time." This is a political question that Congress must answer. Congress has authorized the Administrator of General Services to promulgate amendments when ratified by three fourths of the states; in the case of an amendment that is considered by Congress to have been before the states for more than a reasonable time, Congress could instruct the Administrator to cease counting state ratifications.

Many questions arising out of Article V are political questions; indeed, it is probable that the present Court would, if occasion arose, accept Justice Black's statement of a few years ago that "Congress, possessing exclusive power over the amending process, cannot be bound by and is under no duty to accept the pronouncements upon that exclusive power by this Court. . . ." [71]

Between 1789 and 1970 over 5000 amendments have been introduced in Congress, but only thirty have actually been proposed. Twenty-five of these have been ratified. Two of the rejected amendments were proposed along with the ten that were finally ratified as the Bill of Rights (see page 104). Another that was not ratified (1810) would have withdrawn citizenship from any person who accepted a title of nobility or who received without the consent of Congress an office or emolument from a foreign power. On the eve of the Civil War, Congress proposed an amendment that would have prohibited any amendment to the Constitution interfering with slavery in any of the states. In 1924, Congress proposed an amendment that would have given it the power to regulate child labor. Only twenty-eight states have ratified, no state having done so since 1937.

The formal amendatory procedures have been criticized as "undemocratic." One fourth of the states plus one state (which could be much less than one fourth of the people) could block amendments desired by a large majority of the country. It is also possible for amendments to be adopted without a direct expression of popular opinion. The latter criticism would be largely met were Congress to require ratification by state conventions called for that purpose rather than by state legislatures chosen to deal with other issues.

Other Methods of Constitutional Development

The Constitution, written before the industrial and democratic revolutions had made their impress on the nation, continues to be a living fundamental law for our powerful industrial democracy. Obviously, the Constitution has had to change as the nation changed. Although the framework is the same, fundamental alterations have been made in the operation of the government within that framework. The formal amending process has been relatively unimportant in this development; less formal, more subtle methods have been employed.

Congressional Elaboration   The framers were wise and humble men who doubted that they had either the moral right or the necessary wisdom to prescribe the details of how the nation should be governed for future generations. They knew that a rigid, detailed, and restrictive Constitution would have little chance to endure. They painted in broad strokes, made their grants of power general, and left to Congress the development of the structure of government by ordinary legislation. Congress determines the organization and functions of all executive officials subordinate to the President. It also determines the size, jurisdiction, and organization of the federal court system.

Judicial Interpretation   As we have already seen, the courts are the authoritative interpreters of the Constitution. The words of the Constitution are sufficiently broad to accommodate divergent interpretations. As conditions have changed, so have judicial interpretations of the Constitution. In the words of Woodrow Wilson, "The Supreme Court is a constitutional convention in continuous session." At one time the Supreme Court ruled that the national government could not regulate child labor.[72] Today the national government does so with the approval of the Supreme Court. The Supreme Court's response to a persistent public demand made formal amendment unnecessary.[73]

Presidential Practices   The President has great discretion in developing the nature and role of his office. There has been no change in his formal constitutional position, but the President participates in the making of legislative policy to an extent not anticipated by the Founding Fathers. With the growth of political parties, the President became a national party leader and an active participant in party battles. In response to crises, the Presidency has grown into the pivotal office of our national government.

Customs and Usages   The President's Cabinet and the local residence requirement for congressmen are examples of constitutional customs. A more significant example is the custom of presidential electors pledging themselves to support the candidates of their party, a practice that has transformed the electoral college into an automatic transmitter of the electorate's choice.

The Unwritten Constitution: Summary

We can see that surrounding the formal document are customs and usages, congressional statutes, judicial decisions, and presidential practices that supplement the written Constitution. These rules are sometimes called the "Unwritten Constitution." It has been primarily through the use of the informal methods of development and alterations in the "Unwritten Constitution" itself that our governmental system has grown. The Constitution was democratized by the extension of the suffrage within the states and by the extraconstitutional development of national political parties. The national government has been strengthened to meet the emergencies of a national economy and an interdependent world without fundamentally changing the written Constitution. In short, our Constitution provides for a living, organic, and growing governmental system.

> *[continued] Provided that no Amendment which may be made prior to the Year One thousand eight hundred and eight shall in any Manner affect the first and fourth Clauses in the Ninth Section of the first Article;*

This provision referred to the importation of slaves and possesses only historical interest today.

> *[continued] and [provided] that no State, without its Consent, shall be deprived of its equal Suffrage in the Senate.*

Some consider this provision unamendable, and others contend that there are ways in which even it can be changed. It could be repealed, they say, by amendment and then another amendment adopted by the regular procedure that would permit unequal representation in the Senate.

Article VI

The Supremacy Article

> *1. All Debts contracted and Engagements entered into, before the Adoption of this Constitution, shall be as valid against the United States under this Constitution, as under the Confederation.*

At the time of the Constitutional Convention, the securities and currency issued by the Confederation and the several states had depreciated in value. Later, Alexander Hamilton, Washington's brilliant Secretary of the Treasury, proposed that the national government assume the debts of the several states and pay in full the debts of the Confederation. Adoption of this proposal did much to strengthen the new Union—at a handsome profit to speculators in Confederation securities.

> *2. This Constitution, and the Laws of the United States which shall be made in Pursuance thereof; and all Treaties made, or which shall be made, under the authority of the United States, shall be the supreme Law of the Land; and the Judges in every State shall be bound thereby, any Thing in the Constitution or Laws of any State to the Contrary notwithstanding.*

This clause lays down one of the key principles of the Constitution. It makes federalism work. *The powers of the national government are limited, but within the field of its powers it is supreme, and the state courts are bound to uphold this supremacy.* Any provision of a state constitution or any state law is null and void if it conflicts with the Constitution, with a federal law passed in pursuance of the Constitution, or with a treaty made under the authority of the United States. To take a single example out of scores, in 1956, the Supreme Court held that a Pennsylvania law punishing the advocacy of sedition against the United States was unenforceable on the ground that it conflicted with a similar federal law.[74]

United States Treaty Power

Treaties are of two types, self-executing and nonself-executing. The former require no implementation by Congress to have internal application as supreme law of the land. If the President, with the consent of two thirds of the Senate, ratifies a self-executing treaty giving foreign nationals certain rights in return for reciprocal concessions for American nationals, the treaty is valid as internal law. It takes precedence over any conflicting state constitutions or laws. Nonself-executing treaties, while bringing into existence a binding international obligation, require action by Congress in the form of implementing legislation; this legislation becomes supreme law of the land, enforceable in the courts.

Treaties, like national laws, must conform to the national Constitution. A treaty or a law implementing a treaty that abridged First Amendment freedoms would be just as unconstitutional as a law that did the same thing. As Justice Black phrased it, "This Court has regularly and uniformly recognized the supremacy of the Constitution over a treaty." [75]

May the national government make treaties regulating matters that otherwise would be subject only to state regulation? In other words, does the fact that the national government is in internal matters restricted to its constitutional grants of authority mean that in making treaties it is also restricted to matters that it can regulate by law? These questions came to the Supreme Court in the famous case of *Missouri* v. *Holland* (1920). After Congress, in 1913, passed a law regulating the hunting of migratory birds, several district judges ruled that the law was unconstitutional because regulation of wild game was not among the powers delegated to the national government. Three years later, the United States became party to a treaty with Canada (via Great Britain) in which the national government promised to protect the birds that migrated between Canada and this country in return for a reciprocal promise by Canada. To fulfill the obligations of the United States under this treaty, Congress passed a law even more stringent than its 1913 enactment. This time the case went to the Supreme Court and Justice Holmes, speaking for a unanimous Court, said:

Acts of Congress are the supreme law of the land only when made in pursuance of the Constitution, while treaties are declared to be so when made under the authority of the United States. . . . We do not mean to imply that there are no qualifications to the treaty-making power; but they must be ascertained in a different way. It is obvious that there may be matters of sharpest exigency for the national well-being that an act of Congress could not deal with but that a treaty followed by such an act could. . . . The only question is whether it is forbidden by some invisible radiation from the general terms of the Tenth Amendment. We must consider what this country has become in deciding what that Amendment has reserved. . . . We see nothing in the Constitution that compels the Government to sit by while a food supply is cut off and the protectors of our forest and our crops are destroyed.[76]

Today, discussions of whether or not the treaty power is broader than the national lawmaking power have lost much of their significance. With the liberal construction of the national government's legislative powers, there are few subjects of national importance that Congress cannot directly regulate. Fears that the President and the Senate will use the treaty power to interfere with states' rights are hard to understand, for if there is ever such a desire, there are other and easier procedures to use to accomplish this goal. Nevertheless, in recent years, some senators have been urging, so far ineffectively, that the Constitution be amended to restrict the treaty power to the same dimensions as the lawmaking power.

3. The Senators and Representatives before mentioned, and the Members of the several State Legislatures, and all executive and judicial Officers, both of the United States and of the several States, shall be bound by Oath or Affirmation, to support this Constitution; but no religious Test shall ever be required as a Qualification to any Office or public Trust under the United States.

This clause makes it clear that the first allegiance of all Americans, including state officials, is to the national Constitution. If a state governor, for example, is ordered by his state constitution or legislature to perform an act that is contrary to the Constitution, his duty is nonetheless to comply with the national Constitution.

Article VII

Ratification of the Constitution

The Ratification of the Conventions of nine States, shall be sufficient for the Establishment of this Constitution between the States so ratifying the Same.

The Constitutional Convention was a revolutionary body. The delegates were representatives of the states acting in response to a call by the Congress of the Confederation. Since the Articles of Confederation could be amended only with the consent of all thirteen state legislatures, and since they created a "perpetual Union," Congress, when it called the Convention, had explicitly stated that no recommendations should be effective until approved by Congress and ratified in accordance with the terms of the Articles—that is, by all thirteen state legislatures. Nevertheless, the delegates to the Convention boldly assumed power to exceed their mandate and to propose an entirely new government that was to go into effect upon the ratification by specially chosen conventions of only nine of the thirteen states.

Done in Convention by the Unanimous Consent of the States present the Seventeenth Day of September in the Year of our Lord one thousand seven hundred and Eighty seven and of the Independence of the United States of America the Twelfth. In Witness whereof We have hereunto subscribed our Names,

(For a discussion of the signing of the Constitution see page 16).

Amendments to the Constitution

THE BILL OF RIGHTS

Much of the opposition to ratification of the Constitution stemmed from its lack of specific guarantees of certain fundamental rights. The Constitutional Convention failed to adopt such guarantees because they were thought to be unnecessary and dangerous—unnecessary because the Constitution itself prohibited bills of attainder, ex post facto laws, and suspension of the writ of habeas corpus except in times of public danger, and required trial by jury in federal criminal cases; dangerous because prohibitions might furnish an argument for claiming powers not granted the new government. Thus to forbid the national government to *abridge* freedom of the press might be thought to imply that it had the power to *regulate* the press if it could do so without abridging it. It was also urged that the protection of fundamental rights ultimately rested not on paper guarantees but in the hearts and minds of the nation's citizen.[1]

Despite these arguments, there was a general demand for a Bill of Rights; the Constitution was adopted with the understanding that the first business of the First Congress would be the consideration of amendments suitable for the purpose. Congress proposed twelve such amendments on September 25, 1789, ten of which were ratified and became part of the Constitution on December 15, 1791. The two that were not ratified prescribed the ratio of representation to population in the House of Representatives and prohibited any increase in congressmen's compensation until an election for representatives had intervened.

The Bill of Rights and the States

By 1789, most state constitutions contained a bill of rights. In general, people were confident that they had sufficient political power to prevent abuse of authority by state and local officials. But the national government was new, distant, and threatening: a Bill of Rights was added to the Constitution to restrict its powers. In *Barron* v. *Baltimore,* John Marshall confirmed the obvious: the Bill of Rights applies only to the national government, and it imposes no restraints on state and local authorities.[2]

The national government, however, responsive to a broadly based political community, did not prove to be as much a threat to civil liberties and civil rights as did state and local governments. Furthermore, the primary responsibility for the administration of justice vests in the states; the failure of the national Constitution to restrain state and local authorities left large segments of governmental activity without federal constitutional limitation. True, state constitutions contain most of the same guarantees as are found in the Bill of Rights; however, state judges, who alone have jurisdiction to construe their respective state constitutions, have seldom applied their state bill of rights so as to restrain state or local officials.

After the adoption of the Fourteenth Amendment, which does apply to state (and local) governments, the Supreme Court was urged to construe the amendment, especially its due process clause, as applying to the states the same limitations that the Bill of Rights applies to the national government. The Supreme Court did read the amendment to prevent state regulation of property in a manner that the justices thought to be unreasonable. The Court also brought within the scope of the due process clause a provision of the Bill of Rights forbidding the taking of private property without just compensation, but for decades it refused to go further.

Then, in 1923, in *Gitlow* v. *New York,* the Supreme Court took the momentous step of holding that the word "liberty" in the due process clause of the Fourteenth Amendment includes liberty of speech.[3] By the early 1940s, the Supreme Court had incorporated within the due process clause all the provisions of the First Amendment. In short, by construction of the Fourteenth Amendment, the major substantive restrictions that the Bill of Rights places on the national government in order to protect freedom of religion, speech, press, petition, and assembly were given national constitutional protection against abridgment by state and local authorities.

What of the other parts of the Bill of Rights? If the due process clause of the Fourteenth Amendment imposes on state governments the same limitations that the First Amendment places on the national government, why does not the rest of the Bill of Rights also come within the scope of the Fourteenth? For some time a persistent minority of the Supreme Court justices have so argued, that is, they would construe the due process clause of the Fourteenth Amendment to mean that the states should follow precisely the same procedures that the Bill of Rights requires of the national government. What national authorities cannot do because of the Bill of Rights, these justices contend, state authorities cannot do because of the due process clause of the Fourteenth Amendment. The Supreme Court still has not gone quite so far as to incorporate totally into the Fourteenth Amendment all the applicable provisions of the Bill of Rights, but it has come very close to doing so.

Until recently the official doctrine of the Court majority was the Doctrine of Selective Incorporation, or Selective Absorption, or, because it was explained by Justice Cardozo in *Palko* v. *Connecticut,* it is also known as the Palko Test.[4] According to this view the Fourteenth Amendment's due process clause does not prescribe any specific procedures for the administration of justice or for the execution of governmental affairs. Rather, it forbids states to adopt procedures that violate the standards of justice of the civilized world or to deprive people of rights fundamental to an ordered scheme of liberty. The application of this general standard of fundamental fairness resulted in the selective incorporation or absorption into the due process clause of some but not of all of the provisions of the Bill of Rights. The distinction between those incorporated and those not incorporated within due process was that the former provisions protect rights such as freedom of speech and the press, which are so fundamental as to be "implicit in the concept of ordered justice," whereas provisions in the latter category, such as that requiring indictment by grand jury which the Fifth Amendment prescribes for the national government, merely provide certain procedures that will secure justice, but these are not the only procedures that will do so. States could indict persons other than by grand jury and still do justice.

Beginning in the 1930s and accelerating after 1964, the Supreme Court selectively incorporated provision after provision of the Bill of Rights into the requirements of the due process clause of the Fourteenth Amendment. Moreover, in 1968 the Court majority revised the Palko Test to permit the incorporation of additional provisions: Instead of asking if a particular procedure is necessary in order to conform to the requirements of a civilized society, the Supreme Court now asks if it is considered fundamental for an Anglo-American regime of ordered liberty, with the emphasis on the American part of the regime. Using this standard, the Supreme Court ruled that trial by jury for serious offenses is essential for due process. The Court conceded that in some societies justice is secured without using juries (in England most criminal trials take place before judges without juries), but "in the American states, as in the federal judicial system . . . a general grant of jury trial for serious offenses is a fundamental right, essential for preventing miscarriages of justice and for assuring that fair trials are provided for all defendants." [5]

By 1970, for all practical purposes, the Bill of Rights has been incorporated into the Fourteenth Amendment. Today, except for the Second, Third, and Tenth Amendments, which are not applicable to the states, the Fourteenth Amendment imposes on states all the requirements that the Bill of Rights imposes on the national government *except* those calling for indictment for serious crimes by a grand jury and for trial by jury in all civil cases involving more than $20.

What does it mean to say that the Bill of Rights, or at least most of it, has been absorbed into the Fourteenth Amendment? It has three major consequences: the Supreme Court has jurisdiction to review cases involving the application of these provisions and to establish standards to guide the behavior of state and local as well as national authorities; the federal district judges, through habeas corpus petitions, have enlarged jurisdiction to hear complaints by persons alleging that they are being held contrary to the commands of the Constitution; Congress has the power to pass whatever laws are necessary and proper to implement constitutional guarantees.

The "nationalization" of the Bill of Rights has not, however, ended constitutional debate or resulted in each provision of the Bill of Rights being treated in the same fashion. The old battles are emerging in new forms. For example, the Supreme Court is now distinguishing between some "constitutional rights so basic to a fair trial that their infraction can never be treated as a harmless error," and on the other hand, "some constitutional errors which in the setting of a particular case are so unimportant and insignificant that they may consistent with the Federal Constitution, be deemed harmless, not requiring the automatic reversal of the conviction." Examples of the former are use of coerced confessions, denial of the right to counsel, lack of an impartial judge. An example of the latter might be passing comments by a prosecutor about a defendant's failure to take the stand. Such comment violates the right against self-incrimination, but if the state reviewing courts find that it was "harmless beyond a reasonable doubt," the Supreme Court might not insist on reversal.[6]

The Supreme Court has also distinguished among provisions in terms of whether its decisions incorporating them are to be applied prospectively or retroactively. For example, on May 20, 1968, the Supreme Court held for the first time that the Fourteenth Amendment requires states to try persons for serious crimes before juries, but it subsequently held that persons tried without benefit of juries before May 20, 1968, need not be retried. At the time of their original trials states were following the then authoritative construction of the Constitution, and it cannot be said that all convictions made in the absence of jury are so inherently unfair that they should be upset years after imposed.[7] The Court has ruled otherwise, however, with respect to other "incorporations," for example, after bringing the Sixth Amendment guarantee of the right to the assistance of counsel into the Fourteenth Amendment, the Supreme Court held that any person presently under sentence imposed without the assistance of counsel is entitled to a retrial even though at the time of his original trial the state was following the then authoritative construction of the Constitution. No trial held without the assistance of counsel, the Court has decided, can be considered fair.[8]

Whereas one of the major constitutional debates of the 1960s was whether all the provisions of the Bill of Rights should be incorporated into the due process clause of the Fourteenth Amendment, one of the major constitutional debates of the 1970s may well be whether the due process clause of the Fourteenth Amendment is confined to the specific provisions of the Bill of Rights. Justice Black, presently representing only a minority point of view, contends that unless the Bill of Rights specifically forbids authorities from doing something, they are free to do it. He is suspicious of a general standard of due process and of tests such as those of "fundamental fairness" which allow justices to roam at will "in their own notions of what policies outside the Bill of Rights are desirable and what are not."[9] The majority view, however, is that there are no superfluous words in the Constitution. The due process requirements of the Fifth and Fourteenth Amendments are additional limitations on national and state governments beyond those enumerated in the other provisions of·the Bill of Rights, and in addition to the specific rights listed in the Bill of Rights, the due process clauses protect other fundamental rights, such as the right of privacy (see page 138).

Amendment I

Religion, Speech, Assembly, and Petition

Congress shall make no law respecting an establishment of religion,

The First Amendment is directed specifically to Congress. The Fourteenth Amendment, as now interpreted, imposes the same restrictions on the states.

God is not mentioned in the Constitution, and the word *religion* occurs in only one other place—in the prohibition of any religious test as a qualification for office. The framers of the Constitution were not irreligious. Several of them came from states with established religions, but all probably agreed that religious matters ought not to fall to the jurisdiction of the national government.

Some have argued that the Establishment Clause does not forbid governmental support for religion but merely governmental favoritism toward a particular church. The Supreme Court has unequivocally rejected this narrow construction of the prohibitions of the Establishment Clause.[10] All levels of government must be completely neutral, neither aiding a particular religion nor all religions. But as Justice White has said, "the line between state neutrality to religion and state support of religion is not easy to locate. . . . The problem, like many problems in constitutional law, is one of degree." [11] The test fashioned by the Supreme Court to distinguish between forbidden involvements of the State with religion and those contracts which the Establishment Clause permits, focuses on the purpose and primary effect of the enactment. "To withstand the strictures of the Establishment Clause there must be a secular legislative purpose and a primary effect that neither advances nor inhibits religion." [12] In applying the Establishment Clause the absence of a coercive impact of an enactment makes no constitutional difference: Any governmental act that advances or inhibits religion exceeds the scope of power as circumscribed by the Constitution.

The Establishment Clause forbids states to introduce devotional exercises of any variety into the public school curriculum, including denominationally neutral prayers, devotional reading of the Bible, or recitation of the Lord's Prayer.[13] A state may not proscribe from its school curriculum the teaching of Darwin's theory of evolution because of "its supposed conflict with the Biblical account, literally read." [14] School authorities may not permit religious instructors to come into the public school buildings during the school day to provide religious instruction, even on a voluntary basis.[15] On the other hand, the Constitution does not prevent the study of the Bible or religion in public schools when presented as part of a secular program of education. And a 1952 decision permitting schools to release students from part of the compulsory school day in order to secure religious instruction, provided it takes place outside of the school building, has not been reversed despite what appears to be a conflict between the reasoning in support of this ruling and the since-proclaimed construction of the Establishment Clause.[16]

Laws requiring business establishments to close on Sunday have passed the Supreme Court's test: The Court majority reasoned that whatever the original purpose of these Sunday closing laws, now they have taken on a secular cast as a measure to promote family living by providing a common day of rest and recreation.[17] Also permissible is the use of tax funds to furnish textbooks, lunches, and transportation to pupils of parochial schools, along with similar benefactions to pupils of the public schools.[18] These holdings were based on the view that these programs are in the interest of promoting health, safety, and education of students, not in promoting their instruction in religion. The parochial school, in short, is regarded as a distributing agent for welfare services.

For decades governments have provided tax exemptions for property owned by churches or used for religious purposes, and public funds have been spent for chaplains for legislatures and the armed forces. The first case involving the constitutionality of tax exemptions for church-owned property is presently before the Court.

or prohibiting the free exercise thereof;

Since there can be no compulsion by law of any form of worship, and since the government recognizes neither orthodoxy nor heresy, everyone has an absolute right to believe whatever he wishes. A state may not compel a religious belief nor deny any person any right or privilege because of his beliefs or lack of them. Such things as religious oaths as a condition of public employment are unconstitutional.

Although carefully protected, the right to act in accordance with one's belief is not, and cannot be, absolute. Religion may not be used to justify action or refusal to act that is contrary to a nondiscriminatory law properly enacted to promote the public safety, morals, health, or general welfare of the community. No one has a right to refuse "to bear arms," * to refuse to pay taxes, to practice polygamy, or to invade the rights of others even in the name of religion. Persons may be required to comply with Sunday closing laws in the interest of providing a common day of rest and recreation even if Sunday is not their sabbath.[19] Parents may be compelled to have their children vaccinated as a condition for attending public schools, despite the fact that vaccination violates their religious beliefs.[20] The Supreme Court, however, will scrutinize closely laws that infringe on religious practices and insist upon some compelling public purposes. For example, the Supreme Court did not feel that a state's interest in promoting patriotism justified it in requiring public school pupils to salute the flag, which is to the Jehovah's Witnesses a symbol of the Evil One.[21] Nor would the Court permit a state to deny unemployment compensation to Sabbatarians who refused to accept positions requiring them to work on Saturday.[22] Nor may states require parents to send their children to public schools who wish to educate them in religious schools.[23]

* Congress exempts from military duty persons who by reason of religious belief are conscientiously opposed to participation in war. This privilege is one granted by Congress but not required by the Constitution.

or abridging the freedom of speech, or of the press;

The right of freedom of speech and press is essential to the preservation and operation of democracy, but even this right is not absolute. Anyone (except a congressman or the President) who slanders or libels another may be penalized. Furthermore, "obscene" speech is not entitled to constitutional protection nor are "fighting words," words that by their very utterance injure and provoke others to attack. Constitutional problems are involved, however, in the definition and determination of which speech is libelous, obscene, or considered as fighting words. The Supreme Court is suspicious of definitions that cast their net too wide. It carefully scrutinizes procedures used to apply these laws to preserve the maximum freedom against the sometimes overzealous police and prosecutors and those to whom these officials respond.[24]

Libel prosecutions have often been a favorite weapon to suppress criticism of governmental officials and to prevent discussion of public issues. In seventeenth-century England, for example, seditious libel was defined to include criticism of the king or his ministers, whether true or false, and the stirring up of public discontent. Under our Constitution, however, only statements deliberately made with a high degree of awareness of their probable falsity are outside the scope of constitutional protection. And in the case of public officials or public figures, it is not sufficient to sustain a conviction for libel merely to prove that the comments made about them are false. Before any person may be subject either to civil damages or criminal conviction because of comments made about a *public official,* there must be proof that the comments were made with "actual malice—that is, with knowledge that it was false or with reckless disregard of whether it was false or not." [25] The proof required to sustain a libel conviction against those who make comments about *public figures,* for example, football coaches and other prominent individuals, is only slightly less stringent: "highly unreasonable conduct constituting an extreme departure from the standards of investigation and reporting ordinarily adhered to by a responsible publisher." [26] Even private individuals who become involved in newsworthy matters, for example, robbery victims, may not collect damages against publishers under state statutes designed to protect persons from invasion of privacy or under libel laws (although there is no direct ruling on this) unless they can demonstrate that the publisher knew he was publishing "false materials or acted in reckless disregard for the truth." [27]

What of obscenity? The production or sale of obscene matter is not entitled to constitutional protection, although its mere possession cannot be made a crime.[28] The Supreme Court has had the same difficulty as has everybody else who has tried to define "obscenity." But the standard that appears to be emerging is that no material is to be considered constitutionally obscene unless three essential criteria are present: It must be established that (1) the average person applying contemporary community (national, not local) standards would judge the dominant theme of the materials, taken as a whole, to be an appeal to a prurient interest in sex; (2) the material is patently offensive because it affronts contemporary standards; and (3) the material is "utterly without redeeming social value." [29] A person may be punished, however, for suggestively promoting materials even if the materials considered apart from the manner of their sale could not be constitutionally adjudged obscene.[30] In short, so long as materials are discreetly promoted, governments must stay their hand against those who sell or publish for sale to adults all but hardcore pornography—itself difficult to define, but as Justice Stewart wrote, "I know it when I see it." [31]

What of the knowing sale of obscene materials to children or to teenagers? The Supreme Court has approved what is known as the "variable obscenity" doctrine, which in effect means that materials that could not be held to be constitutionally obscene if offered for sale to adults may be so considered if offered for sale to juveniles.[32] Even so, states are not free to define "juvenile obscenity" at will: they must adopt precise and clear standards.[33] So far the only law that has been approved by the Supreme Court is one that on its face comes very close to meeting the standard as applied to "adult obscenity," although the particular transaction involved was the sale of "girlie magazines" to teenagers, which if sold to adults would not be considered sufficient to sustain a conviction.

What about seditious speech, that is, advocacy of the use of violence as a political tactic or as a means to overthrow the government? Since World War I the Supreme Court has considered this question a number of times in a variety of contexts. In 1951 in *Dennis* v. *United States* the Supreme Court upheld the Smith Act, which makes it a crime to advocate violent overthrow of the government, as applied to the leaders of the Communist Party who were accused of conspiring to do so.[34] The Dennis decision was cited by the Court as good law as recently as 1969, but in an opinion that so "explained" the Dennis ruling as in effect to overrule it. Said the Supreme Court, "constitutional guarantees of free speech and free press do not permit a State to forbid or proscribe advocacy of the use of force or of law violation except where such advocacy is directed to inciting or producing imminent lawless action and is likely to incite or produce such action. . . . The mere abstract teaching . . . of the moral propriety or even moral necessity for a resort to force and violence is not the same as preparing a group for violent action and steeling it to such action. . . . A statute which fails to draw this distinction impermissibly intrudes upon the freedoms guaranteed by the First and Fourteenth Amendments." [35]

The Supreme Court has elaborated a whole series of doctrines to measure the constitutionality of laws that appear to restrict freedom of expression. The Court requires a state to demonstrate a very compelling interest before it will be allowed to place any restraints on freedom of expression. Even indirectly, and even if the state can show a legitimate and compelling justification for its enactment, it must adopt measures to accomplish these goals which do not have an undue impact on First Amendment freedoms. Furthermore, broadly drawn regulations that have a "chilling effect upon First Amendment rights" may well be declared unconstitutional on their face without waiting for their particular enforcement. To illustrate from a substantial number of decisions adverse to state action: Louisiana was enjoined from enforcing its Subversive Activities and Communist Control Law because of its sweeping, vague, and overbroad terms; [36] New York's attempts to ban "sacrilegious movies" and publications of "criminal deeds of bloodshed or lust . . . so massed as to become vehicles for inciting violent and depraved crimes" were declared unconstitutional because no one could know what was or was not allowed; [37] the Board of Education of Will County, Illinois, acted unconstitutionally when it fired a teacher for publishing a letter in a local paper critical of the board, even conceding that the letter contained information that was false and that the board had authority to regulate the flow of communications between teachers and the board; [38] Arkansas could not inquire into the qualifications of its teachers in such a way as to impose restraints on their rights to express political convictions; [39] the Georgia Legislature violated the Constitution when it denied a seat to a duly elected member because of his comments critical of the American participation in the Vietnam War.[40]

In summary, the Warren Court has come very close to the view that "pure speech" unconnected with action is constitutionally protected from governmental regulation.

When speech becomes bracketed with action, it may lose its constitutional immunity. "We cannot accept the view," wrote Chief Justice Warren, "that an apparently limitless variety of conduct can be labeled speech whenever the person engaged in the conduct intends thereby to express an idea." [41] Even so the "Court has repeatedly warned States and governmental units that they cannot regulate conduct connected with [First Amendment freedoms] through the use of sweeping, dragnet statutes that may, because of vagueness, jeopardize these freedoms. . . . [However the Court has been] careful to point out that the Constitution does not bar enactment of laws regulating conduct, even though connected with speech, press, assembly, and petition, if such laws specifically bar only the conduct deemed obnoxious and are carefully and narrowly aimed at that forbidden conduct." [42]

The line, of course, between speech and conduct is not easy to draw. A majority of the justices, after carefully distinguishing between questions such as length of skirts, type of clothing, hair style, deportment, group demonstrations, held that school authorities had violated the Constitution when they suspended two students who had defied their principal by quietly and passively wearing black armbands to school to protest the Vietnam war. Justice Black, long a champion of free speech, wrote a vigorous dissent, "I think . . . . that the armbands did exactly what the elected school officials and principal foresaw they would, that is, took the students' minds off their class work. . . . One does not need to be a prophet or the son of a prophet to know that after the Court's holding today that some students . . . will be ready, able, and willing to defy their teachers on practically all orders. . . . [G]roups of students all over the land are already running loose, conducting break-ins, sit-ins, lie-ins, and smash-ins." [43] The Supreme Court had less difficulty in unanimously sustaining the constitutionality of a 1965 amendment to the Selective Service Act which makes it a crime knowingly to destroy or mutilate draft cards.[44] What of laws that make it a crime to deliberately desecrate the American flag? The Court sidestepped the question on the ground that in the case being considered the defendant might have been punished for what he said rather than for what he did.[45]

Does the Constitution protect speech via the mails, radio, television, motion pictures, picketing? It does, but for each of these media there are special problems that result in different degrees of protection.

Fifty years ago, Justice Holmes wrote: "The United States may give up the Post Office when it sees fit, but while it carries it on the use of the mails is almost as much a part of free speech as the right to use our tongues." [46] Justice Holmes, however, wrote in dissent and the prevailing doctrine was that the use of the mails was a privilege that the federal government could freely condition. Then, in 1965, the Supreme Court, in *Lamont* v. *Postmaster General,* adopted Justice Holmes' position and ruled unconstitutional a 1962 congressional act that directed the Postmaster General to detain unsealed foreign mailings of "communist political propaganda" and to deliver it only upon the addressee's request. In striking down the first act of Congress ever to be held in conflict with the First Amendment, Justice Douglas said for the Court, "The Act sets administrative officials astride the flow of mail to inspect it, appraise it, write the addressee about it, and await a response before dispatching the mail. . . . The regimen of this Act is at war with the 'uninhibited, robust, and wide-open' debate and discussion that are contemplated by the First Amendment." [47]

Broadcasters use publicly owned air waves, and no one has a constitutional right to use these facilities.[48] A license must be secured from the

Federal Communications Commission (FCC), the facilities must be used, not merely for private profit or purposes but also in the public interest as defined by the FCC, subject to congressional policy and judicial supervision. As Justice White said for the Court, "This is not to say that the First Amendment is irrelevant to public broadcasting. . . . But it is the right of the viewers and listeners not the right of the broadcasters, which is paramount. . . . Congress need not stand idly by and permit those with licenses to ignore the problems which beset the people or to exclude from the airways anything but their own views of fundamental questions." [49] Federal licensing, however, does give broadcasters some protection from state regulations. State laws requiring the licensing of motion pictures may not be applied to pictures shown over television.

The Constitution tolerates more regulation of motion pictures than of printed media. A state or city may require all motion pictures to be licensed prior to being shown to the public whereas such prior censorship is not permitted in the case of printed media.[50] However, even with respect to motion pictures the Supreme Court is suspicious of prior restraint; it insists that procedures must be established to insure prompt judicial determination that a particular picture is unfit to be shown.[51] And the only permissible grounds on which a license might be withheld is obscenity, as constitutionally defined.[52]

The right to picket unaccompanied by threats or violence is protected by the Constitution, but since picketing involves "elements of both speech and conduct, i.e., patrolling . . . this intermingling of protected and unprotected elements, picketing can be subjected to controls that would not be constitutionally permissible in case of pure speech." [53] Even peaceful picketing can be restricted by a state if it is conducted for an illegal purpose, that is, designed to pressure someone to do something that the law forbids him to do.[54] However, the Constitution forbids sweeping statutes or court injunctions that are not narrowly and clearly drawn. Moreover, states may not interfere with picketing that federal legislation protects under the Taft-Hartley or other laws.

or the right of the people peaceably to assemble, and to petition the government for a redress of grievances

People who wish to protest have no constitutional right to do so "whenever and however and wherever they please." [55] No one has a right to incite riots, to hold meetings that block traffic, to take over a school, to seize and hold the office of a mayor (or a university chancellor), to hold parades or to make speeches in the public streets during rush hours. State and local governments have the power to make reasonable regulations to preserve order. However, the Constitution protects the right to assemble peaceably in public places, and the courts will look carefully at regulations or police action that trench on this right, especially in circumstances that raise the suspicion that the law is not being applied even-handedly. The Supreme Court is unwilling to sanction regulations authorizing authorities to determine, at their own discretion, which groups will be allowed to hold public meetings, to participate in parades or to uphold laws that are so broad that they give police wide discretion to determine whom to arrest and courts latitude to determine whom to convict. Regulations designed to preserve the public peace must be precisely drawn and fairly administered. For example, the Court sustained a Louisiana statute that forbids parading near a court house with the intent to influence a judge, juror, or witness,[56] but it struck down the application of another Louisiana law that defined disturbing the peace so broadly that it would permit arrest merely for holding a meeting on a public street or public highway.[57] Similarly, the Court declared unconstitutional a Birmingham ordinance requiring permission from the city commission before participating in any parade on the city streets because the ordinance gave unbridled discretion to the commission and failed to provide for expeditious judicial review of the commission's refusal to issue a permit.[58]

Does the Constitution require police officers to protect unpopular groups whose peaceful public meetings and demonstrations arouse others to violence? If the answer were no, then the right of unpopular minorities to hold meetings would be seriously curtailed. It is almost always easier for the police to maintain order by curbing the peaceful meetings of the unpopular minority than to move against those threatening the violence. But if police were never to have the right to order a group to disperse, public order is at the mercy of those who may resort to street demonstrations just to create public tensions and provoke street battles.

The Supreme Court has refused to give a categorical answer to this question; the answer depends on the circumstances. In 1951 (*Feiner* v. *New York*) the Court upheld the conviction for "unlawful assembly" of a sidewalk speaker who continued to talk after being ordered to stop by the only two policemen present. There was no evidence that the police interfered because of objection to what was being said. But in view of the hostile response of the audience, the police were fearful a riot might ensue that they could not contain or prevent.[59] The Feiner case has never been overruled, but since then the Supreme Court has tended to emphasize the need for governments to move under more precisely drawn statutes. The Supreme Court, for example, in *Edwards* v. *South Carolina* (1963) reversed the conviction of 187 Negro students who held a mass meeting in front of the South Carolina State House to protest denial of their civil rights. A crowd of about three hundred onlookers watched the demonstration and the police provided protection for about forty-five minutes. Then the police gave the students fifteen minutes in which to disperse. They refused to do so and were arrested and subsequently convicted for breach of the peace. The Supreme Court stressed that this was not a prosecution for violation of a precise and narrowly drawn statute limiting or prescribing specific conduct, such as interfering with traffic. All that had happened was that the opinions being expressed had been sufficiently opposed by a majority of the community so as to attract a crowd and necessitate police protection. "The Fourteenth Amendment," said the Court, "does not permit a State to make criminal the peaceful expression of unpopular views." [60] Justice Clark, the lone dissenter, argued that the right to express views does not include the right to do so under circumstances where law-enforcement officers conclude in good faith that a dangerous disturbance is imminent.

In 1969 the Supreme Court followed the Edwards rather than the Feiner precedent when it reversed the conviction under a disorderly conduct statute of Dick Gregory and other demonstrators who had marched in a peaceful and orderly procession, under police protection, from city hall to the Mayor of Chicago's residence to press their claims for desegregation of the schools. As they marched in front of the Mayor's home a large and growing number of onlookers became unruly toward the demonstrators. For some time the police tried to maintain order, but when they concluded that there was an imminent threat of violence they demanded that the demonstrators disperse. The command was not obeyed and Gregory and his followers were arrested and subsequently convicted of disorderly conduct. Although the Supreme Court reversed the decision, the Court made it clear that the situation would have been different if Chicago had acted under ordinances specifically forbidding demonstrations after certain hours in residential areas or under ordinances making it an offense to disobey a police officer when there is an imminent threat of violence and the police have made all reasonable efforts to protect the demonstrators from hostile bystanders. The Supreme Court's objection was to the fact that Gregory and his followers had been charged with and convicted of disorderly conduct when there was no evidence that they had been acting disorderly. Justices Douglas and Black concurred, but they went out of their way to emphasize: "Speech and press are, of course, to be free. . . . But picketing and demonstrating can be regulated like other conduct of men. We believe that the homes of men, sometimes the last citadel of the tired, the weary and the sick, can be protected by government from noisy, marching, trampling, threatening picketers and demonstrators bent on filling the minds of men, women, and children with fears of the unknown." [61]

What of public facilities such as libraries, courthouses, schools, or swimming pools that are designed to serve purposes other than public assembly? As long as persons use such facilities within the normal bounds of conduct, they may not be constitutionally restrained from doing so. But if they attempt by sit-ins or other kinds of demonstrations to interfere with programs or try to appropriate facilities for their own use, a state has constitutional authority to punish, provided it does so under laws that are not applied in a discriminatory fashion and that properly limit the discretion of those enforcing them. To illustrate the application of these general rules: a small group of protestors who quietly remained in a library for ten to fifteen minutes in order to protest racial discrimination, but who did not interfere with the operations of the library, could not constitutionally be charged with breach of the peace;[62] a large group of students who marched to and around a jailhouse to protest the arrest of fellow students and to protest segregation within the jail could be convicted for trespass when they refused to leave the jail upon order of the sheriff.[63]

The right to associate for the peaceful promotion of political causes derives from the rights of free speech and assembly and is equally entitled to constitutional protection. For example, the Supreme Court ruled that Alabama could not demand from the NAACP a list of all its members, ostensibly in connection with a judicial proceeding to determine if the NAACP was violating the state's foreign corporation registration law. The NAACP contended that in Alabama if it were made known that a person belonged to the NAACP, he might lose his job, be subjected to other types of economic coercion, perhaps even suffer bodily harm. If the NAACP could be forced to publicize its membership, many would hesitate to join. Under the circumstances, the Supreme Court held, the state had failed to show an interest in learning the names sufficient to justify the restraint on the right of NAACP members to associate that would result from publication.[64] The Supreme Court has also struck down laws restraining the right of organizations to make legal services available to members.[65] The Court conceded that a state has a legitimate interest in regulating the practice of law, but it must do so by means that do not impinge on the right to associate for peaceful purposes.

What of the freedom not to associate? May a state compel lawyers to join a bar association or allow unions to make membership in the union a condition for securing or retaining employment? To oversimplify a complex problem, the Supreme Court has been willing to sustain such laws provided arrangements are made to insure that no individual is required to give his financial support to the political activity of the association. A member is entitled to receive a reimbursement for that portion of his dues used for political purposes.[66]

A troublesome question grows out of the conflict between the constitutional right to engage in political activity and to join political organizations and the right of government to regulate the conditions of public employment. Persons may be disqualified from public employment who are actively attempting to overthrow the state or the United States by force, but neither the national nor the state governments may condition all employment in their respective services on the abandonment by its employees of their constitutional rights of association (but see below). The Supreme Court has struck down state loyalty oath requirements, especially as applied to teachers, that bring within their net persons who are members of an organization that may have unlawful purposes, but who themselves do not participate in its unlawful activities or share its unlawful purposes.[67] And in 1967 in *United States* v. *Robel* the Supreme Court for the second time in our history declared an act of Congress to be in conflict with the First Amendment. The case involved a provision of the Internal Security Act of 1950 that made it unlawful for any member of a Communist-action organization "to engage in any employment in any defense facility." The provision trapped within its proscription persons who might be inactive members of a designated organization, unaware of its unlawful aims, and working in positions where they would be most unlikely to be able to endanger the national security. Said the Court majority, the provision contains "the fatal defect of overbreadth because it seeks to bar employment both for association which may be proscribed and for association which may not be proscribed consistently with First Amendment rights." [68]

Still "on the books," however, is a decision of the Supreme Court upholding the Hatch Act, which forbids most federal employees to engage in active political party affairs.[69] Presumably, governments may condition public employment on nonparticipation in the affairs of any political party, but if it singles out a particular kind of political activity, it must show with respect to employees in "nonsensitive positions" that the individual is engaging in illegal activity beyond the mere fact of joining an organization.

Amendment II

Militia and the Right to Bear Arms

A well regulated Militia, being necessary to the security of a free State,* the right of the people to keep and bear Arms, shall not be infringed.

This amendment's sole purpose is to prevent Congress from disarming the state militias. It provides no constitutional right for a private citizen to retain weapons. Congress could use its several delegated powers —taxation, interstate commerce, postal, and so on—to regulate private ownership of firearms. Furthermore, the amendment provides no protection against regulation by state and local governments.

* This refers to "state" in the generic sense rather than to states of the Union.

Amendment III

Quartering of Soldiers

No Soldier shall, in time of peace be quartered in any house, without the consent of the Owner, nor in time of war, but in a manner to be prescribed by law.

Certain remarks of Justice Miller are appropriate here: "This amendment seems to have been thought necessary. It does not appear to have been the subject of judicial exposition; and it is so thoroughly in accord with all our ideas, that further comment is unnecessary." [70]

Amendment IV

Searches and Seizures

The right of the people to be secure in their persons, houses, papers, and effects, against unreasonable searches and seizures, shall not be violated, and no Warrants shall issue, but upon probable cause, supported by Oath or affirmation, and particularly describing the place to be searched, and the persons or things to be seized.

Since the Fourth Amendment has been incorporated into the due process clause, the limitation against unreasonable searches and seizures now applies to state and local as well as to federal police officers. In this highly technical area, where the Supreme Court has had difficulty in determining what the Constitution means, it is difficult to summarize, but as the result of the most recent decisions it is somewhat easier to do so.

In general, any search without a warrant is unreasonable. The only exceptions are the following:

1. Searches of moving vehicles that the police have probable cause to believe contain evidence of crimes or are being used to commit crimes.

2. When making a lawful arrest, police may make contemporary warrantless searches, but they may not go beyond the person of the arrestee except to the limited area into which he might reach to obtain weapons or to destroy evidence.[71]

3. A police officer may stop and frisk a suspect if he has reason to believe that he is dealing with an armed and dangerous person, regardless of whether he has probable cause to arrest the individual for a crime. The search must be confined to that which is designed to find hidden weapons that could be used to assault the officer.[72]

With the above exceptions, prior to engaging in a search, police must appear before a magistrate and under oath demonstrate that they have probable cause to believe that the search will produce criminal evidence. The warrant issued must specify the premises to be searched and the property to be seized. The magistrate must "perform his 'neutral and detached function and not serve merely as a rubber stamp for the police.' " [73] The premises protected against unreasonable searches and seizures include any place a person has a legitimate right to be, including hotel rooms, rented homes, apartments of friends, or even telephone booths.

The Fourth Amendment also protects persons against arrests or police detentions, although the police may make arrests without warrants whenever they have probable cause to believe that a person has committed or is about to commit a crime. Since people, like automobiles, are movable the courts are somewhat more lenient in permitting warrantless arrests than warrantless searches.

Recently the Supreme Court extended the Fourth Amendment to cover searches by health inspectors and similar officials, and now they must secure warrants if occupants refuse to allow them to make the inspections required by law. However, it is not necessary for the inspector to demonstrate to a magistrate that he has probable cause to believe that a particular dwelling contains violations of the standards prescribed, but only that the particular inspection is authorized by law. With respect to administrative inspections of commercial establishments, the Court stated: "We do not decide whether warrants to inspect business premises may be issued only after access is refused; since surprise may often be a crucial aspect of routine inspection of business establishments, the reasonableness of warrants issued in advance of inspection will necessarily vary with the nature of the regulation involved and may differ from standards applicable to private homes." [74]

The gadgets of science have confronted judges with novel problems in applying the prohibition against unreasonable searches and seizures. Obviously, the framers of this amendment had in mind physical objects such as books, papers, letters, and other kinds of documents that they felt should not be seized by police officers except on the basis of limited search warrants issued by magistrates. But what of tapping phone wires or using electronic devices to eavesdrop? In *Olmstead* v. *United States,* decided in 1928, a bare majority of the Supreme Court held that there is no unconstitutional search unless there is seizure of physical objects or an actual physical entry into a premise.[75] Justices Holmes and Brandeis wrote vigorous dissents in which they argued that the Constitution should be kept abreast of modern times and that the "dirty business" of wire tapping produced the same evil invasions of privacy that the framers had in mind when they adopted the Fourth Amendment.

Forty years later in *Katz* v. *United States,* the Supreme Court adopted the Holmes-Brandeis position: "The Fourth Amendment protects people —and not simply 'areas'—against unreasonable searches and seizures and the use by police officers of electronic devices to overhear a conversation inside a public telephone booth is a 'search and seizure' within the meaning of the Constitution. Wherever a man may be, he is entitled to know that he will remain free from unreasonable searches and seizures." [76] Conversations, along with physical things, are now protected by the Fourth Amendment. There is no violation of the Constitution, however, if one confides to a friend and he in turn informs the police or if the "friend" is "wired-for-sound" so that what one says is amplified back to police officers.[77]

The Crime Control Act of 1968 makes it a federal offense for any unauthorized person to tap telephone wires or to use electronic bugging devices or to sell such devices in interstate commerce, but at the same time Congress established procedures whereby federal police, by specifying the identity of the persons, the nature of the conversations, and the crime they expect to uncover may secure warrants from federal judges to "search and seize" evidence by electronic means and by wiretaps for a whole range of specified federal offenses. Congress even authorized police to make emergency intercepts for a forty-eight hour period without warrants with respect to investigations relating to national security or involving organized crime. And the President is authorized without going through court procedures to allow bugging and tapping in behalf of national security. (Justice Stewart has made a point of the fact that the question is still open as to the "standards governing the constitutionality of electronic surveillance relating to the gathering of foreign intelligence information—necessary for the conduct of international affairs and for the protection of national defense secrets and installations from foreign espionage and sabotage." [78]) Congress also authorized state and local police and prosecutors to secure warrants from state courts for bugging to detect evidence of crimes punishable by imprisonment for more than one year.[79] Undoubtedly the Supreme Court will be asked before too long to determine whether the Crime Control Act of 1968 creates warrant procedures consistent with the Fourth Amendment. It has already held a New York statute unconstitutional for its failure to establish precise standards for judges to apply or to limit sufficiently the conditions under which intercepts might take place.[80]

The prohibition against unreasonable searches and seizures is combined with the Fifth Amendment prohibition against self-incrimination (see pages 126–128) to forbid the introduction into any court proceeding of unconstitutional evidence secured by the police from the accused. To permit the use of such evidence not only compels the accused to testify against himself, but the Supreme Court has concluded that exclusion of such evidence is the only effective means to discourage police from violating constitutional procedures. Since the Fourth Amendment "now affords protection against the uninvited ear, oral statements, if illegally overheard, and their fruits are also subject to suppression." [81] Unconstitutionally obtained evidence, however, may be submitted in a trial against persons whose Fourth Amendment rights have not been violated. For example, the Fourth Amendment secures conversations of those who participate in them and of the legal occupants of the premises in which the conversation takes place. But if in overhearing these conversations police uncover evidence against other persons, the evidence can be introduced at the trial of such third persons, since their Fourth Amendment rights have not been violated.[82]

Electronic police investigations may also run afoul of other provisions of the Constitution; for example, when police officers secretly installed a radio transmitter in an automobile to overhear a conversation between a person out on bail but under indictment and a supposed confederate who gave police permission to install the transmitter, the Supreme Court held that the police had deprived the suspect of his rights to the assistance of counsel.[83] Evidence elicited in this fashion cannot be used at the trial.

The Supreme Court adopted the exclusionary rule for federal courts in 1914.[84] Although the Court in 1949 ruled that the Fourth Amendment ban on unreasonable searches and seizures applies to state and local police,[85] it was not until 1961 in *Mapp* v. *Ohio* that the Court held that state courts, too, must exclude evidence from trials taken in violation of the Fourth Amendment.[86] Since the Mapp decision, the Supreme Court has ruled that state searches and seizures are to be judged by the same standards as apply in the federal courts.[87]

Amendment V

Grand Juries, Double Jeopardy, Self-Incrimination, Due Process, and Eminent Domain

No person shall be held to answer for a capital, or otherwise infamous crime, unless on a presentment or indictment of a Grand Jury,

The Fifth Amendment introduces us to the oldest institution known to the Constitution, the grand jury. It hails from the days of William the Conqueror; the trial, or petty (also spelled *petit*), jury is an offshoot from it (see Sixth Amendment). Like its English forerunner, the grand jury is composed of not more than twenty-three members of whom twelve are sufficient to make a "presentment" or return an "indictment"—that is, to accuse some person or persons of an offense against the laws of the United States, on the basis either of evidence gathered by itself or of evidence laid before it by a prosecuting officer. Since the "accused" is not being tried, the grand jury's proceedings are secret and one-sided (ex parte), only the government being represented.

> *except in cases arising in the land or naval forces or in the Militia, when in actual service in time of War or public danger;*

This clause, along with Article I, Section 8, giving Congress the power to make "rules for the government and regulations of the land and naval forces," means that persons subject to trial before military courts are not entitled to the same protections as are civilians. Recently, however, the Supreme Court has progressively narrowed the exception and limited the jurisdiction of military tribunals. Neither civilian employees of the Armed Forces overseas nor civilian dependents of military personnel accompanying them overseas may be tried by court-martial.[88] The military lack jurisdiction to try ex-soldiers for cimres committed while they were in service.[89] And in 1969 the Court went so far as to hold that, at least during peacetime and while serving in the United States, even military personnel may not be subject to court-martial for "non-service connected crimes." Hence a soldier stationed in Hawaii could not be tried by the military on the charge of attempted rape alleged to have been committed while he was on leave with an evening pass and dressed in civilian clothes.[90]

> *nor shall any person be subject for the same offense to be twice put in jeopardy of life or limb;*

The guarantee against double jeopardy consists of three separate constitutional protections. "It protects against a second prosecution for the same offense after acquittal. It protects against a second prosecution for the same offense after conviction. And it protects against multiple punishments for the same offense."[91] A person has been put in jeopardy as soon as he is brought to trial under a valid indictment before a judge or a properly constituted jury. Once a trial has begun and the prosecution is unwilling to proceed or a verdict of acquittal has been entered, even if the judge mistakenly orders such a verdict, the defendant cannot be tried again for the same offense.[92] If, however, a jury is unable to agree upon a verdict or a mistrial is declared by the judge on the motion of, or in the interest of, the defendant or if the jury is dismissed because it is composed of persons not competent to serve, the accused may be subject to another trial. He may also be retried if on the motion of the defendant a court sets aside the original conviction because of error in the proceedings. However, on retrial, the double jeopardy guarantee requires that credit be given to the defendant for any part of the sentence already served.[93]

The restriction on double jeopardy does not prevent civil and criminal proceedings or the placing of a person in jeopardy for each of several offenses that may arise from a single act. The test as to whether an offense is the same offense is that the same evidence is required to sustain conviction.

Within the recent (1969) incorporation of the double jeopardy provision into the Fourteenth Amendment,[94] the Supreme Court may reconsider its earlier holdings that the clause does not prevent prosecution by both federal and state governments for the same offense.[95] A single act, for example, robbing a bank chartered under federal laws, may be an offense against both the national and state government and trial by one does not prevent subsequent trial by the other, even if the defendant is acquitted of the charge in the courts of the first government to bring him to trial.

nor shall be compelled in any criminal case to be a witness against himself;

Originally construed to mean only that a person on trial might not be forced to testify against himself, the provision has been broadened in a variety of highly significant ways.

The privilege now protects persons from being compelled to answer incriminating questions put by any governmental agency—the House Committee on Internal Security (formerly known as the Committee on Un-American Activities) or the Federal Trade Commission, for example. Furthermore, the Supreme Court has extended the privilege to exempt persons from payment of certain kinds of federal taxes when compliance with the tax laws would expose them to a "real and appreciable" risk of self-incrimination because it would give governments evidence of their illegal activities. In effect these decisions have rendered unenforceable federal laws imposing taxes on professional gamblers and gambling, possession and sale of certain kinds of unregistered firearms, and on persons who are unauthorized to possess or buy marijuana.[96]

Although a person is not entitled to refuse to answer questions merely because his answers might be embarrassing, lead to public ridicule, or incriminate others, he is entitled to refuse to answer questions that may furnish the police with links to evidence that could result in prosecution even if the ultimate outcome would be acquittal. To illustrate: the Supreme Court held unconstitutional a provision of the Subversive Activities Control Act of 1950 that required communist organizations to list their members with the Attorney General. Admission of membership in the Communist Party exposes one to risk of prosecution for violating several federal laws. Congress had stipulated that the fact of registration and admission of Party membership should not per se constitute a violation of a federal law or be received in evidence; but this stipulation did not save the Act. The immunity granted was not broad enough—it did not preclude the use of the admission as an investigatory lead.[97]

Another significant change in the application of the self-incrimination provision is its inclusion within the Fourteenth Amendment as a limitation of the states,[98] and permitting a person to claim the right in order to avoid the risk of prosecution by either national or state authorities.[99] Until these recent constructions, a witness before a federal agency could not invoke the Fifth Amendment to avoid prosecution by a state agency, and a witness before a state agency could not claim the Fourteenth Amendment to refuse to answer questions that might lead to prosecution by the national (or state) government.

What if a government grants immunity from prosecution? If the immunity is as broad as the protection provided by the self-incrimination clause, a witness may be compelled to respond under pain of fine or imprisonment.[100] However, although the national government may confer sweeping immunity against both national and *state* prosecutions, a state may not confer such sweeping protection against national prosecution. National authorities may not use the evidence produced under a grant of state immunity, but they are free to prosecute for federal crimes uncovered as the result of compelled response to an investigation by a state.[101] Some thorny questions still lurk in this area of the self-incrimination clause.

Complex questions remain with respect to the application of the self-incrimination clause to public employees. In a series of closely divided decisions the Supreme Court has held that: answers of police officers under threat of discharge for failure to answer cannot be used in subsequent criminal prosecutions; police officers may not be dismissed merely for invoking the self-incrimination clause; public employees may be dismissed if they refuse to answer questions of their superiors directly relating to the performance of their official duties, provided they are not required to relinquish their constitutional immunity not to have such compelled evidence used against them in subsequent criminal prosecutions.[102] In view of the complexity of the problems and the closely divided nature of the decisions, it is still not clear what all these decisions add up to.

It is in the areas of protection for those accused of crime that the self-incrimination clause has had its most important and controversial extensions. Traditionally, the right to refuse to incriminate applied only at the trial. But what good was this constitutional protection, or the guarantee of the right to assistance of counsel, or the presumption of innocence, if long before the accused were brought before a judge, he was detained and without help of an attorney forced to prove his innocence to the police? Do not such procedures reduce the courtroom proceedings to a mere formality?

In the 1930s, the Supreme Court began to move against these tactics. At first it used the more general due process standards (see pages 128–130) to reverse convictions obtained by using evidence secured by torture, by prolonged psychological coercion, or by involuntary confession. It acted not so much because these practices amount to self-incrimination but because such brutal procedures and the use of such unreliable evidence offend the due process clause.[103]

In 1966, in *Miranda* v. *Arizona,* the Supreme Court abandoned case-by-case determination of where police interrogation has gone too far; by a five-to-four vote, it brought the self-incrimination clause into play.[104] The Court announced that henceforth no conviction could stand if evidence introduced at the trial had been obtained by the police as the result of "custodial interrogation" unless: (1) the suspect had been notified that he is free to remain silent, (2) warned that what he says may be used against him in court, (3) told that he has a right to have his attorney present during the questioning, (4) informed that if he cannot afford to hire his own lawyer, an attorney would be provided for him, (5) permitted at any stage of the police interrogation to terminate it. If the suspect answers questions in the absence of his attorney, the prosecution must be prepared to demonstrate that the suspect knowingly and intelligently waived his rights to remain silent and to have his own lawyer present. Failure to comply with these requirements will lead to reversal of a conviction even if other independent evidence would be sufficient to establish guilt.

The Supreme Court has also liberalized the construction of the self-incrimination clause as it applies within the courtroom. A defendant always has had the right to refuse to take the stand to answer any questions, incriminating or not. For many decades in the federal courts, neither prosecutor nor judge could comment about the defendant's silence. The same rule now is a constitutional requirement for state courts.[105] If, however, a defendant does take the stand, the prosecution may cross-examine him on all his testimony.

In short, as a result of the Supreme Court's liberal construction of the self-incrimination clause, it now applies to all governments, serves to protect persons in all settings in which their freedom of action is curtailed, and has become an essential mainstay of our adversary system. A government seeking to punish an individual must produce the evidence against him by its own independent labors and cannot force the suspect to contribute to his own conviction. Needless to say, many police officers are highly critical of these Supreme Court decisions, since they restrict the police's ability to question suspects, an ability they believe to be essential for the solution of many crimes.

Congress responded to the criticism of the Miranda decision in the Crime Control Act of 1968 when it stipulated for *federal* courts much less stringent rules for the introduction of evidence than those laid down by the Court in Miranda and other cases, especially as to the admissibility of confessions. The Supreme Court has not as yet ruled on the constitutionality of these provisions, but it has not been dissuaded from extending the Miranda decision to interrogations by income tax investigators in circumstances where they have fixed on an individual for possible criminal prosecution, or to any kind of police interrogation wherever a person is "deprived of his freedom of action in any way," whether in custody at a police station or otherwise, for example, when he is subject to police questioning in his own home.[106]

Somewhat anomalously, a week after the Miranda decision, the Supreme Court reconfirmed an earlier precedent and allowed a police officer to direct a physician to withdraw blood from a person arrested for driving while under the influence of intoxicating liquor.[107] The five-man majority stressed that the drawing of the blood sample was done in a hospital according to accepted medical practices when the officer had reasonable grounds to believe that the suspect was drunk, and the policeman had had no time to secure a search warrant. The dissenting justices could not accept the distinction that the self-incrimination clause prevents police from compelling a suspect to answer questions but that it does not prevent the police from compelling a suspect to give his own blood sample.

A police "line-up," either before or after indictment, does not violate the self-incrimination clause, but if it takes place without the presence of counsel it may violate the Sixth Amendment (see page 135).[108] Similarly, the taking of fingerprints or handwriting exemplars does not violate the self-incrimination requirement.[109]

nor be deprived of life, liberty, or property, without due process of law;

A parallel clause is found in the Fourteenth Amendment as a limitation on the states. The due process clauses of the Fifth and Fourteenth Amendments have resulted in more cases and controversies than any other in the Constitution except possibly the commerce clause and, earlier, the obligation of contracts clause. Even so, it is impossible to give these clauses any exact, final, and completely satisfactory explanation. Indeed, the Supreme Court itself has refused to give them precise definition, stating that it preferred to rely upon "the gradual process of judicial inclusion and exclusion." [110] Certain things concerning it may, nevertheless, be said with some assurance.

There are two kinds of due process—*procedural* and *substantive*. Procedural due process refers to the methods by which the law is enforced. It requires, to paraphrase Daniel Webster's famous definition, a procedure that "hears before it condemns, proceeds upon inquiry, and renders judgment only after [a] trial" in which the essentials of justice have been preserved.

There are several ways in which a law itself may violate procedural due process: (1) If it fails to establish a definite standard of guilt or in the words of the Supreme Court, "A statute which either forbids or requires the doing of an act in terms so vague that men of common intelligence must necessarily guess at its meaning and differ as to its application, violates the first essential of due process of law." [111] (2) If it creates a statutory presumption of guilt where there is no "rational connection between the facts proved and the facts presumed." For example, the Court has declared unconstitutional a law that created a presumption that a firearm in the possession of a person convicted of a crime of violence had been transported or received in violation of the law, and it also declared unconstitutional a provision that possession of marijuana created a presumption that it had been illegally imported and the possessor was aware of the illegal importation.[112] (3) If the application of a statute results in deprivation of liberty or property without adequate notice or opportunity to be heard. For example, the Supreme Court declared unconstitutional a prejudgment garnishment procedure that allowed creditors to freeze a portion of wages in possession of an employer, but did not give the wage-earner adequate notice and chance to be heard prior to the "freezing." [113]

For the most part, procedural due process has its application in the courtroom. For the federal courts, procedural due process requires as a minimum the careful observance of the provisions of the Bill of Rights as outlined in Amendments Four through Eight. With the absorption into the due process clause of the Fourteenth Amendment of most of the provisions of the Bill of Rights, the Constitution sets about the same minimum due process standard for both national and state courts.

Procedural due process applies to all governmental proceedings— not just to courtrooms: hearings before congressional committees, administrative tribunals, juvenile hearings, disbarment proceedings, and so on.[114] But the same procedures that are essential for criminal prosecutions are not necessarily essential in order for there to be due process in noncriminal proceedings. What is due process varies with the kind of procedure and is difficult to generalize, but at a minimum, before there can be a deprivation of liberty or property as the result of any governmental action there must be adequate notice and opportunity for an appropriate hearing.

If the procedure is akin to a determination of criminal culpability, in addition there may have to be right of confrontation, cross-examination of witnesses, and right to present evidence (see pages 134–135).

Whereas procedural due process places limits on the manner in which governmental power may be exercised, substantive due process withdraws certain subjects from the full reach of governmental power regardless of the procedures used. Substantive due process, which began to be import int in the United States Supreme Court about 1890, requires that the Court be convinced that the law—not merely the procedures by which the law would be enforced but its very purpose—is fair, reasonable, and just.

Along with substantive due process, the Supreme Court has also expanded the meaning of "property" and of "liberty," but especially of the latter. Originally "liberty" had meant "freedom from physical restraint"; now it has been expanded to denote "not merely freedom from bodily restraint but also the right of the individual to contract, to engage in any of the common occupations of life, to acquire useful knowledge, to marry, establish a home and bring up children, to worship God according to the dictates of his own conscience, and generally to enjoy those privileges long recognized at common law as essential to the orderly pursuit of happiness by free men.[115]

Prior to 1937, the most important phase of this "new liberty" protected by the Supreme Court was "liberty of contract," that is, business liberty. Indeed, the adoption of the doctrine of substantive due process and the simultaneous expansion of the meaning of liberty rendered the Supreme Court, for a time, the final arbiter of our economic and industrial life. During this period, the Court struck down many laws—laws regulating hours of labor, establishing minimum wages, regulating prices, forbidding employers to discharge workers for union membership, and so on—on the ground that they were unreasonable interferences with the liberty of employers and employees to contract with one another.

Since 1937, however, the Supreme Court has largely abandoned the doctrine of "liberty of contract" and in general has refused to apply the doctrine of substantive due process to laws regulating the American economy. This action did not presage a return to the old narrow conception of liberty or the abandonment of substantive due process. Quite to the contrary: since 1937 the word *liberty* of the Fifth and Fourteenth Amendments has been expanded to include the basic "civil liberties," and substantive due process has been given new life as a limitation of governmental power in the field of those liberties.

nor shall private property be taken for public use, without just compensation.

This clause places a restriction on the government's power of eminent domain—that is, the power to take private property for public use—a power existing in all governments; even in those that are organized on the principle of private ownership, the rights of society are paramount to those of any one owner. Private property may, however, be taken under the eminent-domain power only for *public* use; the owner must be fairly compensated. In cases of disagreement between the government and the individual about what price is just, decision is referred to a disinterested body.

The "taking" mentioned in the clause must be direct. The clause does not require compensation for property losses incidental to the exercise of governmental powers. For example, the passage of a rent-control measure would deprive persons of the right to charge what the traffic will bear and so decrease, presumably, the value of their property; the government is not required to award compensation. Nor does the government have to pay damages when it temporarily occupies a building in the course of restoring order in a riot situation.[116] Nor is it required to reimburse people for the losses they may suffer because Congress lowers the tariff or declares war. However, even where title is left in the hands of the owners, sometimes the courts will rule that the government has "taken" property. For example, where airplanes take off over land adjacent to airports at such low levels that the land is no longer suitable for other uses, this is a "taking" for which the government must compensate.[117]

These limits on the power of eminent domain were the first provisions of the Bill of Rights to be incorporated within the Fourteenth Amendment and thus to be made applicable to the states.[118]

Amendment VI

Criminal Court Procedures

In all criminal prosecutions, the accused shall enjoy the right to a speedy [trial]

A trial may be "speedy" in a legal sense that admits of considerable delays, especially those caused by the counsel of the accused. As the Supreme Court has said, "This guarantee is an important safeguard to prevent undue and oppressive incarceration prior to trial, to minimize anxiety and concern accompanying public accusation, and to limit the possibilities that long delay will impair the ability of an accused to defend himself. However, because of the many procedural safeguards provided an accused, the ordinary procedures for criminal prosecution are designed to move at a deliberate pace." [119] But, when Texas refused for six years to bring to trial a prisoner in a federal penitentiary who had so requested, the Supreme Court held that Texas had failed to meet the constitutional requirement and must dismiss the charge.[120]

and public trial,

Under special circumstances, the judge may order the general public from the courtroom, but the defendant by timely objections may safeguard his right not to be tried in secret. A public trial, the Supreme Court has held, is essential to due process and therefore is a right secured to defendants in state as well as in federal courts.[121]

The right to a public trial belongs to defendants and not to television or newsreel cameramen, photographers, or newspaper reporters. More constitutional questions have been raised by too much rather than too little public involvement in trials. Too public a trial may lead to conditions in which calm deliberation by a jury considering only the evidence presented in open court becomes impossible. Televising trials may—in the opinion of four justices, always does—create such distractions that it will deny the defendant due process.[122] Even in the absence of television cameras, if a judge allows newsmen to hound witnesses or permits the prosecutor to make statements to the press, it may deprive the defendant of his right to have a trial by an impartial jury free from outside influences. As the Supreme Court said, "Trial courts must take strong measures to ensure that the balance is never weighted against the accused." [123]

by an impartial jury

Despite the fact that Article III requires a trial by jury of all federal crimes in the state in which the crime was committed, the right was considered so important that it was further guaranteed again by the Sixth Amendment, and since 1968 the Fourteenth Amendment "guarantees a right of jury trial in all [state] criminal cases which, were they tried in a federal court, would come within the Sixth Amendment's guarantee of trial by jury." [124]

Trial by jury is a constitutional requirement for serious but not petty crimes. "The boundaries of the petty offense category have always been ill-defined, if not ambulatory," but the definition followed within the federal courts, and now also presumably applicable to the states, is that petty offenses are those punishable by no more than six months in prison and a $500 fine.[125]

The jury trial requirement now also applies to convictions for criminal contempt if the penalty imposed exceeds imprisonment for six months.[126] It does not apply to civil contempts nor to other noncriminal proceedings such as deportation or loyalty-security hearings.

Trial by jury includes all the elements recognized by the common law at the time the Constitution was adopted, the most important being a jury consisting of no more and no less than twelve and the requirement of a unanimous verdict for conviction.

A defendant may waive his right to a jury trial, in fact he can, by a plea of guilty, waive his right to any kind of trial. But the record must clearly show that the defendant knows what he is doing and is fully aware of the consequences of his action.[127] A judge may insist on a jury trial even against the wishes of the defendant for there is no constitutional right *not* to be tried by a jury.[128] But if a statute gives the accused the choice between pleading guilty subject only to a maximum sentence of life imprisonment or standing trial before a jury which can vote for the imposition of a death penalty, the death penalty may not be imposed. Such a choice places an unconstitutional coercive impact on the accused to waive his right to a trial by jury.[129]

Two decades ago, the Supreme Court refused to reverse convictions imposed by blue ribbon juries chosen to consist of educated persons because no connection had been shown to exist between such juries and discrimination against any race, class, or occupation.[130] The thrust of more recent opinion calls into question the continuing validity of this ruling. In *Witherspoon* v. *Illinois,* for example, although faced with a different issue, the Court majority placed great stress on the requirement that a jury be representative of all the views of a community. In that decision the Court ruled that although a jury from which persons had been excluded because of general objections to the death penalty or because of scruples against its infliction could be impartial with respect to determining innocence or guilt, it could not be impartial with respect to choosing between a sentence of life or death.[131]

> of the State and district wherein the crime shall have been committed, which district shall have been previously ascertained by law,

The early English juries were always from the neighborhood of the accused, which was sometimes an advantage, sometimes the contrary. One of the grievances against George III was that his government had forced American colonists to stand trial in England for offenses alleged to have been committed in America. To prevent the national government from using such procedures, both Article III and the Sixth Amendment require trial to be held in the state in which the crime was committed (the Sixth Amendment adds district). A defendant may, however, petition for removal of the trial from the district on the grounds that the community has been so inflamed and prejudiced against him that it would be impossible to select a fair and impartial jury in the district in which the crime was committed.

and to be informed of the nature and cause of the accusation;

There are no common-law offenses against the United States, and the only federal criminal acts are those that Congress has forbidden and for which penalties are imposed. A statute must state precisely the acts that are forbidden and must include all the ingredients essential to a proper judgment of guilt of the crime. A law that is so vague as to provide no clear standard by which alert men may know what actions have been made criminal and by which judge and jury may be guided in determining guilt violates this requirement. Moreover, the defendant must be furnished with a copy of the indictment and a bill of the particular charges.

to be confronted with the witnesses against him;

All testimony (certain deathbed statements are an exception) must be presented in open court, since the defendant has the right to be confronted with the witnesses against him and to cross-examine them. The same standards are now applied to state courts.[132] Convictions have been reversed where those in charge of a jury, such as bailiffs, made adverse comments about the defendant in the presence of the jury or where deputy sheriffs who are in charge of the jury were also prosecution witnesses.[133] A co-defendant's confession cannot be introduced if the co-defendant refuses to take the stand because it deprives his fellow defendant of the right of cross-examination.[134] It is, however, only in criminal prosecutions that the Supreme Court has held that a person has a constitutional right to be confronted by his accusors and to cross-examine them. Aliens have been deported and governmental employees have been dismissed on the basis of the testimony of unidentified informers. The Supreme Court has hinted in recent decisions, however, that proceedings which lack confrontation may run afoul of the due process requirements, as well as of this particular provision, if the proceedings could result in substantial deprivation of liberty or property.[135]

to have the compulsory process for obtaining witnesses in his favor,

In the eighteenth century under the English common-law, persons accused of felonies or treason were not allowed to introduce any witnesses in their own defense. England abolished this general disqualification in 1787, but retained a number of restrictions on the kinds of witnesses that could be called. For a time the Supreme Court held that the rules of evidence for federal courts were to be those in force in the various states at the time of the passage of the Judiciary Act of 1789, but in 1918 the Supreme Court declared that defendants should be allowed to call in their behalf all persons of competence who may have knowledge of the facts involved in the case.[136] In 1967 the Supreme Court brought this provision into the due process requirement of the Fourteenth Amendment when it set aside a Texas statute based on the common law that disqualified an alleged accomplice from testifying in behalf of the accused.[137] Unaffected by the Court's holding are the common-law testimonial privileges, such as those against self-incrimination, lawyer-client, husband-wife or the disqualification of persons accused of mental infirmity or those who are in their infancy.

Of course, a state has no authority to compel the attendance in its court proceedings of witnesses who are outside its jurisdiction. Nonetheless, it must make a good-faith effort to try to secure witnesses for the defense wherever they are located.[138]

and to have the Assistance of Counsel for his defence.

What was once a right of a defendant to be represented by an attorney during his trial, provided he could afford to obtain such assistance, has now become a positive obligation on authorities to see to it that all persons subject to any kind of custodial interrogation are represented by a lawyer. Nowadays when authorities place a person in a setting in which his freedom of action is curtailed, they have a positive duty to inform him of his right to be represented by an attorney and to secure legal counsel for him if he is unable to do so himself: "Where assistance of counsel is a constitutional requirement, the right to be furnished counsel does not depend on request." [139] Unless the record clearly shows that the defendant, in full awareness of what he was doing, waived his right to counsel, the absence of such counsel will render criminal proceedings unconstitutional.

The right begins at the time the police take a person into custody, including placing him in a "line-up." The Supreme Court's insistence upon the presence of legal counsel at every stage of criminal proceedings where substantial rights may be affected—interrogation, trial, sentencing, probation hearings, and appeals—is not only because of the Sixth Amendment but also as a means to enforce compliance with the requirement that no person be compelled to testify against himself (see page 127).

Since the adoption of the Fourteenth Amendment no state could constitutionally deny a defendant the right to be represented by counsel, but for many years the Supreme Court held that only in capital cases did a state have a constitutional duty to furnish counsel for indigent defendants. In other cases there was no such requirement unless special circumstances

—such as the youthfulness of the defendant—made legal assistance essential to due process. Then in 1963, in *Gideon* v. *Wainwright,* the Supreme Court made the federal rule applicable to the states.[140]

The several jurisdictions vary in the way in which they provide counsel for indigents. In some, judges assign counsel, but the growing practice in the larger states and cities is to create and support from tax funds an Office of Public Defender. Not until the Criminal Justice Act of 1964 did Congress provide for the appointment and compensation of legal counsel for indigents accused of federal crimes. Prior to that time attorneys served without fee on appointment by the judge. Congress is presently considering the appointment of full-time federal defenders in certain district courts.

Amendment VII

Trial by Jury in Common-Law Cases

In Suits at common law, where the value in controversy shall exceed twenty dollars, the right of trial by jury shall be preserved, and no fact tried by a jury, shall be otherwise re-examined in any Court of the United States, than according to the rules of the common law.

This provision refers to litigation in federal courts and has *not* been incorporated into the due process requirement of the Fourteenth Amendment. It concerns suits at common law and does not prevent the two parties from dispensing with a jury with the consent of the court. It does not apply to equity proceedings, which are seldom before a jury, nor to suits arising out of statutory law.

Amendment VIII

Bail and Cruel and Unusual Punishments

Excessive bail shall not be required, nor excessive fines imposed,

It is a basic principle of American justice that no man is guilty until pronounced so after a fair trial. Moreover, persons accused of crime are to be given the opportunity to prepare their defense. But if an accused person is thrown in jail prior to conviction and excessive bail imposed, he may be denied the full opportunity to prepare for his trial and may be detained prior to determination of his guilt. For these reasons, the Supreme Court has ruled that bail set at a figure higher than might reasonably be calculated to assure the presence of a defendant at his trial is "excessive." [141] Much depends upon the nature of the offense, the reputation of the offender, and his ability to pay. Bail of a larger amount than is usually set for a particular crime must be justified by evidence.

For some crimes, accused persons may be denied bail. For example, if the person is accused of a crime for which the penalty may be death, he may constitutionally be denied freedom on bail because of the fear that no amount of money would be sufficient to insure his presence at trial.

Congress provided a substantial implementation of the Eighth Amendment by the adoption of the Bail Reform Act of 1966, the first significant federal bail legislation since the Judiciary Act of 1789. Until Congress acted, impoverished defendants often stayed in jail for days: In a case cited by President Johnson when he signed the bill into law, a man spent 101 days in jail because he could not raise bail on a false complaint. Another man who was unable to raise bail waited fifty-four days for trial on a traffic offense in the District of Columbia for which he could have been sentenced to no more than five days.

The Bail Reform Act of 1966, applying only to federal courts, allows magistrates to release persons without bail if after taking into account such factors as past record, family and community ties, seriousness of offense charged, weight of evidence, and character of the accused, bail seems unnecessary to assure appearance at time of the trial. President Nixon, expressing concern about crimes committed by persons released pending trial, has recommended an amendment to the Act: He would have Congress authorize federal judges, after a hearing, to detain and refuse bail to "dangerous" suspects where the evidence suggests a high probability of guilt, where the crime for which the person stands accused is of a serious nature, and where release pending trial may impose substantial risks to the community. If Congress enacts such a pre-trial detention law, it will raise serious constitutional questions and may conflict with the Eighth Amendment.

Although there is no specific Supreme Court decision on the point, almost by definition, imposition by a state of an excessive bail or an excessive fine would violate the due process requirement of the Fourteenth Amendment.

nor cruel and unusual punishments inflicted.

The historic punishments that are banned are burning at the stake, crucifixion, breaking on the wheel, the race and thumbscrew, and in some circumstances, solitary confinement. An increasing number of states have abolished capital punishment, and opposition to it appears to be intensifying. But so far the Supreme Court has not ruled that capital punishment is an unconstitutionally cruel and unusual punishment. At the moment, capital punishment inflicted by hanging, electrocution, lethal gas, or a firing squad is constitutionally permissible. Several years ago a divided Supreme Court ruled that there was no constitutional inhibition against electrocuting a prisoner after a first attempt failed because of a power breakdown.[142]

Punishment may be cruel and unusual if it is out of all proportion to the offense, for example, capital punishment for a petty crime. Nor may the mere act of being addicted to drugs be made a criminal offense, for this would inflict punishment simply for being ill.[143] On the same grounds, a state could not make the act of being a chronic alcoholic a crime. However, a closely divided Court held that a chronic alcoholic could be punished for violating a statute against appearing drunk in a public place: Such a statute does not punish for being ill but imposes a criminal sanction upon public behavior.[144]

Amendment IX

Rights Retained by the People

The enumeration in the Constitution, of certain rights, shall not be construed to deny or disparage others retained by the people.

This amendment embodies the dominant political thought of eighteenth-century America, which taught that before the establishment of government men existed in a state of nature and lived under the natural law, which endowed them with certain natural rights. When, by mutual consent, men created government, they granted to it their natural right of judging and executing the natural law but retained the rest of their natural rights. In accordance with this theory, the Bill of Rights did not *confer* rights but merely *protected* those already granted by the natural law. The Ninth Amendment made it clear that the enumeration of rights to be protected did not imply that the other natural rights not mentioned were abandoned.

Although the Supreme Court had recognized that the right to engage in political activity is protected by this amendment against unreasonable national regulation,[145] until 1965, no law had even been declared unconstitutional because of a disparagement of any of these unenumerated rights, nor had there been any suggestion that this amendment limited the powers of the states. Then, in 1965, a majority of the Supreme Court ruled that a Connecticut law forbidding the use of contraceptives violated the right of marital privacy. The right of privacy, it stated, is "within the penumbra of specific guarantees of the Bill of Rights," and it is one of the fundamental rights reserved by the Ninth Amendment to the people against disparagement by a *state* or the national government.[146]

With the incorporation of most of the specific provisions of the Bill of Rights into the Fourteenth Amendment, the "glittering generalities" of the Ninth Amendment may become the next constitutional battleground.[147] Some of the justices appear to be looking to this amendment as the source for protecting from governmental intrusion what they consider to be basic rights. In addition to the right of privacy, which the Court has developed by combining the Fourth and Ninth Amendments, it has already secured a right to travel by combining the commerce clause, the privileges and immunities clause of the Fourteenth Amendment (see page 148), and the Ninth Amendment.

Amendment X

Reserved Powers of the States

The powers not delegated to the United States by the Constitution, nor prohibited by it to the States, are reserved to the States respectively, or the people.

This amendment was adopted to assuage fears, and it does not alter the distribution of powers between the national and state governments. It adds nothing to the Constitution; in the words of Justice Stone, "it is merely a truism." However, for one hundred years after John Marshall's death, the Supreme Court from time to time held that some of the "reserved" powers to the states were sovereign powers and hence set a limit to the delegated powers of the national government. Thus, when the national government used its specifically granted taxing and spending powers in such a way that agricultural production was regulated, its action was held by the Supreme Court, in 1937, to be repugnant to this amendment, since the regulation of agriculture is a power reserved to the states.[148]

Earlier, the Supreme Court ruled that since the power to regulate conditions of employment is reserved to the states, Congress could not use its powers to regulate interstate commerce or to tax for the purpose of driving employers of children out of the interstate market. In short, under what was known as the doctrine of Dual Federalism, the Supreme Court used the Tenth Amendment to limit some of the enumerated powers of the national government.

Subsequently, however, the Court has returned to Marshall's view that the Tenth Amendment and the reserved powers of the states do not limit the national government in exercising the powers given to it by the

Constitution. Today it makes no constitutional difference whether or not an act of Congress touches or governs matters otherwise subject to state regulation.

Note that the Tenth Amendment does not say that powers not *expressly* delegated to the United States are reserved to the states. The framers of the Tenth Amendment specifically rejected such a statement, for its adoption would have seriously curtailed the scope of national powers. Moreover, it should be emphasized that the states must exercise their reserved powers subject to the national government's supremacy and national constitutional limitations. For example, states have the reserved power to establish public schools, but they may not exercise this power contrary to the Fourteenth Amendment or to any other constitutional limit. Nor can they exercise it in such a way as to conflict with national regulations— for example, by compelling eighteen-year-olds who are subject to the national draft to attend schools. The national power to raise and support armies and navies takes precedence over the state power to educate.

PRE-CIVIL WAR AMENDMENTS

Amendment XI

Suits against States

The Judicial power of the United States shall not be construed to extend to any suit in law or equity, commenced or prosecuted against one of the United States by Citizens of another State, or by Citizens or Subjects of any Foreign State.

This amendment was proposed March 4, 1794 and proclaimed January 8, 1798.

Article III, Section 2, paragraph 1, among other things, extends the judicial power of the United States to "cases and controversies between a state and citizens of another state." During the struggle over ratification of the Constitution, many persons objected to this clause on the ground that it would permit a private individual to hale a state before a federal court; they were assured by Hamilton and others that because of the doctrine of "sovereign immunity," no state could ever be sued without its own consent. In 1792, however, the Supreme Court applied the literal terms of the Constitution and upheld the right of the federal courts to take jurisdiction in a case commenced by a citizen of South Carolina against Georgia.[149] Since many states were in default on their debts, there was a great alarm lest a series of similar suits should result. Immediately after the Supreme Court's decision, the Eleventh Amendment was proposed, and its ratification in effect "recalled" the decision.

The Supreme Court has always recognized that the amendment immunizes a nonconsenting state from federal court suits brought by its own citizens as well as by citizens of another state.[150] But Congress exercising its delegated powers may condition state participation in some activities on willingness to waive immunity. For example, in the Federal Employers Liability Act, Congress made railroads financially responsible for personal injuries sustained by their employees. When a state operates a railroad, it consents to the provisions of this act, including amenability to suit in a federal court.[151]

The Eleventh Amendment does not prevent an appeal from the highest state court to which a particular case may be carried to the Supreme Court in cases arising under the Constitution, laws, and treaties of the United States. Nor does it prevent federal courts, on the application of private individuals in appropriate proceedings, from restraining state officers who are acting unconstitutionally; by the principle of "the rule of law," an officer who acts beyond the law ceases to be an officer and thus ceases to be a representative of his state. However, when state officers act beyond the law, the Fourteenth Amendment applies, and their actions are considered to be those of the state (see page 158).

Amendment XII

Election of the President

The Electors shall meet in their respective states and vote by ballot for President and Vice-President, one of whom, at least, shall not be an inhabitant of the same state with themselves; they shall name in their ballots the person voted for as President, and in distinct ballots the person voted for as Vice-President, and they shall make distinct lists of all persons voted for as President, and of all persons voted for as Vice-President, and of the number of votes for each, which lists they shall sign and certify, and transmit sealed to the seat of the government of the United States, directed to the President of the Senate; —The President of the Senate shall, in the presence of the Senate and House of Representatives, open all certificates and the votes shall then be counted;—The person having the greatest number of votes for President, shall be the President, if such number be a majority of the whole number of Electors appointed; and if no person have such majority, then from the persons having the highest numbers not exceeding three on the list of those voted for as President, the House of Representatives shall choose immediately, by ballot, the President. But in choosing the President, the votes shall be taken by states, the representation from each state having one vote; a quorum for this purpose shall consist of a member or members from two-thirds of the states, and a majority of all the states shall be necessary to a choice. **And if the House of Representatives shall not choose a President whenever the right of choice shall devolve upon them, before the fourth day of March next following, then the Vice-President shall act as President, as in the case of the death or other constitutional disability of the President.**—*The person having the greatest number of votes as Vice-President, shall be the Vice-President, if such number be a majority of the whole number of Electors appointed, and if no person have a majority, then from the two highest numbers on the list, the Senate shall choose the Vice-President, a quorum for the purpose shall consist of two-thirds of the whole number of Senators, and a majority of the whole number shall be necessary to a choice. But no person constitutionally ineligible to the office of President shall be eligible to that of Vice-President of the United States. [emphasis added]*

This amendment was proposed December 8, 1803 and declared in force by the Secretary of State September 25, 1804.

The emphasized portion of this amendment has been superseded by the Twentieth Amendment and modified by the Twenty-fifth.

The presidential electoral system is the classic example of how custom and usage have amended and democratized the Constitution. As previously mentioned (see page 74), the authors of the Constitution expected electors to be distinguished citizens who would in fact, as well as in form, choose the President and the Vice President. Their expectations were not fulfilled because of the rise of national political parties. By the election of 1800, electors had come to be party puppets, pledged in advance to vote for the candidates nominated by their respective parties. In this election, the Republican-Democratic electors were in a majority. Since, under the original provisions for selecting the President and the Vice President each elector voted for two individuals without indicating which was his choice for President and which for Vice President, Aaron Burr, the Republican-Democratic candidate for Vice President, secured the same number of electoral votes as Thomas Jefferson, the Republican-Democratic candidate for President. This circumstance transferred the election to the House of Representatives, where the Federalists were in control. Although many Federalists favored Burr as the lesser of two evils, Hamilton threw his great influence on the side of Jefferson, who was finally elected on the thirty-sixth ballot. The Twelfth Amendment was designed to prevent such a situation from occurring again.

The two major differences between the Twelfth Amendment and the original provisions of the Constitution, which were repealed by it, are as follows: today electors are required to cast separate votes for President and Vice President, clearly designating which is their choice for President and which for Vice President. In the event no person receives a majority of the electoral votes for President, the House of Representatives chooses from the three persons with the most electoral votes (the original provision was from the five highest). If no person receives a majority of the electoral vote for Vice President, the Senate chooses between the two persons with the most electoral votes.

Today, presidential and vice-presidential candidates are chosen by political parties in national nominating conventions. On the first Tuesday after the first Monday in November, the voters select the electors, who are morally pledged to cast their electoral votes for the candidates chosen by their particular national convention. In some states, the electors' names do not even appear on the ballot; only the names of the candidates to whom they are pledged appear. Thus the electors have been reduced to automata and "the Electoral College," as the electors are known collectively, to an automatic registering device.

The development of the two-party system had another consequence for the Electoral College that the framers did not anticipate. It greatly lessened the probability that the House of Representatives would be called upon to make the final selection. Only once since 1801 has the House exercised this duty. In the election of 1824, before the full development of our party system, Andrew Jackson, John Quincy Adams, and William Crawford received the most electoral votes, but not one of them had a majority. The House, voting by states, chose John Quincy Adams. The only time the Senate has been called upon to make the final selection for the Vice Presidency was in 1837, when it favored Richard M. Johnson over Francis Granger. With only two major political parties there is no dispersion of the vote, and one party is assured of a majority of the electoral votes. Whenever a strong third party develops, as was the case in the 1968 election, the probability of final selection by the House and Senate is greatly increased.

All the state legislatures except Maine now provide for the selection of electors on a general statewide straight-ticket basis. Each voter casts one vote for the Democratic, Republican, American Independence, or other party electors. This means that the party that receives the most popular votes in a state receives *all* that state's electoral votes. For example, in 1968 Nixon (that is, the Republican electors) received 1,325,467 votes in New Jersey and Humphrey received 1,264,206, a modest plurality for Nixon of 61,261 votes; nevertheless, President Nixon received all 17 of New Jersey's electoral votes. It is even possible for a person to receive a majority of the popular vote without receiving a majority of the electoral vote. Let us take a hypothetical case involving two states to illustrate this point:

State X—15 electoral votes: Republican popular votes 255,000
                                      Democratic popular votes 250,000
State Y— 5 electoral votes: Republican popular votes 20,000
                                        Democratic popular votes 50,000

Results: Republican popular vote 275,000—Republican electoral vote
15
         Democratic popular vote 300,000—Democratic electoral vote
5

This very thing happened in 1876, when Tilden received more popular votes but lost the electoral vote to Hayes, and again in 1888, when Cleveland, despite his larger popular vote, was defeated by Harrison.

The present system helps to preserve one-party domination in that anything less than a plurality of a state popular vote does not count. A party that believes that it has little chance of winning a plurality of the popular vote is not likely to spend much time or effort campaigning in that state. Furthermore, men from states with few electoral votes and from states in which one party dominates have less chance of being nominated for President than those from the more populous states in which the two parties are more evenly divided. Parties favor men from these "pivotal" states because they hope that by nominating candidates from these states they can secure all the state's electoral votes. However, were the President elected by a direct vote of the people or were electoral votes distributed in proportion to the popular vote, a Republican vote in Georgia or a Democratic vote in South Dakota would be just as important as votes elsewhere; there would be an incentive for both parties to campaign throughout the United States instead of concentrating on the pivotal states.

Despite the generally recognized and widely supported view that the electoral college needs to be reformed, it has been difficult to secure any agreement about what reforms should be made. The 1968 elections revived and intensified the concerns about the risks inherent in our present arrangements: If George Wallace had secured enough electoral votes to keep both major party candidates from obtaining a majority, electors might have been tempted to exercise some discretion, or more probably, the election would have been thrown into the House of Representatives where the Wallace supporters might have had the votes necessary to determine the presidential choice between the two major party candidates. The chaos that could result from the installation of a President selected through such procedures is hard to exaggerate.

Whether the "near miss" of the 1968 elections will provide sufficient incentive to develop a consensus about electoral reform remains to be determined. For many years, amendments have been introduced in Congress to change the procedures for electing the President and the Vice President. In the past, the voters in the less populous states have opposed substituting direct popular election. Since states have as many electoral votes as they have senators and representatives, the smaller states carry greater weight in the Electoral College than they would in a nationwide direct election. Some people have proposed that we do away with the individual electors but retain the system of electoral votes and distribute a state's electoral vote in the same ratio as its popular vote. Such a change would obviate any danger of an elector's disregarding the wishes of the voters (as happened in 1956, 1960, and 1968), lessen the influence of strategically located minorities, weaken the one-party system where it now exists, and insure the election of the candidate with the largest popular vote. This change has been opposed by those who fear it would weaken the influence of people living in large cities who often have the balance of power in presidential elections. Since these urban voters have, in the past, been discriminated against by the gerrymandering of Congress, it is argued, it is only fair that they have more influence in the selection of the President. The same objections hold even more strongly against proposals to have electors chosen by congressional districts rather than on statewide tickets.

Reform of the electoral college remains a lively issue in Congress with the choice narrowing down to some kind of direct election with a specified minimum vote. Whether any such drastic reform can be accomplished prior to the 1972 election is doubtful, but not impossible. The operation of the Electoral College for the 1972 elections can also be altered if more states, especially those with a large number of electoral votes, should follow the lead of Maine, which in 1969 adopted a new law providing that one presidential elector is to be chosen from each of its two congressional districts with the state's remaining two electors chosen at large.

CIVIL WAR AMENDMENTS

The Thirteenth, Fourteenth, and Fifteenth Amendments were adopted after and as a result of the Civil War. Their purpose was to free the Negro slaves, grant them citizenship, and protect their rights, especially the right to vote, against infringement by the states. As Justice Miller wrote, "No one can fail to be impressed with the one pervading purpose of them all, lying at the foundation of each . . . we mean the freedom of the slave race, the security and firm establishment of that freedom, and the protection of the newly-made freeman and citizen from the oppressions of those who formerly exercised unlimited dominion over him." [152] Clearly the purpose of these amendments was to deprive the states of the "right" to impose any disabilities upon the Negroes because of their race, color, or previous condition of servitude. It was to take almost three quarters of a century, however, before the Civil War amendments were to be used primarily for this purpose.

Amendment XIII

Slavery

Section 1

Neither slavery nor involuntary servitude, except as a punishment for crime whereof the party shall have been duly convicted, shall exist within the United States, or any place subject to their jurisdiction.

This amendment was proposed January 31, 1865 and declared in force by the Secretary of State December 18, 1865.

Before the adoption of this amendment, each state could determine for itself whether or not slavery should be permitted within its borders. The Thirteenth Amendment deprived both the states and the national government of that power.

The amendment was aimed at Negro slavery. Persons may still be compelled to help build public roads,* to pay alimony, or to serve on a jury, in the militia, or in the armed forces, all without violating the amendment.

Several state laws that made failure to work after receiving money prima-facie evidence of intent to defraud have been held to be contrary to the Thirteenth Amendment. In effect, these laws made it a crime punishable by imprisonment to fail to work after securing money on the promise to do so.[153]

The Thirteenth Amendment is one of the two provisions of the Constitution (the other is the Twenty-first Amendment) that an individual can violate directly. It is "self-executing"—that is, it does not require action by Congress to put it into effect, although, in fact, Congress has implemented it and attached penalties to its violation.

Section 2

Congress shall have power to enforce this article by appropriate legislation.

* Under the common law, men could be drafted for a certain number of days every year for this purpose. In some cases, payment of taxes exempted them from such duties.

Not until a century after its adoption did Section 2 have much significance. Prior to 1968 the prevailing construction was that the Thirteenth
Amendment prohibited only slavery narrowly defined, and that racial discrimination against Negroes by private individuals was not to be regarded
as imposing on them the badges of slavery or as keeping them in servitude.[154] Hence, Congress had no power under Section 2 to legislate against
racial discrimination. Except for some Reconstruction legislation that
makes it a crime to hold another in slavery or peonage—involuntary
servitude forced upon a person in order to work off a debt—Congress
did not attempt to exercise what little power Section 2 was thought to give
it.

Then in 1968 in *Jones* v. *Mayer* the Supreme Court construed Section 2 in a significantly new way, or some would say the Court finally got
around to interpreting the Section as its framers intended. The case grew
out of a suit filed by Mr. and Mrs. Joseph Lee Jones against a developer
in St. Louis County who refused to sell them a home because Mr. Jones is
black. The Joneses cited an almost unused section of the Civil Rights Act
of 1866 which reads, "All citizens of the United States shall have the same
right, in every State and Territory, as is enjoyed by white citizens thereof
to inherit, purchase, lease, sell, hold, and convey real and personal property." Few thought that the Joneses had a good case: under prevailing doctrine Congress lacks power under the Fourteenth Amendment (see page
157) to legislate against discrimination unless it is imposed or supported by
governmental action. The Thirteenth Amendment was thought to cover
only slavery; the Civil Rights Act of 1866 had always been construed to
cover only state imposed discrimination. Besides, Congress in 1968 had
just passed the Civil Rights Act covering discrimination in housing that
many thought superseded any impact the 1866 law might have had.

As anticipated, the district court dismissed the complaint, and the
court of appeals affirmed, both courts concluding that the Civil Rights
Act of 1866 applies only to state action and does not reach private refus-
als to sell. But the Supreme Court, with only two justices dissenting, reversed. Significant beyond the immediate facts of this case was the Supreme Court's interpretation of Section 2 of the Thirteenth Amendment.
Mr. Justice Stewart, speaking for the Court, proclaimed:

> The Thirteenth Amendment authorized Congress to do more than merely
> dissolve the legal bond by which the Negro slave was held to his master;
> it gave Congress the power rationally to determine what are the badges
> and the incidents of slavery and the authority to translate that determina-
> tion into effective legislation. . . .
> When racial discrimination herds men into ghettos and makes their abil-

ity to buy property turn on the color of their skin, then it too is a relic of slavery. . . .
At the very least, the freedom that Congress is empowered to secure under the Thirteenth Amendment includes the freedom to buy whatever a white man can buy, the right to live wherever a white man can live. If Congress cannot say that being a free man means at least this much, then the Thirteenth Amendment made a promise the Nation cannot keep.[155]

In short, Section 2, as now construed, gives Congress the authority to enact whatever legislation is necessary and proper to overcome all incidents and badges of slavery no matter from what source they may be imposed.

Amendment XIV

Privileges and Immunities of United States Citizenship, Due Process, and Equal Protection of the Laws

Section 1
All persons born or naturalized in the United States, and subject to the jurisdiction thereof, are citizens of the United States and of the State wherein they reside.

This amendment was proposed June 13, 1866 and declared in force by the Secretary of State July 28, 1868.
In the famous, perhaps infamous, Dred Scott Case (1857), Chief Justice Taney had declared that the framers did not include Negroes as part of the sovereign "people of the United States" and he wrote: " [Negroes] were not intended to be included, under the word 'citizen' in the Constitution, and can therefore claim none of the rights and privileges which that instrument provides for and secures to citizens of the United States. On the contrary, they were at that time considered as a subordinate and inferior class of beings, who had been subjugated by the dominant race, and, whether *emancipated or not* [italics added], yet remained subject to their authority, and had no rights or privileges but such as those who held the power and the government might choose to grant them." [156] The opening sentence of the Fourteenth Amendment reversed this decision.
Persons born in the United States but not subject to the jurisdiction thereof are children of foreign diplomats and children born of alien enemies in the event of a hostile occupation of the United States. Although the Indian tribes are subject to the jurisdiction of the United States, they have been considered in a special category, as "wards of the nation," and the Fourteenth Amendment did not directly confer citizenship upon them.

However, all Indians are now citizens of the United States by act of Congress. All other children born in the United States become citizens even if their parents are aliens.

The clause confers citizenship on the principle of *jus soli*—by reason of place of birth; it does not prevent Congress from conferring citizenship by *jus sanguinis*—by reason of blood. For example, by law of Congress, children born outside the United States to American citizens are citizens of the United States "from birth." Citizenship may also be acquired by naturalization (see page 58).

The Constitution confers citizenship on all persons born or naturalized in the United States. Although naturalization secured by fraud may be cancelled through proper judicial action and persons may under certain conditions voluntarily renounce their citizenship, what the Constitution confers, Congress cannot constitutionally take away.

Congress has listed some fourteen acts which it has declared are to be construed as incompatible with undivided allegiance to the United States, and it has stipulated that a person who commits one of these acts is to be deprived of his American nationality. Four of these expatriation provisions have been challenged before the Supreme Court. It has declared all of them unconstitutional: to be court-martialed and dishonorably discharged for desertion during wartime;[157] to leave the United States during time of war or national emergency to avoid the draft;[158] to be a naturalized citizen living abroad for a stipulated number of years;[159] to vote in the elections of other nations.[160] A few years earlier the Supreme Court had sustained the constitutionality of this last provision,[161] but in 1967 four justices joined with Justice Black to declare: "We hold that the Fourteenth Amendment was designed to, and does, protect every citizen of the Nation against a congressional forcible destruction of his citizenship." [162]

Since there is a constitutional right to remain a citizen unless it is voluntarily relinquished, it would appear that most of the other provisions of the expatriation laws are also unconstitutional, although the question remains open whether some of them cover acts that will be considered a voluntary relinquishment of citizenship, for example, becoming a naturalized citizen of another nation.

Section 1
[continued] No State shall make or enforce any law which shall abridge the privileges or immunities of citizens of the United States;

After the adoption of the Thirteenth Amendment, several southern states that were restored by President Johnson promptly adopted legislation that, in the words of Justice Miller, "imposed upon the colored race onerous disabilities and burdens, and curtailed their rights in the pursuit of life, liberty, and property to such an extent that their freedom was of little value. . . ." These laws convinced those in control of Congress, again to quote Miller, "that something more was necessary in the way of constitutional protection to the unfortunate race who had suffered so much." [163] Accordingly, they insisted upon the ratification of the Fourteenth Amendment as a condition of restoring southern state governments to full participation in the government of the Union.

Despite the obvious purpose of the Fourteenth Amendment to protect the Negro from "oppressions of those who had formerly exercised unlimited dominion over him," it was not until the 1940s that the amendment was used primarily for this purpose. And it has not been the "privileges or immunities" clause that has been used but rather the due process and equal protection clauses (see pages 151–156).

The Supreme Court, in the *Slaughter House Cases,* so narrowly construed the privileges or immunities clause in the very first case in which the Fourteenth Amendment came before it that it has never had much significance. The Court held that there are two distinct citizenships, state and federal and that the "fundamental" civil and political rights that we enjoy are privileges or immunities stemming from *state,* not *United States,* citizenship. In other words, this clause conferred no new rights upon United States citizens but merely made explicit a federal guarantee against state abridgment of already established rights.

The privileges or immunities of United States citizens (which this clause forbids states to abridge) are those that owe their existence to the Constitution, the laws and treaties of the United States, such as the right to travel in the United States, the right to engage in interstate and foreign commerce, the right to protection of the national government on the high seas and in foreign countries, the right to vote in primaries and general elections in which congressmen and presidential electors are chosen and to have that vote properly counted. And while the Supreme Court in past decisions has held some important rights are not privileges or immunities of United States citizens—such as the right to be secure in one's home, the right to refuse to give self-incriminatory evidence in state courts, the right to engage in a legal occupation, the right to attend public schools, the right to vote in state elections—the significance of these decisions has been substantially undermined by more recent rulings.[164] These may not be privileges of United States citizens as such, but today they are protected by the due process and equal protection clauses of the Fourteenth Amendment (see below). Furthermore, with the expansion of federal civil rights laws, there are a large number of such rights that owe their existence to federal laws and thus are protected from state (or private, for that matter) abridgment.

Section 1
[continued] nor shall any State deprive any person of life, liberty, or property, without due process of law;

It should be emphasized that this clause, as well as the privileges and immunities clause and the equal protection of laws clause (see below), is directed to the states, their officials, and local governments. Private wrongs—wrongful acts of private individuals—if not sanctioned in some way by a state, do not violate the Fourteenth Amendment. In brief, the Fourteenth Amendment protects individuals against *state,* not *private,* action.

As has been noted (see pages 105–107), after the Supreme Court's interpretation of the privileges or immunities clause rendered it ineffective as a protector of the "fundamental rights," an attempt was made to make the due process clause serve this purpose, an attempt that was not completely successful until the 1960s. The Supreme Court still has not gone so far as to make the due process clause of the Fourteenth Amendment a mirror image of the Bill of Rights, although in fact most provisions of the Bill of Rights have been incorporated into the due process clause.

Section 1
[continued] nor deny to any person within its jurisdiction the equal protection of the laws.

This clause forbids states to make "unreasonable" and "arbitrary" classifications, but it does not rule out "reasonable" classifications that affect alike all persons similarly situated and that have some relation to permissible ends. For example, to classify persons for tax purposes (but not for voting, see below) on the basis of wealth is reasonable; so is classification on the basis of age for the purpose of voting. Likewise, the Supreme Court sustained an Ohio law forbidding any women other than the wife or daughters of the owner of a tavern to serve as barmaids. A majority of the justices felt that this "discrimination" against women owners and other ladies who were denied such employment was justified by the widely recognized difference between men and women.[165]

Recently the Supreme Court appears to have adopted a new standard to test laws that it conceives to touch on fundamental rights such as the right to vote or the right to travel in the United States. If laws appear to the Supreme Court to have a discriminatory impact on these rights, the normal presumption of constitutionality is reversed and the state must demonstrate a "compelling governmental interest." Applying this standard the Supreme Court has declared unconstitutional: laws making persons who have resided in a state for less than a year ineligible to receive public assistance;[166] suffrage requirements making ineligible persons residing in a state because of military duty;[167] requirements denying nontaxpayers the right to vote for bond issues;[168] requirements denying nontaxpayers and nonparents the right to vote in school board elections;[169] requirements that petitions to get on a statewide ballot must contain signatures of a certain number of persons in a certain number of counties;[170] laws that make it difficult for minor parties to obtain places on a ballot.[171]

In the same fashion, classifications based on race, religion, or national origin, are "odious" to our system, "constitutionally suspect," "subject to the most rigid scrutiny," and "in most instances irrelevant." The Supreme Court has come very close to ruling that any such classification is necessarily unreasonable.[172] Some of the justices have stated flatly that they cannot conceive of any compelling governmental interest that would justify a racial classification.[173] However, the Supreme Court has not made a blanket prohibition of all such classifications. During the Second World War the Supreme Court reluctantly sustained the right of the military to force American citizens of Japanese ancestry to leave their homes and jobs on the West Coast and go to "relocation camps." The Court agreed that during an emergency period, when a Japanese invasion was threatened, there was justification for classifying persons by their ancestry.[174] However, once the military had conceded that particular persons were loyal, the government could not, the Court made clear, impose any restraints on the freedom of movement of such persons of Japanese ancestry that were not imposed on all persons.[175]

Since 1954 when the Supreme Court in *Brown* v. *Board of Education* reversed *Plessy* v. *Ferguson* and set aside the separate-but-equal formula it has gone a long way toward depriving racial classifications of any constitutional support. In the Plessy case (1896) the Supreme Court had held that a state could compel racial segregation in the use of public facilities provided equal facilities were available to all races.[176] State-imposed segregation, said the Supreme Court, was not state discrimination. Under the guise of this formula, "Jim Crow" laws, as segregation laws are known, were passed in southern states to cover all phases of life from birth to death, from hospitals to burial grounds. For many decades, the facilities provided for Negroes were separate but they were not equal. Beginning in the 1940s the Supreme Court started to insist that states must either stop requiring segregation or start providing blacks with exactly equal facilities.

Finally, in the spring of 1954 (*Brown* v. *Board of Education*), the Supreme Court reversed its 1896 holding as applied to public schools and ruled that "separate but equal" is a contradiction in terms and that segregation is itself discrimination.[177] A year later, the Court ordered school boards to proceed with deliberate speed to desegregate public schools at the earliest practicable date.[178]

Since the Brown Decision, the Supreme Court has declared unconstitutional laws applying segregation to recreational facilities, public transportation, places of public accommodation, and courthouses.[179] The Supreme Court now agrees with first Justice Harlan dissenting in *Plessy* v. *Ferguson,* "The Constitution is color-blind."

In the years since the Brown Decision, federal courts have struck down a whole battery of schemes designed to circumvent the consequences of it. In the Little Rock Decision (*Cooper* v. *Aaron,* 1958)—in an opinion signed individually by each member of the Supreme Court in order to emphasize the justices' unanimity and the strength of their convictions— the Court held that community opposition, even violent protest, does not justify delaying public school desegregation. Said the Court, "The constitutional rights of children not to be discriminated against in school admission on grounds of race or color . . . can neither be nullified openly and directly by state legislators or state executives or judicial officers, nor nullified indirectly by them through evasive schemes for segregation whether attempted 'ingeniously or ingenuously.' " [180] In 1963, nine years after the first Brown Decision, the Supreme Court pointedly stated, "Brown never contemplated that the concept of 'deliberate speed' would countenance indefinite delay in elimination of racial barriers in schools." [181] In 1966, the Supreme Court twice emphasized, "Delays in desegregating school systems are no longer tolerable." [182] Finally in 1968 the Supreme Court stated, "The time for more mere 'deliberate speed' has run out. . . . Delays in desegregating school systems are no longer tolerable. . . . The burden on a school board today is to come forward with a plan that promises realistically to work and promises realistically to work now." [183]

Since 1964 the Department of Justice has been authorized to take an active role in filing of school desegregation suits, and perhaps of even greater significance, federal funds may be denied to school districts that refuse to desegregate. Desegregation of public schools, North or South, in both law and fact remains to be accomplished, but those who oppose integration no longer have the constitutional cards stacked in their favor.

Since the end of the Second World War the Supreme Court has refused to sustain any law based on a racial classification for whatever purpose, whether it be related to marriage, schools, parks, prisons, etc. (Perhaps there is one exception: The Supreme Court upheld a judicial decree that ordered the assignment of black teachers to each school on a quota basis as a means of forcing a school district to move faster toward dismantling its racially separated school system.) [184]

The equal protection clause also covers courtroom procedures. Any indictment or conviction of a Negro by a jury from which Negroes have been excluded because of their race, whether by law or by administrative practices, is a denial of equal protection. Discrimination on the basis of national origin in jury selection elicits the same ruling, and the Supreme Court would undoubtedly so rule if the issue of religious discrimination were presented.[185] Exclusion of persons from a jury because of race, religion, or national origin (but not because of attitude toward the death penalty, see page 133) through peremptory challenges will pass constitutional challenge, if it is not a pattern of systematic official discrimination.[186] The use of peremptory challenges is common in most states in which both the prosecution and the defense are allowed to have removed from the jury a certain number of persons without having to explain why.

Exclusion of women from juries does not violate the equal protection clause, since classifications on the basis of sex for certain purposes, in contrast with those based on race or national origin, may be reasonable.[187] Today, however, the common practice is to call women for jury service on the same terms as men. A female defendant obviously has the same constitutional rights as a man.

The Supreme Court has applied the equal protection clause to impose on the states not only a duty to avoid discrimination against indigents in the administration of justice, but also a positive obligation to see to it that those without funds have treatment equal to those who can afford proper legal counsel, appeals, and so on. If a state, for example, makes a transcript a requirement for an appeal, it must furnish transcripts to those unable to afford them.[188]

Racial, religious, and class minorities are not the only groups protected by the equal protection clause. Except where the Constitution specifically provides otherwise, as it does with respect to the apportionment of United States senators and electoral votes among the states, any electoral scheme that makes one man's vote weigh less than another's denies him the equal protection of the laws. The Supreme Court struck down Georgia's county unit system for counting votes because it gave rural voters a much greater voice in the selection of statewide executive officers than those living in cities.[189] An Illinois law suffered the same fate since it gave more weight to rural than to urban signatories by requiring that of the 25,000 signatures needed on petitions to secure a place on statewide ballots that at least 200 must come from each of 50 of the state's 102 counties.[190]

In somewhat the same vein, a state may not impose a poll tax as a condition of eligibility to vote, even if there is no showing that the poll tax discriminates against blacks; it establishes an unreasonable classification of wealth. Justice Douglas wrote for the Court, "Wealth, like race, creed, or color, is not germane to one's ability to participate intelligently in the electoral process. . . . Lines drawn on the basis of wealth or property, like those of race are traditionally disfavored."[191] Along a similar line, the Supreme Court declared unconstitutional a Texas law that disqualified from the suffrage all servicemen, unless they had been residents of Texas at the time of their induction into the armed forces.[192] On the other side, the Supreme Court concluded that Illinois' absentee ballot provisions, the effect of which was to deny such ballots to persons in jail within their home county but not to persons in jail outside their home counties, was not unconstitutional. Chief Justice Warren emphasized that the classification was not based on a suspect criteria of race or wealth, and that the law touched not the right to vote but the right to an absentee ballot. Therefore, the exacting requirements of a "compelling state interest" were not necessary: the classification could not be called unreasonable.[193]

Discrimination by private individuals, although it may violate a law, does not violate the equal protection clause unless aided, supported, or positively encouraged by state action. Persons who wish to do so may place covenants in deeds restricting the use of their property to persons of particular races or religions and such covenants by themselves are not prohibited by the equal protection clause (although they may conflict with federal and state laws.) But no court or other officer may help to enforce such covenants.[194] Similarly, if owners of places of accommodation refuse to serve Negroes, such conduct may violate the laws of the state and the Civil Rights Act of 1964 that covers firms affecting interstate commerce, but it does not violate the equal protection clause. However, in communities where laws or customs require proprietors to provide service to Negroes on a segregated basis, the police may not arrest nor the courts convict Negroes merely for peacefully insisting on service in places open to the general public. Where laws and state-enforced customs prevent proprietors from exercising a free choice, the whole procedure for denying Negroes nonsegregated service is so infused with state support and state aid that the equal protection clause comes into play.[195] In like manner, private schools may exclude Negroes; if the schools receive any kind of financial or other public support, their conduct becomes subject to the limitation of the equal protection clause.

The Supreme Court inspects closely whenever there is a suspicion of state involvement in discriminatory conduct. For example, the Court declared unconstitutional an amendment to the California Constitution that in effect rendered unenforceable previously enacted legislation forbidding racial discrimination in the sale of real estate. By so amending its Constitution, California was not merely being neutral, but was encouraging discrimination and making it more difficult for blacks than for whites to buy homes. No one has a constitutional or legal right to discriminate against others because of race and a state may not use its powers to protect this right.[196] Similarly, a charter amendment of Akron, Ohio, requiring open housing—but no other—ordinances to be submitted to popular referendum came into conflict with the equal protection clause: Here again the power of government was being used to make it more difficult for those who favor open housing legislation to secure its enactment than for those who favor other kinds of legislation.[197]

There is no equal protection clause limiting the national government; however, just as the due process clause of the Fourteenth Amendment has been used to apply provisions of the Bill of Rights to the states, so has the due process clause of the Fifth Amendment been used to prevent national discriminatory legislation. Hence segregation in the public schools in the District of Columbia and the use of national courts to enforce racially restrictive covenants are also unconstitutional.[198] And a requirement of the District of Columbia that one must reside there for a year to be eligible for public assistance was held to be so "unjustifiable a discrimination against poor people as to be violative of the due process clause." [199]

Section 2
Representatives shall be apportioned among the several States according to their respective numbers, counting the whole number of persons in each State, excluding Indians not taxed.

This section supersedes Article I, Section 2, paragraph 3. Slaves were originally counted at three fifths the number of free persons.

Section 2
[continued] But when the right to vote at any election for the choice of electors for President and Vice President of the United States, Representatives in Congress, the Executive and Judicial officers of a State, or the members of the Legislature thereof, is denied to any of the male inhabitants of such State, being twenty-one years of age, and citizens of the United States, or in any way abridged, except for participation in rebellion, or other crime, the basis of representation therein shall be reduced in the proportion which the number of such male citizens shall bear to the whole number of male citizens twenty-one years of age in such State.

This provision has never been enforced by Congress, and may today be regarded as obsolete through disuse and, also, possibly through obvious disharmony with the Nineteenth Amendment.

Section 3
No person shall be a Senator or Representative in Congress, or elector of President and Vice President or hold any office, civil or military, under the United States, or under any State, who, having previously taken an oath, as a member of Congress, or as an officer of the United States, or as a member of any State

legislature, or as an executive or judicial officer of any State, to support the Constitution of the United States, shall have engaged in insurrection or rebellion against the same, or given aid or comfort to the enemies thereof. But Congress may by a vote of two-thirds of each House, remove such disability.

This section politically disabled those who led the southern states into the Confederacy. It was placed in the Fourteenth Amendment by the radical Republicans and was a factor in their struggle with President Johnson. It limited the President's power to pardon the leaders of the Confederacy and thus restore their political and civil rights. Congress removed this disability on June 6, 1898.

Section 4

The validity of the public debt of the United States, authorized by law, including debts incurred for payment of pensions and bounties for services in suppressing insurrection or rebellion, shall not be questioned. But neither the United States nor any State shall assume or pay any debt or obligation incurred in aid of insurrection or rebellion against the United States, or any claim for the loss or emancipation of any slave; but all such debts, obligations and claims shall be held illegal and void.

This section invalidated all the securities and other evidences of debt of the Confederacy and reaffirmed those of the Union.

Section 5

The Congress shall have power to enforce, by appropriate legislation, the provisions of this article.

In the *Civil Rights Cases* (1883), the Supreme Court restricted the power of Congress under this section to the prevention or correction of state (including local) governmental action that abridges the privileges or immunities of a United States citizen, that deprives any person of life, liberty, or property without due process, or that denies him the equal protection of the laws. The Supreme Court held that since the Fourteenth Amendment forbids only *state* action, Section 5 did not authorize Congress to make it a federal crime for innkeepers and other proprietors of public places to deny accommodations to persons because of race. Congress could adopt legislation under Section 5 only to prevent state discrimination, not abridgment of civil rights by private groups or persons.[200]

In view of the Supreme Court's holding in the Civil Rights Cases, Congress relied on the commerce clause when it adopted the Civil Rights

Act of 1964 that forbids discrimination by employers and by operators of places of public accommodation. However, even if Congress had chosen to base the 1964 Act more directly on Section 5, it is likely that the present Supreme Court would have sustained it and would have narrowed the sweep of its earlier 1883 decision. It is not difficult to construct an argument that there is sufficient state action to justify an application of the Fourteenth Amendment when a state stands back and allows those who serve the public to discriminate against persons because of their race. Furthermore, not only does the broader concept of state action cover more and more areas of conduct, but as we noted earlier (see page 147), the current interpretation of Section 2 of the Thirteenth Amendment makes it much less necessary to be concerned about demonstrating state action. For if Congress chooses to move against private racial discrimination, it can do so under the Thirteenth Amendment as well as the Fourteenth.

Even without any liberalization of either Section 5 of the Fourteenth or Section 2 of the Thirteenth Amendments, Congress clearly has authority under Section 5 to regulate the conduct of private individuals who attempt to keep persons from securing the benefits of the Fourteenth Amendment. For example, persons are subject to federal regulation if they threaten children in order to keep them from attending a desegregated public school or for coercing persons in order to keep them from entering a state park. Congress has started to use its powers under Section 5: it has, for example, authorized the Department of Justice to initiate suits in federal courts to prevent public officials or *private* persons from depriving persons of the right not to have a *state* deny them equal protection of the laws.[201]

There is no doubt about the constitutionality of federal civil rights laws that make it a federal offense for persons acting under the color of law willfully to deprive a person of a right secured to him by the Constitution or federal laws.[202] These laws apply even to officials who, in the course of their daily duties, commit acts that are not authorized by state or local law. For example, a police officer who subjects blacks to different treatment from whites may be prosecuted by the federal authorities. Such action may also lead to civil damage suits in federal courts by those who have been deprived of their rights.[203]

In 1966, the Supreme Court gave Section 5 a most interesting "new" significance. The Court held that Section 5 authorizes Congress to do whatever it thinks is necessary and proper in order to enforce the rights guaranteed by the Fourteenth Amendment, even to the extent of superseding state regulations that are not themselves an unconstitutional denial of Fourteenth Amendment rights! This ruling came about in a challenge to a section of the Voting Rights Act of 1965 that stipulates that no person who has had a sixth-grade education under the American flag shall be denied the right to vote because he is not literate in English. This section was adopted to set aside a requirement of New York that was keeping many American citizens from Puerto Rico from voting. Although Justices Douglas and Fortas thought that the New York law was unconstitutional, a majority of the justices thought otherwise. Even so, the Court majority held, Congress is empowered by Section 5 to use its own judgment in determining what legislation is needed to keep states from denying persons equal protection of the laws. Justices Harlan and Stewart dissented on the grounds that Congress was exercising judicial power. So long as a state is not denying any person the equal protection of the laws and is operating within its constitutional sphere, according to the dissenting justices, Congress has no power to act under Section 5.[204]

Independently of Section 5 and the Fourteenth Amendment, Congress has ample constitutional authority to protect persons in the exercise of rights that flow from federal laws and directly from the Constitution, regardless of the source of the threat to these rights. For example, the right to travel freely in interstate commerce, the right to the privileges that flow from federal labor laws, from federal civil rights acts or the right not to have the badges of slavery imposed are rights that Congress can secure against abridgment by private citizens as well as by public officials.[205]

Amendment XV
The Right to Vote

Section 1
The right of the citizens of the United States to vote shall not be denied or abridged by the United States or by any State on account of race, color, or previous condition of servitude.

This amendment was proposed February 26, 1869 and declared in force by the Secretary of State March 30, 1870.

"The Fifteenth Amendment," wrote Justice Frankfurter, "nullifies sophisticated as well as simple-minded modes of discrimination."[206] Yet, for many decades, white Southerners in charge of registration and voting readily circumvented the Fifteenth Amendment. They had an arsenal of discriminatory schemes. Since the end of the Second World War, the Supreme Court has declared unconstitutional most of the devices used to keep Negroes from registering and voting. The first to go was the white primary. Under the pretense that there was no state action involved, blacks were kept from voting in the Democratic party primaries, in many areas the only elections that really mattered. But in *Smith* v. *Allwright* (1944), the Supreme Court said, "When primaries become a part of the machinery for choosing officials . . . the same tests to determine the character of discrimination . . . would be applied to the primary as are applied to the general election." [207] The discriminatory use of understanding and good character tests have also been enjoined.[208] The Constitution has been amended to forbid the requirement of a poll tax payment as a condition for voting for presidential electors or for congressmen (see pages 169–170), and the Constitution has been construed by the Supreme Court to forbid the requirement of a poll tax payment as a condition for voting in any public election (see page 170). In lawsuit after lawsuit, the federal courts have struck down one discriminatory scheme after another.

Section 2
The Congress shall have power to enforce this article by appropriate legislation.

Until the Voting Rights Act of 1965, Congress used its power under Section 2 very little, and what little it did do was to open federal courts for legal action against discriminatory state practices. This case-by-case litigation was inadequate to combat widespread and persistent discrimination because of the inordinate amount of time and energy required to overcome the obstructionist tactics invariably encountered in these lawsuits. Even after a lawsuit was won, there was no assurance that blacks would be permitted to vote. So, in 1965, Congress, using its authority under this Section to do whatever is necessary and proper to insure that no state shall deprive any person of the right to vote because of race, adopted a new approach. By the Voting Rights Act of 1965, Congress set aside literacy and other tests in those states and counties that have had a persistent history of violating the Fifteenth Amendment. In these areas of persistent discrimination, the Attorney General, without first having to win a lawsuit, may send federal registrars to enroll voters if state and local officials fail to do so. He may also send federal authorities to supervise elections and the counting of ballots whenever he thinks it is necessary. As a result of the Voting Rights Act of 1965, for the first time in almost a hundred years, the Fifteenth Amendment became an operating reality in many parts of the United States. Blacks were permitted to register and vote. More than 800,000 Negroes have been registered and more than 50 percent of eligible Negroes are currently registered in every southern state. The Act is due to expire in 1970 and Congress is presently deliberating whether and how to extend the Act. President Nixon has recommended that its prohibitions against literacy tests be extended to the entire nation: Leaders of most civil rights organizations prefer to maintain the Act in its present form and believe that any alterations could lead to a dilution of efforts.

In *South Carolina* v. *Katzenbach,* the Supreme Court by a unanimous vote sustained the most important provisions of the Voting Right Act of 1965 (Justice Black dissented with respect to one provision). Said Chief Justice Warren for the Court, "Congress may use any rational means to effectuate the constitutional prohibition of racial discrimination in voting." [209] In another case involving the Act, the Supreme Court ruled that in a county with a past history of separate but unequal schools even the "impartial" administration of literacy tests would be discriminatory.[210] This ruling would seem to suggest that even absent the Voting Rights Act, a literacy test in such a county would be unconstitutional.

TWENTIETH-CENTURY AMENDMENTS

Amendment XVI

Income Taxes

The Congress shall have power to lay and collect taxes on incomes, from whatever source derived, without apportionment among the several States, and without regard to any census or enumeration.

This amendment was proposed July 12, 1909, and declared in force by the Secretary of State February 25, 1913.

During the Civil War, an income tax was levied as part of the war financing program. As was generally expected, the Supreme Court upheld the national government's right to levy such a tax. In 1894, the Wilson-Gorham Tariff levied a 2 per cent tax on incomes over $4000. The year following, after hearing the tax assailed as the opening wedge of "populism," "communism," and the like, the Supreme Court held, by a five-to-four decision, that a tax on income from property was tantamount to a tax on the property itself and hence a "direct tax" that had to be apportioned among the several states according to population (see Article I, Section 2, paragraph 3).[211] The levying of an income tax was thus rendered impracticable until the adoption of the Sixteenth Amendment in 1913.

Amendment XVII

Direct Election of Senators

1. The Senate of the United States shall be composed of two Senators from each State, elected by the people thereof for six years; and each Senator shall have one vote. The electors in each State shall have the qualifications requisite for electors of the most numerous branch of the State legislatures.

This amendment was proposed May 13, 1912 and declared in force by the Secretary of State May 31, 1913.

The adoption of universal suffrage and the growing strength of the democratic spirit made it inevitable that United States senators should be chosen directly by the people. During the last half of the nineteenth century, the dissident labor and farmer parties had called for direct election. The revelation of certain senators' great wealth and of their obligations to various large economic interests reinforced these demands. By the turn of the century, all the major parties supported proposals for direct election; the House of Representatives several times passed resolutions proposing an amendment to make the change. Finally in 1912, the Senate capitulated. As a matter of fact, by that date the voters in half of the states had obtained the right to indicate their preference for senator in the party primaries; the state legislatures normally followed the wishes of the voters. The adoption of the Seventeenth Amendment merely rounded out a reform that had been long under way.

2. When vacancies happen in the representation of any State in the Senate, the executive authority of such State shall issue writs of election to fill such vacancies: Provided, That the legislature of any State may empower the executive thereof to make temporary appointments until the people fill the vacancies by election as the legislature may direct.

Most vacancies are filled by temporary appointments.

3. This amendment shall not be so construed as to affect the election or term of any Senator chosen before it becomes valid as part of the Constitution.

Amendment XVIII

Prohibition

Section 1
After one year from the ratification of this article the manufacture, sale, or transportation of intoxicating liquors within, the importation thereof into, or the exportation thereof from the United States and all territory subject to the jurisdiction thereof for beverage purposes is hereby prohibited.

This amendment was proposed December 18, 1917, and declared in force by the Acting Secretary of State January 29, 1919.

There have always been those who have waged war upon the demon rum. As long ago as 1842 the State of Maine went dry, and the Prohibition party has had a candidate on the ballot in at least a few states in every presidential election since 1872. But it was the Anti-Saloon League—a pressure group deluxe, formed in 1895—that gave the prohibition movement its greatest impetus. During the First World War, the necessity of saving grain lent prohibition the guise of patriotism. Although the Eighteenth Amendment was ultimately ratified by all the states except Rhode Island and Connecticut, it always lacked the support of large groups of citizens, especially in the large cities. Bootlegging, lax enforcement, and general disregard for the amendment impaired respect for the entire Constitution. The "noble experiment," as it was called, demonstrated that it is almost impossible to regulate personal conduct by legal machinery when the law is contrary to the mores of large sections of the country. National prohibition was finally repealed in 1933 by the Twenty-first Amendment.

Section 2
The Congress and the several States shall have concurrent power to enforce this article by appropriate legislation.

The Volstead Act went into effect January 17, 1920. By 1929, three states *repealed* their enforcement acts; most states left the national government alone to implement this amendment.

Section 3
This article shall be inoperative unless it shall have been ratified as an amendment to the Constitution by the legislatures of the several States, as provided in the Constitution, within seven years from the date of the submission hereof to the States by the Congress.

Amendment XIX
Woman Suffrage

1. The right of citizens of the United States to vote shall not be denied or abridged by the United States or by any State on account of sex.

The Nineteenth Amendment was proposed June 4, 1919, and declared in force by the Secretary of State August 26, 1920.

This amendment was the culmination of a struggle that began in the 1840s. In 1890, women were admitted to full suffrage rights in Wyoming; by the time the amendment was adopted, fifteen states and Alaska had given them full suffrage, fourteen states had given them "presidential suffrage," and two states had given them the right to take part in the primaries. Many of the arguments advanced against woman suffrage sound ludicrous today. Much of the opposition came from certain business groups (especially the liquor industry) who feared that women would vote for regulation. Actually, their votes have not materially changed our politics. Since the adoption of this amendment, there seem not to have been any issues that divided voters along the lines of sex. As a class, men vote in higher proportion to their numbers than women. But, as a class, a higher proportion of the better educated and economically secure vote than do those with little education and less of the world's goods. Almost all of the educated and economically favored women vote, but many of the lower-income and less-educated women still do not cast a ballot. Thus it may be that the Nineteenth Amendment introduced a slight political advantage for the values represented by the "upper classes."

The Nineteenth Amendment does not affect state laws dealing with ownership of property, jury service, and so forth. Therefore many organizations are now advocating an "equal-rights amendment" to confer upon women full equality with men. Opponents of the proposed amendment argue that it would jeopardize women's special privileges concerning hours of work, minimum wages, maternity benefits, and the like.

2. Congress shall have power to enforce this article by appropriate legislation.

Amendment XX

The Lame-Duck Amendment

Section 1
The terms of the President and Vice President shall end at noon on the 20th day of January, and the terms of Senators and Representatives at noon on the 3d day of January, of the years in which such terms would have ended if this article had not been ratified; and the terms of their successors shall then begin.

This amendment was proposed March 3, 1932, and declared in force by the Secretary of State February 6, 1933.

This amendment was eventually ratified by all the states. Senator George W. Norris of Nebraska was the moving force behind the amendment, which sometimes bears his name. Its adoption brought to a close the Progressive Movement's contribution to constitutional reform, a movement that led to the Sixteenth through the Twentieth Amendments.

Before the adoption of the Twentieth Amendment, congressmen and the President elected in November did not take office until the following March, and newly elected congressmen did not (unless called into special session) actually begin their work until the following December— thirteen months after their election. Meanwhile, congressmen defeated in the November elections ("lame ducks") continued to serve until the following March 4 and, although repudiated at the polls, continued to represent their constituencies in the December-to-March session.

Section 2

The Congress shall assemble at least once in every year, and such meeting shall begin at noon on the 3d day of January, unless they shall by law appoint a different day.

This section supersedes Article I, Section 4, paragraph 2, which called for Congress to meet on the first Monday in December and so necessitated every other year a short, ineffective December-to-March, "lame-duck" session. The Twentieth Amendment does away with this session, which was frequently featured in the Senate by filibusters.

Section 3

If, at the time fixed for the beginning of the term of the President, the President elect shall have died, the Vice President elect shall become President. If a President shall not have been chosen before the time fixed for the beginning of his term, or if the President elect shall have failed to qualify, then the Vice President elect shall act as President until a President shall have qualified; and the Congress may by law provide for the case wherein neither a President elect nor a Vice President elect shall have qualified, declaring who shall then act as President, or the manner in which one who is to act shall be selected, and such person shall act accordingly until a President or Vice President shall have qualified.

It should be noted that within the meaning of the Constitution there is no President-elect or Vice President-elect until the electoral votes have been counted by Congress or, in the event that no person has a majority of the electoral votes, until the House of Representatives and the Senate make their choice.

Congress has now made the same provision for succession in the event of the disability or disqualification of the President-elect and Vice President-elect as in the case of the President and Vice President (see page 76).[212]

Section 4
The Congress may by law provide for the case of the death of
any of the persons from whom the House of Representatives
may choose a President whenever the right of choice shall
have devolved upon them, and for the case of the death of any
of the persons from whom the Senate may choose a Vice Presi-
dent whenever the right of choice shall have devolved upon
them.

Congress has failed to act under this section, but see the Twenty-fifth
Amendment.

Section 5
Sections 1 and 2 shall take effect on the 15th day of October
following the ratification of this article.

Section 6
This article shall be inoperative unless it shall have been rati-
fied as an amendment to the Constitution by the legislatures of
three-fourths of the several States within seven years from the
date of its submission.

Amendment XXI

Repeal of Prohibition

Section 1
The eighteenth article of amendment to the Constitution of the
United States is hereby repealed.

This amendment was proposed February 20, 1933 and declared in
force by the Secretary of State December 5, 1933.

It soon became apparent that the Eighteenth Amendment failed to
diminish the amount of liquor consumed; instead, it diverted taxes and
profits from legitimate interests into the hands of bootleggers and criminals
and was endangering respect for the Constitution and the laws of the land.
The demand for repeal became insistent. In 1928, Alfred Smith, the Democratic candidate for President, advocated repeal; by 1932, the platforms
of both major parties were, in the phrase of the day, "dripping wet."

Section 2
The transportation or importation into any State, Territory, or
possession of the United States for delivery or use therein of
intoxicating liquors, in violation of the laws thereof, is hereby
prohibited.

This section gives states greater authority to regulate intoxicating beverages than any other item of interstate commerce. States may impose restrictions on the transportation or importation of intoxicating liquors and regulate its distribution or sale in ways that would be an unconstitutional interference with commerce among the states for any other commodity. Even so, state regulations may be set aside by Congress under the commerce clause and must be "reasonable" in the judgment of the Court. For example, in 1964, the Supreme Court set aside a Kentucky tax on each gallon of whiskey imported from Scotland as a violation of the Export-Import Clause (see page 70). Justice Black, in dissent, quipped, "Although I was brought up to believe that Scotch whiskey would need a tax preference to survive in competition with Kentucky bourbon, I never understood the Constitution to require a State to give such preference." [213]

Section 3
This article shall be inoperative unless it shall have been ratified as an amendment to the Constitution by conventions in the several States, as provided in the Constitution, within seven years from the date of the submission hereof to the States by the Congress.

Amendment XXII
The Number of Presidential Terms

Section 1
No person shall be elected to the office of the President more than twice, and no person who has held the office of President, or acted as President, for more than two years of a term to which some other person was elected President shall be elected to the office of the President more than once. But this Article shall not apply to any person holding the office of President when this Article was proposed by the Congress,

This amendment was proposed March 24, 1947, and certified as adopted by the Administrator of General Services March 1, 1951.

The maximum period that a man could serve would be ten years, two years by elevation to the office through death or disability of the elected President, and two elected terms of four years each—in some cases it might be only six years since elevation for two years and a day, through death or disability of the elected President, would make a person eligible for only one elected term of four years.

Section 1

[continued] and shall not prevent any person who may be hold-
ing the office of President, or acting as President, during the
term within which this Article becomes operative from holding
the office of President or acting as President during the re-
mainder of such term.

Section 2

This article shall be inoperative unless it shall have been rati-
fied as an amendment to the Constitution by the legislatures of
three-fourths of the several States within seven years from the
date of its submission to the States by the Congress.

Within four years after submission, forty-one state legislatures ratified this amendment. There was very little discussion of its significance; in some instances, the legislators voted for ratification without debate.

What effect will the Twenty-second Amendment have on the influence of the President? In the past, when it was possible that the President might seek another term, he had considerably more influence than when he made known his decision not to run again. Congressmen, governors, and politicians were much less inclined to oppose the man who might be the head of their ticket than the man who was about to retire to the role of elder statesman. The adoption of this amendment eliminated even the outside possibility of a second-term President's running again.

Amendment XXIII

Presidential Electors
for the District of Columbia

Section 1

The District constituting the seat of Government of the United
States shall appoint in such manner as the Congress may di-
rect;

A number of electors of President and Vice-President
equal to the whole number of Senators and Representatives in
Congress to which the District would be entitled if it were a
State, but in no event more than the least populous State;
there shall be in addition to those appointed by the States, but
they shall be considered, for the purposes of the election of
President and Vice-President, to be electors appointed by a
State; and they shall meet in the District and perform such du-
ties as provided by the twelfth article of amendment.

This amendment was proposed June 16, 1960 and ratified March 29, 1961.

Congress set a seven-year time limit for ratification when it submitted the amendment to the state legislatures. Although Tennessee was the only southern state to ratify, it took only nine months to secure approval of the legislatures in three fourths of the states—thirty-eight of them—the fastest ratification of any amendment since the approval of the Twelfth.

Since the least populous state, Alaska, has only three electoral votes, this is all that will be assigned to the District of Columbia, despite the fact that it has more residents than twelve of the states, in fact more than Alaska, Nevada, and Wyoming combined.

In the event a presidential election is thrown into the House of Representatives, the voters of the District will have no voice in the deliberations since the District is not a state and has no representation in the House.

Section 2
The Congress shall have power to enforce this article by appropriate legislation.

Congress has set the voting age under the Twenty-third Amendment at twenty-one, created a one-year residence requirement, and provided for registration every four years.

Amendment XXIV
The Anti-Poll Tax Amendment

Section 1
The right of citizens of the United States to vote in any primary or other election for President or Vice-President, for electors for President or Vice-President, or for Senator or Representative in Congress shall not be denied or abridged by the United States or any State by reason of failure to pay any poll tax or other tax.

Section 2
The Congress shall have power to enforce this article by appropriate legislation.

This amendment proposed August 27, 1962, was readily ratified within the seven years stipulated by Congress and became part of the Constitution on January 23, 1964. At the time it was submitted, only five states imposed a poll tax as a requirement for voting.

The Anti-Poll Tax Amendment by its own terms forbids payment of a poll tax as a condition for voting for presidential electors and congressmen. It was rendered superfluous by the Supreme Court decision of 1966, *Harper* v. *Virginia Board of Electors,* that the Equal Protection Clause precludes a state from imposing a poll tax as a requirement to vote in *any* election.[214] Earlier, the Supreme Court had held that under the Twenty-fourth Amendment a state could not give voters the choice of either paying a poll tax or filing a certificate of residence six months prior to an election. Such a requirement erects an obstacle to voting for those who assert their constitutional exemption from the poll tax.[215]

Amendment XXV

Presidential Disability—
Vice Presidential Vacancies

Section 1
In the case of the removal of the President from office or of his death or resignation, the Vice President shall become President.

At the time Congress submitted this proposal on July 6, 1965, it stipulated that ratification would have to take place within seven years to be effective. It was ratified February 10, 1967.

This section merely confirms what has been consistent practice (see page 76) of the eight Vice Presidents who acceded to the presidency on the death of the President. It does deal, however, with the additional situation that has as yet never occurred, resignation of a President. It would preclude a man from resigning and then after doing so attempting to return to office.

Presumably a resignation would be effective if submitted in writing to the Speaker of the House and President pro tempore of the Senate, but the proposed Amendment does not deal with the matter.

Section 2
Whenever there is a vacancy in the office of the Vice President, the President shall nominate a Vice President who shall take office upon confirmation by a majority vote of both Houses of Congress.

The Vice Presidency has been vacant sixteen times, the most recent being created when Lyndon Johnson became President on November 22, 1963, after the assassination of President Kennedy. This situation dramatized the unsatisfactory situation of leaving the line of presidential succession open to the Speaker of the House, a man not chosen because of his suitability to serve as Acting President of the United States.

The procedure for filling the vacancy has some resemblance to the procedure for selecting a Vice President. Once a party selects its presidential candidate, that candidate chooses his vice-presidential running mate who, subject to confirmation by the national convention of his party and election along with the President, becomes Vice President. Between elections, Congress will serve in lieu of the electorate to confirm the presidential choice.

Section 3
Whenever the President transmits to the President pro tempore of the Senate and the Speaker of the House of Representatives his written declaration that he is unable to discharge the powers and duties of his office, and until he transmits to them a written declaration to the contrary, such powers and duties shall be discharged by the Vice President as Acting President.

Until this amendment, Congress had never established procedures to determine how it should be judged whether or not the President is unable to discharge his duties. Five times in our history, this question has caused difficulty: when President Garfield suffered a lingering death from an assassin's bullet; when President Wilson had a physical breakdown during the closing years of his second term; when there was concern about President Roosevelt's health prior to his fatal attack; and when President Eisenhower was temporarily disabled, first by a heart attack and later by a serious operation.

Section 4
Whenever the Vice President and a majority of either the principal officers of the executive departments or of such other body of Congress may by law provide, transmit to the President pro tempore of the Senate and the Speaker of the House of Representatives their written declaration that the President is unable to discharge the powers and duties of his office, the Vice President shall immediately assume the powers and duties of the office as Acting President.

Section 4 deals with the situation in which a President may be unable to declare his own inability to discharge his duties. The responsibility then vests in the Vice President and the Cabinet to so declare. Upon such a declaration, the Vice President would *immediately* become Acting President.

It is interesting to note that in this section there is the first constitutional mention of them collectively—the Cabinet. Heretofore the composition of the Cabinet has varied from President to President, and there has been no very precise definition of its membership. Vesting this constitutional responsibility in the Cabinet as an entity suggests the need for some more formal definition of the composition of the Cabinet.

Section 4

[continued] Thereafter, when the President transmits to the President pro tempore of the Senate and the Speaker of the House of Representatives his written declaration that no inability exists, he shall resume the powers and duties of his office unless the Vice President and a majority of either the principal officers of the executive departments or of such other body as Congress may by law provide, transmit within four days to the President pro tempore of the Senate and the Speaker of the House of Representatives their written declaration that the President is unable to discharge the powers and duties of his office. Thereupon Congress shall decide the issue, assembling within forty-eight hours for that purpose, if not in session. If the Congress, within twenty-one days after receipt of the latter written declaration, or, if Congress is not in session, within twenty-one days after Congress is required to assemble, determines by two-thirds vote of both Houses that the President is unable to discharge the powers and duties of his office, the Vice President shall continue to discharge the same as Acting President; otherwise, the President shall resume the powers and duties of his office.

In case of a conflict between the President, Vice President and a majority of the Cabinet over the issue of the President's fitness to assume his duties, Congress decides. However, the presumption is in favor of the President; a two-thirds vote of both Houses is required to retain the Vice President as Acting President in the face of a declaration by the President that he is able to resume his duties.

Contingencies still not covered are methods to fill vacancies caused by the death or resignation of presidential candidates before the election, or a method to fill post-election vacancies caused by the death of the winners of the election before there is in a constitutional sense a President-elect or a Vice President-elect. If an amendment is proposed to alter the electoral college, (see page 145) it is likely that Congress will include provisions authorizing Congress to cover such contingencies.

The Constitution of the United States

We the People of the United States, in Order to form a more perfect Union, establish Justice, insure domestic Tranquility, provide for the common defence, promote the general Welfare, and secure the Blessings of Liberty to ourselves and our Posterity, do ordain and establish this Constitution for the United States of America.

Article I

Section 1

All legislative Powers herein granted shall be vested in a Congress of the United States, which shall consist of a Senate and House of Representatives.

Section 2

The House of Representatives shall be composed of Members chosen every second Year by the People of the several States, and the Electors in each State shall have the Qualifications requisite for Electors of the most numerous Branch of the State Legislature.

No Person shall be a Representative who shall not have attained to the Age of twenty five Years, and been seven Years a Citizen of the United States, and who shall not, when elected, be an Inhabitant of that State in which he shall be chosen.

Representatives and direct Taxes shall be apportioned among the several States which may be included within this Union, according to their respective Numbers, which shall be determined by adding to the whole Number of free Persons, including those bound to Service for a Term of Years, and excluding Indians not taxed, three fifths of all other Persons. The actual Enumeration shall be made within three Years after the first Meeting of the Congress of the United States, and within every subsequent Term of ten Years, in such Manner as they shall by Law direct. The Number of Representatives shall not exceed one for every thirty Thousand, but each State shall have at Least one Representative; and until such enumeration shall be made, the State of New Hampshire shall be entitled to chuse three, Massachusetts eight, Rhode-Island and Providence Plantations one, Connecticut five, New-York six, New Jersey four, Pennsylvania eight, Delaware one, Maryland six, Virginia ten, North Carolina five, South Carolina five, and Georgia three.

When vacancies happen in the Representation from any State, the Executive Authority thereof shall issue Writs of Election to fill such Vacancies.

The House of Representatives shall chuse their speaker and other Officers; and shall have the sole Power of Impeachment.

Section 3

The Senate of the United States shall be composed of two Senators from each State, chosen by the Legislature thereof, for six Years; and each Senator shall have one Vote.

Immediately after they shall be assembled in Consequence of the first Election, they shall be divided as equally as may be into three Classes. The Seats of the Senators of the first Class shall be vacated at the Expiration of the second Year, of the second Class at the Expiration of the fourth Year, and of the third Class at the Expiration of the sixth Year, so that one third may be chosen every second Year; and if Vacancies happen by Resignation, or otherwise, during the Recess of the Legislature of any State, the Executive thereof may make temporary Appointments until the next Meeting of the Legislature, which shall then fill such Vacancies.

No Person shall be a Senator who shall not have attained to the Age of thirty years, and been nine Years a Citizen of the United States, and who shall not, when elected, be an Inhabitant of that State for which he shall be chosen.

The Vice President of the United States shall be President of the Senate, but shall have no Vote, unless they be equally divided.

The Senate shall chuse their other Officers, and also a President pro tempore, in the Absence of the Vice President, or when he shall exercise the Office of President of the United States.

The Senate shall have the sole Power to try all Impeachments. When sitting for that Purpose, they shall be on Oath or Affirmation. When the

President of the United States is tried, the Chief Justice shall preside: And no Person shall be convicted without the Concurrence of two thirds of the Members present.

Judgment in Cases of Impeachment shall not extend further than to removal from Office, and disqualification to hold and enjoy any Office of honor, Trust or Profit under the United States: but the Party convicted shall nevertheless be liable and subject to Indictment, Trial, Judgment and Punishment, according to law.

Section 4

The Times, Places and Manner of holding Elections for Senators and Representatives, shall be prescribed in each State by the Legislature thereof; but the Congress may at any time by Law make or alter such Regulations, except as to the Places of chusing Senators.

The Congress shall assemble at least once in every Year, and such Meeting shall be on the first Monday in December, unless they shall by Law appoint a different Day.

Section 5

Each House shall be the Judge of the Elections, Returns and Qualifications of its own Members, and a Majority of each shall constitute a Quorum to do Business; but a smaller Number may adjourn from day to day, and may be authorized to compel the Attendance of absent Members, in such Manner, and under such Penalties as each House may provide.

Each House may determine the Rules of its Proceedings, punish its Members for disorderly Behaviour, and, with the Concurrence of two thirds, expel a Member.

Each House shall keep a Journal of its Proceedings, and from time to time publish the same, excepting such Parts as may in their Judgment require Secrecy; and the Yeas and Nays of the Members of either House on any question shall, at the Desire of one fifth of those Present, be entered on the Journal.

Neither House, during the Session of Congress, shall, without the Consent of the other, adjourn for more than three days, nor to any other Place than that in which the two Houses shall be sitting.

Section 6

The Senators and Representatives shall receive a Compensation for their Services, to be ascertained by Law, and paid out of the Treasury of the United States. They shall in all Cases, except Treason, Felony and Breach of the Peace, be privileged from Arrest during their Attendance at the Session of their respective Houses, and in going to and returning from the same; and for any Speech or Debate in either House, they shall not be questioned in any other Place.

No Senator or Representative shall, during the Time for which he was elected, be appointed to any civil Office under the Authority of the United States, which shall have been created, or the Emoluments whereof shall have been encreased during such time; and no Person holding any Office under the United States, shall be a Member of either House during his Continuance in Office.

Section 7

All Bills for raising Revenue shall originate in the House of Representatives; but the Senate may propose or concur with Amendments as on other Bills.

Every Bill which shall have passed the House of Representatives and the Senate, shall, before it become a Law, be presented to the President of the United States; If he approve he shall sign it, but if not he shall return it, with his Objections to that House in which it shall have originated, who shall enter the Objections at large on their Journal, and proceed to reconsider it. If after such Reconsideration two thirds of that House shall agree to pass the Bill, it shall be sent, together with the Objections, to the other House, by which it shall likewise be reconsidered, and if approved by two thirds of that House, it shall become a Law. But in all such Cases the Votes of both Houses shall be determined by yeas and Nays, and the Names of the Persons voting for and against the Bill shall be entered on the Journal of each House respectively. If any Bill shall not be returned by the President within ten Days (Sundays excepted) after it shall have been presented to him, the Same shall be a Law, in like Manner as if he had signed it, unless the Congress by their Adjournment prevent its Return, in which Case it shall not be a Law.

Every Order, Resolution, or Vote to which the Concurrence of the Senate and House of Representatives may be necessary (except on a question of Adjournment) shall be presented to the President of the United States; and before the Same shall take Effect, shall be approved by him, or being disapproved by him, shall be repassed by two thirds of the Senate and House of Representatives, according to the Rules and Limitations prescribed in the Case of a Bill.

Section 8

The Congress shall have Power To lay and collect Taxes, Duties, Imposts and Excises, to pay the Debts and provide for the common Defence and general Welfare of the United States; but all Duties, Imposts and Excises shall be uniform throughout the United States;

To Borrow Money on the Credit of the United States;

To regulate Commerce with foreign Nations, and among the several States, and with the Indian Tribes;

To establish an uniform Rule of Naturalization, and uniform Laws on the subject of Bankruptcies throughout the United States;

To coin Money, regulate the Value thereof, and of foreign Coin, and fix the Standard of Weights and Measures;

To provide for the Punishment of counterfeiting the Securities and current Coin of the United States;

To establish Post Offices and post Roads;

To promote the Progress of Science and useful Arts, by securing for limited Times to Authors and Inventors the exclusive Right to their respective Writings and Discoveries;

To constitute Tribunals inferior to the supreme Court;

To define and punish Piracies and Felonies committed on the high Seas, and Offences against the Law of Nations;

To declare War, grant Letters of Marque and Reprisal, and make Rules concerning Captures on Land and Water;

To raise and support Armies, but no Appropriation of Money to that Use shall be for a longer Term than two Years;

To provide and maintain a Navy;

To make Rules for the Government and Regulation of the land and naval Forces;

To provide for calling forth the Militia to execute the Laws of the Union, suppress Insurrections and repel Invasions;

To provide for organizing, arming, and disciplining, the Militia, and for governing such Part of them as may be employed in the Service of the United States, reserving to the States respectively, the Appointment of the Officers, and the Authority of training the Militia according to the discipline prescribed by Congress;

To exercise exclusive Legislation in all Cases whatsoever, over such District (not exceeding ten Miles square) as may, by Cession of particular States, and the Acceptance of Congress, become the Seat of the Government of the United States, and to exercise like Authority over all Places purchased by the Consent of the Legislature of the State in which the Same shall be for the Erection of Forts, Magazines, Arsenals, dock-Yards, and other needful Buildings;—And

To make all Laws which shall be necessary and proper for carrying into Execution the foregoing Powers, and all other Powers vested by this Constitution in the Government of the United States, or in any Department or Officer thereof.

Section 9

The Migration or Importation of such Persons as any of the States now existing shall think proper to admit, shall not be prohibited by the Congress prior to the Year one thousand eight hundred and eight, but a Tax or duty may be imposed on such Importation, not exceeding ten dollars for each Person.

The Privilege of the Writ of Habeas Corpus shall not be suspended, unless when in Cases of Rebellion or Invasion the public Safety may require it.

No Bill of Attainder or ex post facto Law shall be passed.

No Capitation, or other direct, Tax shall be laid, unless in Proportion to the Census or Enumeration herein before directed to be taken.

No Tax or Duty shall be laid on Articles exported from any State.

No Preference shall be given by any Regulation of Commerce or Revenue to the Ports of one State over those of another: nor shall Vessels bound to, or from, one State, be obliged to enter, clear, or pay Duties in another.

No Money shall be drawn from the Treasury, but in Consequence of Appropriations made by Law; and a regular Statement and Account of the Receipts and Expenditures of all public Money shall be published from time to time.

No Title of Nobility shall be granted by the United States: And no Person holding any Office or Profit or Trust under them, shall, without the Consent of the Congress, accept of any present, Emolument, Office, or Title, of any kind whatever, from any King, Prince, or foreign State.

Section 10

No State shall enter into any Treaty, Alliance, or Confederation; grant Letters of Marque and Reprisal; coin Money; emit Bills of Credit; make any Thing but gold and silver Coin a Tender in Payment of Debts; pass any Bill of Attainder, ex post facto Law, or Law impairing the Obligation of Contracts, or grant any Title of Nobility.

No State shall, without the Consent of the Congress, lay any Imposts or Duties on Imports or Exports, except what may be absolutely necessary for executing it's inspection Laws: and the net Produce of all Duties and Imposts, laid by any State on Imports or Exports, shall be for the Use of the Treasury of the United States; and all such Laws shall be subject to the Revision and Controul of the Congress.

No State shall, without the Consent of Congress, lay any Duty of Tonnage, keep Troops, or Ships of War in time of Peace, enter into any Agreement or Compact with another State, or with a foreign Power, or engage in War, unless actually invaded, or in such imminent Danger as will not admit of delay.

Article II

Section 1

The executive Power shall be vested in a President of the United States of

America. He shall hold his Office during the Term of four Years, and, together with the Vice President, chosen for the same term, be elected, as follows

Each State shall appoint, in such Manner as the Legislature thereof may direct, a Number of Electors, equal to the whole Number of Senators and Representatives to which the State may be entitled in the Congress: but no Senator or Representative, or Person holding an Office of Trust or Profit under the United States, shall be appointed an Elector.

The Electors shall meet in their respective States, and vote by Ballot for two Persons, of whom one at least shall not be an Inhabitant of the same State with themselves. And they shall make a List of all the Persons voted for, and of the Number of Votes for each; which List they shall sign and certify, and transmit sealed to the Seat of the Government of the United States, directed to the President of the Senate. The President of the Senate shall, in the Presence of the Senate and House of Representatives, open all the Certificates, and the Votes shall then be counted. The person having the greatest Number of Votes shall be the President, if such Number be a Majority of the whole Number of Electors appointed; and if there be more than one who have such Majority, and have an equal Number of Votes, then the House of Representatives shall immediately chuse by Ballot one of them for President: and if no Person have a Majority, then from the five highest on the List the said House shall in like Manner chuse the President. But in chusing the President, the Votes shall be taken by States, the Representation from each State having one Vote; A quorum for this Purpose shall consist of a Member or Members from two thirds of the States, and a Majority of all the States shall be necessary to a Choice. In every Case, after the Choice of the President, the Person having the greatest Number of Votes of the Electors shall be the Vice President. But if there should remain two or more who have equal Votes, the Senate shall chuse from them by Ballot the Vice President.

The Congress may determine the Time of chusing the Electors, and the Day on which they shall give their Votes; which Day shall be the same throughout the United States.

No Person except a natural born Citizen, or a Citizen of the United States, at the time of the Adoption of this Constitution, shall be eligible to the Office of President; neither shall any Person be eligible to that Office who shall not have attained to the Age of thirty five Years, and been fourteen Years a Resident within the United States.

In Case of the Removal of the President from Office, or of his Death, Resignation, or Inability to discharge the Powers and Duties of the said Office, the Same shall devolve on the Vice President, and the Congress may by Law provide for the Case of Removal, Death, Resignation or Inability, both of the President and Vice President, declaring what Officer shall then act as President, and such Officer shall act accordingly, until the Disability be removed, or a President shall be elected.

The President shall, at stated Times, receive for his Services, a Compensation, which shall neither be encreased nor diminished during the Period for which he shall have been elected, and he shall not receive within that Period any other Emolument from the United States, or any of them.

Before he enter on the Execution of his Office, he shall take the following Oath or Affirmation:—"I do solemnly swear (or affirm) that I will faithfully execute the Office of the President of the United States, and will to the best of my Ability, preserve, protect and defend the Constitution of the United States."

Section 2

The President shall be Commander in Chief of the Army and Navy of the United States, and of the Militia of the several States, when called into the actual Service of the United States; he may require the Opinion, in writing, of the principal Officer in each of the executive Departments, upon any Subject relating to the Duties of their respective Offices, and he shall have Power to grant Reprieves and Pardons for Offences against the United States, except in Cases of Impeachment.

He shall have Power, by and with the Advice and Consent of the Senate, to make Treaties, provided two thirds of the Senators present concur; and he shall nominate, and by and with the Advice and Consent of the Senate, shall appoint Ambassadors, other public Ministers and Consuls, Judges of the supreme Court, and all other Officers of the United States, whose Appointments are not herein otherwise provided for, and which shall be established by Law: but the Congress may by Law vest the Appointment of such inferior Officers, as they think proper, in the President alone, in the Courts of Law, or in the Heads of Departments.

The President shall have Power to fill up all Vacancies that may happen during the Recess of the Senate, by granting Commissions which shall expire at the end of their next Session.

Section 3

He shall from time to time give to the Congress Information of the State of the Union, and recommend to their Consideration such Measures as he shall judge necessary and expedient; he may, on extraordinary Occasions, convene both Houses, or either of them, and in Case of Disagreement between them, with Respect to the Time of Adjournment, he may adjourn them to such Time as he shall think proper; he shall receive Ambassadors and other public Ministers; he shall take Care that the Laws be faithfully executed, and shall Commission all Officers of the United States.

Section 4
The President, Vice President and all civil Officers of the United States, shall be removed from Office on Impeachment for, and Conviction of, Treason, Bribery, or other High Crimes and Misdemeanors.

Article III

Section 1
The judicial Power of the United States, shall be vested in one supreme Court, and in such inferior Courts as the Congress may from time to time ordain and establish. The Judges, both of the supreme and inferior Courts, shall hold their Offices during good Behaviour, and shall, at stated Times, receive for their Services, a Compensation, which shall not be diminished during their Continuance in Office.

Section 2
The judicial Power shall extend to all Cases, in Law and Equity, arising under this Constitution, the Laws of the United States, and Treaties made, or which shall be made, under their Authority;—to all Cases affecting Ambassadors, other public Ministers and Consuls;—to all Cases of admiralty and maritime Jurisdiction;—to Controversies to which the United States shall be a Party;—to Controversies between two or more States; between a State and Citizens of another State;—between Citizens of different States;—between Citizens of the same State claiming Lands under Grants of different States, and between a State, or the Citizens thereof, and foreign States, Citizens or Subjects.

In all Cases affecting Ambassadors, other public Ministers and Consuls, and those in which a State shall be Party, the supreme Court shall have original Jurisdiction. In all the other cases before mentioned, the supreme Court shall have appellate Jurisdiction, both as to Law and Fact, with such Exceptions, and under such Regulations as the Congress shall make.

The Trial of all Crimes, except in Cases of Impeachment, shall be by Jury; and such Trial shall be held in the State where the said Crimes shall have been committed; but when not committed within any State, the Trial shall be at such Place or Places as the Congress may by Law have directed.

Section 3
Treason against the United States, shall consist only in levying War against them, or in adhering to their Enemies, giving them Aid and Comfort. No Person shall be convicted of Treason unless on the Testimony of two Witnesses to the same overt Act, or on Confession in open Court.

The Congress shall have Power to declare the Punishment of Treason, but no Attainder of Treason shall work Corruption of Blood, or Forfeiture except during the Life of the Person attainted.

Article IV

Section 1
Full Faith and Credit shall be given in each State to the public Acts, Records, and judicial Proceedings of every other State. And the Congress may by general Laws prescribe the Manner in which such Acts, Records and Proceedings shall be proved, and the Effect thereof.

Section 2
The Citizens of each State shall be entitled to all Privileges and Immunities of Citizens in the several States.

A Person charged in any State with Treason, Felony, or other Crime, who shall flee from Justice, and be found in another State, shall on Demand of the executive Authority of the State from which he fled, be delivered up, to be removed to the State having Jurisdiction of the Crime.

No Person held to Service or Labour in one State, under the Laws thereof, escaping into another, shall, in Consequence of any Law or Regulation therein, be discharged from such Service or Labour, but shall be delivered up on Claim of the Party to whom such Service or Labour may be due.

Section 3
New States may be admitted by the Congress into this Union; but no new State shall be formed or erected within the Jurisdiction of any other State; nor any State be formed by the Junction of two or more States, or Parts of States, without the Consent of the Legislatures of the States concerned as well as of the Congress.

The Congress shall have Power to dispose of and make all needful Rules and Regulations respecting the Territory or other Property belonging to the United States; and nothing in this Constitution shall be so construed as to Prejudice any Claims of the United States, or of any particular State.

Section 4

The United States shall guarantee to every State in this Union a Republican Form of Government, and shall protect each of them against Invasion; and on Application of the Legislature, or of the Executive (when the Legislature cannot be convened) against domestic Violence.

Article V

The Congress, whenever two thirds of both Houses shall deem it necessary, shall propose Amendments to this Constitution, or, on the Application of the Legislatures of two thirds of the several States, shall call a Convention for proposing Amendments, which, in either Case, shall be valid to all Intents and Purposes, as Part of this Constitution, when ratified by the Legislatures of three fourths of the several States, or by Conventions in three fourths thereof, as the one or the other Mode of Ratification may be proposed by the Congress; Provided that no Amendment which may be made prior to the Year One thousand eight hundred and eight shall in any Manner affect the first and fourth Clauses in the Ninth Section of the first Article; and that no State, without its Consent, shall be deprived of its equal Suffrage in the Senate.

Article VI

All Debts contracted and Engagements entered into, before the Adoption of this Constitution, shall be as valid against the United States under this Constitution, as under the Confederation.

This Constitution, and the Laws of the United States which shall be made in Pursuance thereof; and all Treaties made, or which shall be made, under the Authority of the United States, shall be the supreme Law of the Land; and the Judges in every State shall be bound thereby, any Thing in the Constitution of Laws of any State to the Contrary notwithstanding.

The Senators and Representatives before mentioned, and the Members of the several State Legislatures, and all executive and judicial Officers, both of the United States and of the several States, shall be bound by Oath or Affirmation, to support this Constitution; but no religious Test shall ever be required as a Qualification to any Office or public Trust under the United States.

Article VII

The Ratification of the Conventions of nine States, shall be sufficient for the Establishment of this Constitution between the States so ratifying the Same.

Done in Convention by the Unanimous Consent of the States present the Seventeenth Day of September in the Year of our Lord one thousand seven hundred and Eighty seven and of the Independence of the United States of America the Twelfth. In Witness whereof We have hereunto subscribed our Names,

G^O WASHINGTON—Presid^t
and deputy from Virginia

New Hampshire	⎧ JOHN LANGDON ⎩ NICHOLAS GILMAN
Massachusetts	⎧ NATHANIEL GORHAM ⎩ RUFUS KING
Connecticut	⎧ W^M SAM^L JOHNSON ⎩ ROGER SHERMAN
New York	⎰ ALEXANDER HAMILTON
New Jersey	⎡ WIL: LIVINGSTON ⎢ DAVID BREARLEY. ⎢ W^M PATERSON. ⎣ JONA: DAYTON
Pennsylvania	⎡ B FRANKLIN ⎢ THOMAS MIFFLIN ⎢ ROB^T MORRIS ⎢ GEO. CLYMER ⎢ THO^S FITZSIMONS ⎢ JARED INGERSOLL ⎢ JAMES WILSON ⎣ GOUV MORRIS
Delaware	⎡ GEO: READ ⎢ GUNNING BEDFORD jun ⎢ JOHN DICKINSON ⎢ RICHARD BASSETT ⎣ JACO: BROOM
Maryland	⎡ JAMES M^{C}HENRY ⎢ DAN OF S^T THO^S JENIFER ⎣ DAN^L CARROLL

Virginia $\left\{\begin{array}{l}\text{JOHN BLAIR—}\\ \text{JAMES MADISON Jr.}\end{array}\right.$

North Carolina $\left\{\begin{array}{l}\text{W}^{\text{M}}\text{ BLOUNT}\\ \text{RICH}^{\text{D}}\text{ DOBBS SPAIGHT.}\\ \text{HU WILLIAMSON}\end{array}\right.$

South Carolina $\left\{\begin{array}{l}\text{J. RUTLEDGE}\\ \text{CHARLES COTESWORTH PINCKNEY}\\ \text{CHARLES PINCKNEY}\\ \text{PIERCE BUTLER.}\end{array}\right.$

Georgia $\left\{\begin{array}{l}\text{WILLIAM FEW}\\ \text{ABR BALDWIN}\end{array}\right.$

AMENDMENTS

The first ten Amendments were ratified December 15, 1791, and form what is known as the "Bill of Rights."

Amendment I

Congress shall make no law respecting an establishment of religion, or prohibiting the free exercise thereof; or abridging the freedom of speech, or of the press; or the right of the people peaceably to assemble, and to petition the Government for a redress of grievances.

Amendment II

A well regulated Militia, being necessary to the security of a free State, the right of the people to keep and bear Arms, shall not be infringed.

Amendment III

No Soldier shall, in time of peace be quartered in any house, without the consent of the Owner, nor in time of war, but in a manner to be prescribed by law.

Amendment IV

The right of the people to be secure in their persons, houses, papers, and effects, against unreasonable searches and seizures, shall not be violated, and no Warrants shall issue, but upon probable cause, supported by Oath or affirmation, and particularly describing the place to be searched, and the persons or things to be seized.

Amendment V

No person shall be held to answer for a capital, or otherwise infamous crime, unless on a presentment or indictment of a Grand Jury, except in cases arising in the land or naval forces, or in the Militia, when in actual service in time of War or public danger; nor shall any person be subject for the same offence to be twice put in jeopardy of life or limb; nor shall be compelled in any criminal case to be a witness against himself, nor be deprived of life, liberty, or property, without due process of law; nor shall private property be taken for public use, without just compensation.

Amendment VI

In all criminal prosecutions, the accused shall enjoy the right to a speedy and public trial, by an impartial jury of the State and district wherein the crime shall have been committed, which district shall have been previously ascertained by law, and to be informed of the nature and cause of the accusation; to be confronted with the witnesses against him; to have compulsory process for obtaining witnesses in his favor, and to have the Assistance of Counsel for his defence.

Amendment VII

In Suits at common law, where the value in controversy shall exceed twenty dollars, the right of trial by jury shall be preserved, and no fact tried by a jury, shall be otherwise re-examined in any Court of the United States, than according to the rules of the common law.

Amendment VIII

Excessive bail shall not be required, nor excessive fines imposed, nor cruel and unusual punishments inflicted.

Amendment IX

The enumeration in the Constitution, of certain rights, shall not be construed to deny or disparage others retained by the people.

Amendment X

The powers not delegated to the United States by the Constitution, nor prohibited by it to the States, are reserved to the States respectively, or to the people.

Amendment XI

The Judicial power of the United States shall not be construed to extend to any suit in law or equity, commenced or prosecuted against one of the United States by Citizens of another State, or by Citizens or Subjects of any Foreign State.

Amendment XII

The Electors shall meet in their respective states and vote by ballot for President and Vice-President, one of whom, at least, shall not be an inhabitant of the same state with themselves; they shall name in their ballots the person voted for as President, and in distinct ballots the person voted for as Vice-President, and they shall make distinct lists of all persons voted for as President, and of all persons voted for as Vice-President, and of the number of votes for each, which lists they shall sign and certify, and transmit sealed to the seat of the government of the United States, directed to the President of the Senate;—The President of the Senate shall, in the presence of the Senate and House of Representatives, open all the certificates and the votes shall then be counted;—The person having the greatest number of votes for President, shall be the President, if such number be a majority of the whole number of Electors appointed; and if no person have such majority, then from the persons having the highest numbers not exceeding three on the list of those voted for as President, the House of Representatives shall choose immediately, by ballot, the President. But in choosing the President, the votes shall be taken by states, the representation from each state having one vote; a quorum for this purpose shall consist of a member or members from two-thirds of the states, and a majority of all the states shall be necessary to a choice. And if the House of Representatives shall not choose a President whenever the right of choice shall devolve upon them, before the fourth day of March next following, then the Vice-President shall act as President, as in the case of the death or other constitutional disability of the President.—The person having the greatest number of votes as Vice-President, shall be the Vice-President, if such number be a majority of the whole number of Electors appointed, and if no person have a majority, then from the two highest numbers on the list, the Senate shall choose the Vice-President; a quorum for the purpose shall consist of two-thirds of the whole number of Senators, and a majority of the whole number shall be necessary to a choice. But no person constitutionally ineligible to the office of President shall be eligible to that of Vice-President of the United States.

Amendment XIII

Section 1
Neither slavery nor involuntary servitude, except as a punishment for crime whereof the party shall have been duly convicted, shall exist within the United States, or any place subject to their jurisdiction.

Section 2
Congress shall have power to enforce this article by appropriate legislation.

Amendment XIV

Section 1
All persons born or naturalized in the United States, and subject to the jurisdiction thereof, are citizens of the United States and of the State wherein they reside. No State shall make or enforce any law which shall abridge the privileges or immunities of citizens of the United States; nor shall any State deprive any person of life, liberty, or property, without due process of law; nor deny to any person within its jurisdiction the equal protection of the laws.

Section 2
Representatives shall be apportioned among the several States according to their respective numbers, counting the whole number of persons in each State, excluding Indians not taxed. But when the right to vote at any election for the choice of electors for President and Vice President of the United States, Representatives in Congress, the Executive and Judicial officers of a State, or the members of the Legislature thereof, is denied to any of the male inhabitants of such State, being twenty-one years of age, and citizens of the United States, or in any way abridged, except for participation in rebellion, or other crime, the basis of representation therein shall be reduced in the proportion which the number of such male citizens shall bear to the whole number of male citizens twenty-one years of age in such State.

No person shall be a Senator or Representative in Congress, or elector of President and Vice President, or hold any office, civil or military, under the United States, or under any State, who, having previously taken an oath, as a member of Congress, or as an officer of the United States, or as a member of any State legislature, or as an executive or judicial officer of any State, to support the Constitution of the United States, shall have engaged in insurrection or rebellion against the same, or given aid or comfort to the enemies thereof. But Congress may by a vote of two-thirds of each House, remove such disability.

The validity of the public debt of the United States, authorized by law, including debts incurred for payment of pensions and bounties for services in suppressing insurrection or rebellion, shall not be questioned. But neither the United States nor any State shall assume or pay any debt or obligation incurred in aid of insurrection or rebellion against the United States, or any claim for the loss or emancipation of any slave; but all such debts, obligations and claims shall be held illegal and void.

The Congress shall have power to enforce by appropriate legislation the provisions of this article.

Amendment XV

The right of citizens of the United States to vote shall not be denied or abridged by the United States or by any State on account of race, color, or previous condition of servitude.

The Congress shall have power to enforce this article by appropriate legislation.

Amendment XVI

The Congress shall have power to lay and collect taxes on incomes, from whatever source derived, without apportionment among the several States, and without regard to any census or enumeration.

Amendment XVII

The Senate of the United States shall be composed of two Senators from each State, elected by the people thereof for six years; and each Senator shall have one vote. The electors in each State shall have the qualifications requisite for electors of the most numerous branch of the State legislatures.

When vacancies happen in the representation of any State in the Senate, the executive authority of such State shall issue writs of election to fill such vacancies: *Provided,* That the legislature of any State may empower the executive thereof to make temporary appointments until the people fill the vacancies by election as the legislature may direct.

This amendment shall not be so construed as to affect the election or term of any Senator chosen before it becomes valid as part of the Constitution.

Amendment XVIII

Section 1

After one year from the ratification of this article the manufacture, sale, or transportation of intoxicating liquors within, the importation thereof into, or the exportation thereof from the United States and all territory subject to the juridsdiction thereof for beverage purposes is hereby prohibited.

Section 2

The Congress and the several States shall have concurrent power to enforce this article by appropriate legislation.

Section 3

This article shall be inoperative unless it shall have been ratified as an amendment to the Constitution by the legislatures of the several States, as provided in the Constitution, within seven years from the date of the submission hereof to the States by the Congress.

Amendment XIX

The right of citizens of the United States to vote shall not be denied or abridged by the United States or by any State on account of sex.

Congress shall have power to enforce this article by appropriate legislation.

Amendment XX

Section 1

The terms of the President and Vice President shall end at noon on the 20th day of January, and the terms of Senators and Representatives at noon on the 3d day of January, of the years in which such terms would have ended if this article had not been ratified; and the terms of their successors shall then begin.

Section 2

The Congress shall assemble at least once in every year, and such meeting shall begin at noon on the 3d day of January, unless they shall by law appoint a different day.

Section 3

If, at the time fixed for the beginning of the term of the President, the President elect shall have died, the Vice President elect shall become President. If a President shall not have been chosen before the time fixed for the beginning of his term, or if the President elect shall have failed to qualify, then the Vice President elect shall act as President until a President shall have qualified; and the Congress may by law provide for the case wherein neither a President elect nor a Vice President elect shall have qualified, declaring who shall then act as President, or the manner in which one who is to act shall be selected, and such person shall act accordingly until a President or Vice President shall have qualified.

Section 4

The Congress may by law provide for the case of the death of any of the persons from whom the House of Representatives may choose a President whenever the right of choice shall have devolved upon them, and for the case of the death of any of the persons from whom the Senate may choose a Vice President whenever the right of choice shall have devolved upon them.

Section 5

Sections 1 and 2 shall take effect on the 15th day of October following the ratification of this article.

Section 6

This article shall be inoperative unless it shall have been ratified as an amendment to the Constitution by the legislatures of three-fourths of the several States within seven years from the date of its submission.

Amendment XXI

Section 1

The eighteenth article of amendment to the Constitution of the United States is hereby repealed.

Section 2

The transportation or importation into any State, Territory, or possession of the United States for delivery or use therein of intoxicating liquors, in violation of the laws thereof, is hereby prohibited.

Section 3

This article shall be inoperative unless it shall have been ratified as an amendment to the Constitution by conventions in the several States, as provided in the Constitution, within seven years from the date of the submission hereof to the States by the Congress.

Amendment XXII

Section 1

No person shall be elected to the office of the President more than twice, and no person who has held the office of President, or acted as President, for more than two years of a term to which some other person was elected President shall be elected to the office of the President more than once. But this Article shall not apply to any person holding the office of President when this Article was proposed by the Congress, and shall not prevent any person who may be holding the office of President, or acting as President, during the term within which this Article becomes operative from holding the office of President or acting as President during the remainder of such term.

Section 2

This article shall be inoperative unless it shall have been ratified as an amendment to the Constitution by the legislatures of three-fourths of the several States within seven years from the date of its submission to the States by the Congress.

Amendment XXIII

Section 1

The District constituting the seat of Government of the United States shall appoint in such manner as the Congress may direct:

A number of electors of President and Vice President equal to the whole number of Senators and Representatives in Congress to which the District would be entitled if it were a State, but in no event more than the least populous State; they shall be in addition to those appointed by the States, but they shall be considered, for the purposes of the election of President and Vice President, to be electors appointed by a State; and they shall meet in the District and perform such duties as provided by the twelfth article of amendment.

Section 2

The Congress shall have power to enforce this article by appropriate legislation.

Amendment XXIV

Section 1

The right of citizens of the United States to vote in any primary or other election for President or Vice-President, for electors for President or Vice-President, or for Senator or Representative in Congress shall not be denied or abridged by the United States or any State by reason of failure to pay any poll tax or other tax.

Section 2

The Congress shall have power to enforce this article by appropriate legislation.

Amendment XXV

Section 1

In the case of the removal of the President from office or of his death or resignation, the Vice President shall become President.

Section 2

Whenever there is a vacancy in the office of the Vice President, the President shall nominate a Vice President who shall take office upon confirmation by a majority vote of both Houses of Congress.

Section 3

Whenever the President transmits to the President pro tempore of the Senate and the Speaker of the House of Representatives his written declaration that he is unable to discharge the powers and duties of his office, and until he transmits to them a written declaration to the contrary, such powers and duties shall be discharged by the Vice President as Acting President.

Section 4

Whenever the Vice President and a majority of either the principal officers of the executive departments or of such other body of Congress may by law provide, transmit to the President pro tempore of the Senate and the Speaker of the House of Representatives their written declaration that the President is unable to discharge the powers and duties of his office, the Vice President shall immediately assume the powers and duties of the office as Acting President. Thereafter, when the President transmits to the President pro tempore of the Senate and the Speaker of the House of Representatives his written declaration that no inability exists, he shall resume the powers and duties of his office unless the Vice President and a majority of either the principal officers of the executive departments or of such other body as Congress may by law provide, transmit within four days to the President pro tempore of the Senate and the Speaker of the House of Representatives their written declaration that the President is unable to discharge the powers and duties of his office. Thereupon Congress shall decide the issue, assembling within forty-eight hours for that purpose, if not in session. If the Congress, within twenty-one days after receipt of the latter written declaration, or, if Congress is not in session, within twenty-one days after Congress is required to assemble, determines by two-thirds vote of both Houses that the President is unable to discharge the powers and duties of his office, the Vice President shall continue to discharge the same as Acting President; otherwise, the President shall resume the powers and duties of his office.

Notes

Background of the Constitution

1. Edward Dumbauld, *The Declaration of Independence and What It Means Today* (Norman, Okla.: University of Oklahoma Press, 1950), p. 27.
2. Letter of May 8, 1825, to Henry Lee, from *The Writings of Thomas Jefferson*, ed. P. L. Ford (10 vols., 1892–1899), X, 343.
3. About six weeks before, Virginia adopted a constitution that contained the first American Bill of Rights. In it the same concepts that are found in the Declaration were stated as follows: "That all men are by nature equally free and independent, and have certain inherent rights, of which, when they enter into a state of society, they cannot by any compact deprive or divest their posterity; namely, the enjoyment of life and liberty, with the means of acquiring and possessing property, and pursuing and obtaining happiness and safety."
4. Rhode Island had refused to send delegates, and much of the time New York was unrepresented.

Basic Features of the Constitution

1. *McCulloch* v. *Maryland,* 4 Wheaton 316 (1819).
2. *Ibid.*
3. See *Fed. Radio Comm'n* v. *Nelson Bros.,* 289 U.S. 266 (1933), and *Opp Cotton Mills* v. *Administrator,* 312 U.S. 126 (1944) for examples.
4. *Schecter Poultry Corp.* v. *United States,* 295 U.S. 495 (1935).
5. 1 Cr. 137 (1803).
6. Oliver Wendell Holmes, *Collected Legal Papers* (New York: Harcourt, Brace & World, Inc., 1920), pp. 295–296.

7. *Luther* v. *Borden,* 7 Howard 1 (1849).
8. *Baker* v. *Carr,* 369 U.S. 186 (1962).
9. *Colegrove* v. *Green* and cases cited therein, 328 U.S. 549 (1946).
10. *Gomillion* v. *Lightfoot,* 364 U.S. 339 (1963).
11. *Wesberry* v. *Sanders,* 376 U.S. 1 (1964).
12. *Gray* v. *Sanders,* 372 U.S. 368 (1963).
13. *Avery* v. *Midland,* 390 U.S. 474 (1968).
14. *Williams* v. *Rhodes,* 393 U.S. 23 (1968)
15. *Reynolds* v. *Sims,* 377 U.S. 533 (1964) and companion cases.
16. *Wells* v. *Rockefeller,* 394 U.S. 542 (1969); *Kirkpatrick* v. *Preisler,* 394 U.S. 526 (1969).
17. *Powell* v. *McCormack,* 395 U.S. 486 (1969).
18. See Justice Brandeis' concurring opinion in *Ashwander* v. *TVA,* 297 U.S. 288 (1936).
19. J. W. Peltason, *Federal Courts in the Political Process* (New York: Random House, Inc., 1955).

The Constitution of the United States

1. *McCulloch* v. *Maryland,* 1 Wheaton 316 (1819).
2. *Constitution of Massachusetts,* Part the First, Article XXX.
3. *United States* v. *Curtiss-Wright Export Corp.,* 299 U.S. 304 (1936).
4. *Wesberry* v. *Sanders,* 376 U.S. 1 (1964).
5. *Kirkpatrick* v. *Preisler,* 394 U.S. 526 (1969).
6. *Ex parte Yarbrough,* 110 U.S. 651 (1884).
7. *United States* v. *Classic,* 313 U.S. 299 (1941); *Smith* v. *Allwright,* 321 U.S. 649 (1944); *Terry* v. *Adams,* 345 U.S. 461 (1953).
8. 42 U.S.C. Sec. 1974–1975.
9. *Powell* v. *McCormack,* 395 U.S. 486 (1969).
10. *United States* v. *Johnson,* 383 U.S. 169 (1966).
11. *McCulloch* v. *Maryland,* 4 Wheaton 316 (1819).
12. *Massachusetts* v. *Mellon,* 262 U.S. 447 (1923).
13. *Frothingham* v. *Mellon,* 262 U.S. 447 (1923).
14. *Flast* v. *Cohen,* 392 U.S. 83 (1968).
15. See, for example, *Bailey* v. *Drexel Furniture Co.,* 259 U.S. 20 (1922).
16. *Machetti* v. *United States,* 390 U.S. 39 (1968). *Haynes* v. *United States,* 390 U.S. 85 (1968). *Leary* v. *United States,* 395 U.S. 6 (1969).
17. *Gibbons* v. *Ogden,* 9 Wheaton 1 (1824).
18. *Maryland* v. *Wirtz,* 392 U.S. 185 (1968).
19. *United States* v. *Darby,* 312 U.S. 100 (1941).
20. *Heart of Atlanta Motel* v. *United States,* 379 U.S. 241 (1964), quoted from headnote summary of Justice Clark's opinion for the Court.
21. *Daniel* v. *Paul,* 395 U.S. 298 (1969).
22. *United States* v. *Appalachian Elec. Power Co.,* 311 U.S. 377 (1940).

23. *Southern Pacific Co.* v. *Arizona*, 325 U.S. 761 (1945).
24. *Fireman* v. *Chicago, Rock Island and Pacific R. R. Co.*, 393 U.S. 129 (1968).
25. *Bibb* v. *Navajo Freight Lines*, 359 U.S. 520 (1959).
26. *National Bell Hess* v. *Dept. of Revenue*, 386 U.S. 753 (1967).
27. *Dunbar-Stanley Studios* v. *Alabama*, 393 U.S. 537 (1969).
28. *The Minnesota Rate Cases*, 230 U.S. 352 (1913).
29. For a fuller discussion see N. S. Small, ed., *The Constitution of the United States of America: Analysis and Interpretation* (Washington, D.C.: Government Printing Office, 1964), pp. 150–296. This is the most comprehensive annotation of the Constitution. It was prepared by the Legislative Reference Service of the Library of Congress. The 1964 edition covering annotations of cases decided by the Supreme Court to June 22, 1964, is based on the 1952 edition of which E. S. Corwin was the editor. Hereinafter it will be referred to as *The Constitution Annotated*.
30. For a fuller discussion see, *The Constitution Annotated*, pp. 296–306.
31. *Fong Yue Ting* v. *United States*, 149 U.S. 698 (1893).
32. Charles Evans Hughes, "War Powers under the Constitution," *42 Reports of the American Bar Association*, September 5, 1917; *Minnesota Mortgage Moratorium Case*, 290 U.S. 398 (1934). For a fuller treatment of this subject see Edward S. Corwin, *Total War and the Constitution* (New York: Knopf, 1947).
33. 10 U.S.C. 332–333.
34. For a fuller discussion see *The Constitution Annotated*, pp. 448–455.
35. *McGrain* v. *Daugherty*, 273 U.S. 135 (1927).
36. 2 U.S.C. 192.
37. *Watkins* v. *United States*, 354 U.S. 178 (1957).
38. *Yellin* v. *United States*, 374 U.S. 109 (1963).
39. *GoJack* v. *United States*, 384 U.S. 702 (1966), and *Russell* v. *United States*, 369 U.S. 749 (1962), and cases cited therein.
40. *United States* v. *Lovett*, 328 U.S. 303 (1946).
41. *United States* v. *Brown*, 381 U.S. 437 (1965).
42. *Zschering* v. *Miller*, 389 U.S. 429 (1968).
43. *Fletcher* v. *Peck*, 6 Cranch 87 (1810); *Dartmouth College* v. *Woodward*, 4 Wheaton 518 (1819); *Sturges* v. *Crowninshield*, 4 Wheaton 122 (1819).
44. *Charles River Bridge Co.* v. *Warren Bridge*, 11 Peters 420 (1837); *Stone* v. *Mississippi*, 101 U.S. 814 (1880).
45. John Locke, *Second Treatise*, p. 109.
46. *Youngstown Sheet & Tube Co.* v. *Sawyer*, 343 U.S. 579 (1952).
47. *Williams* v. *Rhodes*, 393 U.S. 23 (1968).
48. *Moore* v. *Ogilvie*, 394 U.S. 814 (1969).
49. James Madison, *The Records of the Federal Convention of 1787*, Max Farrand, ed. (New Haven: Yale University Press, 1937), II, 110.

50. George Mason, *ibid.*, II, 31.
51. 3 U.S.C. 1, 7, 9–11, 15.
52. *Schneider* v. *Rusk*, 377 U.S. 163 (1964).
53. *Korematsu* v. *United States*, 323 U.S. 214 (1944).
54. *Duncan* v. *Kahanamoku*, 327 U.S. 304 (1946).
55. For a fuller discussion see *The Constitution Annotated*, pp. 484–496.
56. *Wiener* v. *United States*, 357 U.S. 349 (1958); *Myers* v. *United States*, 272 U.S. 52 (1926), and *Humphrey's Executor* v. *United States*, 295 U.S. 602 (1935).
57. *Glidden Co.* v. *Zdanok*, 370 U.S. 530 (1962).
58. *State Farm Fire and Cas. Co.* v. *Tashire*, 386 U.S. 523 (1967).
59. *Ex parte McCardle*, 6 Wallace 318 (1868).
60. *Haupt* v. *United States*, 330 U.S. 631 (1947).
61. *Williams* v. *North Carolina*, 325 U.S. 226 (1945).
62. *Johnson* v. *Muelberger*, 341 U.S. 581 (1951).
63. *Shapiro* v. *Thompson*, 394 U.S. 618 (1969); see also *Toomer* v. *Witsell*, 334 U.S. 385 (1948).
64. 18 U.S.C. 1073.
65. Compare *Stearns* v. *Minnesota*, 179 U.S. 223 (1900) with *Coyle* v. *Smith*, 221 U.S. 559 (1911).
66. *Texas* v. *White*, 7 Wallace 700 (1869).
67. *Hawaii* v. *Mankichi*, 190 U.S. 197 (1903) and *Balzac* v. *Porto Rico*, 258 U.S. 298 (1922).
68. The Court made this summary of the decision in the Oregon Case (*Pacific States Tel. & Tel. Co.* v. *Oregon*, 223 U.S. 118 [1912]) in *Colegrove* v. *Green*, 328 U.S. 549 (1946). See also *Baker* v. *Carr*, 369 U.S. 186 (1962).
69. *Luther* v. *Borden*, 7 Howard 1 (1849).
70. *In re Debs*, 158, U.S. 464 (1895).
71. *Coleman* v. *Miller*, 307 U.S. 433 (1939), concurring opinion.
72. *Hammer* v. *Dagenhart*, 247 U.S. 251 (1918).
73. *United States* v. *Darby*, 312 U.S. 11 (1941).
74. *Pennsylvania* v. *Nelson*, 350 U.S. 497 (1956).
75. *Reid* v. *Covert*, 354 U.S. 1 (1957).
76. *Missouri* v. *Holland*, 252 U.S. 416 (1920).

First Amendment

1. Essay No. 84, by Alexander Hamilton, in *The Federalist*.
2. *Barron* v. *Baltimore*, 7 Peters 243 (1843).
3. *Gitlow* v. *New York*, 268 U.S. 652 (1925).
4. *Palko* v. *Connecticut*, 302 U.S. 319 (1932).
5. *Duncan* v. *Louisiana*, 391 U.S. 145 (1968).
6. *Chapman* v. *California*, 386 U.S. 18 (1967).

7. *DeStefano* v. *Woods*, 392 U.S. 631 (1968).
8. *Gideon* v. *Wainwright*, 372 U.S. 335 (1963).
9. *Duncan* v. *Louisiana*, 391 U.S. 145, 171 (1968).
10. *School District* v. *Schempp*, 374 U.S. 203 (1963); *Engel* v. *Vitale*, 370 U.S. 421 (1962).
11. *Board of Education* v. *Allen*, 392 U.S. 237 (1968).
12. *Everson* v. *Board of Education*, 330 U.S. 1 (1947).
13. *School District* v. *Schempp*, 374 U.S. 203 (1963); *Engel* v. *Vitale*, 370 U.S. 421 (1962).
14. *Epperson* v. *Arkansas*, 393 U.S. 97 (1968).
15. *McCollum* v. *Board of Education*, 333 U.S. 703 (1948).
16. *Zorach* v. *Clauson*, 343 U.S. 306 (1952) and *Abington* v. *Schempp*, 374 U.S. 203 (1963).
17. *McGowan* v. *Maryland*, 366 U.S. 420 (1961).
18. *Cochran* v. *State Board*, 281 U.S. 370 (1930), and *Everson* v. *Board of Education*, 330 U.S. 1 (1947); *Board of Education* v. *Allen*, 392 U.S. 237 (1968).
19. *Braunfeld* v. *Brown*, 366 U.S. 599 (1961).
20. *Jacobson* v. *Massachusetts*, 197 U.S. 11 (1905).
21. *State Board of Education* v. *Barnette*, 319 U.S. 624 (1943).
22. *Sherbert* v. *Verner*, 374 U.S. 399 (1963).
23. *Pierce* v. *Society of Sisters*, 268 U.S. 510 (1925).
24. *Roth* v. *United States*, 354 U.S. 476 (1957); *Manual Enterprises* v. *Day*, 370 U.S. 478 (1962).
25. *New York Times* v. *Sullivan*, 376 U.S. 254 (1964); *St. Amant* v. *Thompson*, 390 U.S. 727 (1968).
26. *Curtis Publishing* v. *Butts*, 388 U.S. 130 (1967).
27. *Time Inc.* v. *Hill*, 385 U.S. 374 (1967).
28. *Stanley* v. *Georgia*, 394 U.S. 557 (1969).
29. *Memoirs* v. *Massachusetts*, 383 U.S. 413 (1966); and *Redrup* v. *New York*, 386 U.S. 767 (1967); *Roth* v. *United States*, 354 U.S. 476 (1957).
30. *Ginzberg* v. *United States*, 282 U.S. 463 (1966).
31. *Jacobellis* v. *Ohio*, 378 U.S. 184 at 197 (1964).
32. *Ginsberg* v. *New York*, 390 U.S. 629 (1968).
33. *Interstate Circuit Inc.* v. *City of Dallas*, 390 U.S. 676 (1968); and *Rabeck* v. *New York*, 391 U.S. 462 (1968).
34. *Dennis* v. *United States*, 341 U.S. 494 (1951), and *Yates* v. *United States*, 354 U.S. 298 (1957). See also Martin Shapiro, *Freedom of Speech: The Supreme Court and Judicial Review.* (Englewood Cliffs, N.J.: Prentice-Hall, Inc., 1966).
35. *Brandenburg* v. *Ohio*, 395 U.S. 444 (1969). Also quoting from *Noto* v. *United States*, 367 U.S. 290 (1961).
36. *Dombrowski* v. *Pfister*, 380 U.S. 479 (1965); *Zwickler* v. *Koota*, 387 U.S. 241 (1967).
37. *Burstyn* v. *Wilson*, 343 U.S. 495 (1952); *Winters* v. *New York*, 333 U.S. 507 (1948).

38. *Pickering* v. *Board of Education of Township High School District, Will County, Illinois,* 391 U.S. 563 (1968).
39. *Bates* v. *Little Rock,* 361 U.S. 516 (1960); *Shelton* v. *Tucker,* 364 U.S. 479 (1960).
40. *Bond* v. *Floyd,* 385 U.S. 116 (1966).
41. *United States* v. *O'Brien,* 391 U.S. 367 (1968).
42. *Justice Black concurring, Gregory* v. *Chicago,* 394 U.S. 111 (1969).
43. *Tinker* v. *Des Moines School District,* 393 U.S. 503 (1969).
44. *United States* v. *O'Brien,* 391 U.S. 367 (1968).
45. *Street* v. *New York,* 394 U.S. 576 (1969).
46. *Milwaukee Pub. Co.* v. *Burleson,* 255 U.S. 407 (1921).
47. *Lamont* v. *Postmaster General,* 381 U.S. 301 (1965).
48. *Fed. Radio Comm'n* v. *Nelson,* 289 U.S. 266 (1933).
49. *Red Lion Broadcasting Co.* v. *Federal Communications Commission,* 395 U.S. 367 (1969).
50. *Times Film Corp.* v. *Chicago,* 365 U.S. 43 (1961).
51. *Teitel Film Corp.* v. *Cusack,* 390 U.S. 139 (1968); *Freedman* v. *Maryland,* 380 U.S. 51 (1965).
52. *Burstyn* v. *Wilson,* 343 U.S. 495 (1952); *Superior Films* v. *Department of Education,* 346 U.S. 587 (1954), and *Kingsley Corp.* v. *Regents,* 360 U.S. 684 (1959).
53. *Amalgamated Food Employees Local 590* v. *Logan Valley Plaza, Inc.,* 391 U.S. 308 (1968); and *Thornhill* v. *Alabama,* 310 U.S. 88 (1940).
54. *Building Serv. Employees Union* v. *Gazza,* 339 U.S. 532 (1950).
55. *Justice Black for the Court, Adderly* v. *Florida,* 385 U.S. 39 (1966); also his dissenting opinion in *Tinker* v. *Des Moines Independent Community School District,* 393 U.S. 503 (1969).
56. *Cox* v. *Louisiana,* 379 U.S. 536 (1965).
57. *Cox* v. *Louisiana,* 379 U.S. 559 (1965).
58. *Shuttlesworth* v. *Birmingham,* 394 U.S. 147 (1969).
59. *Feiner* v. *New York,* 340 U.S. 315 (1951).
60. *Edwards* v. *South Carolina,* 372 U.S. 229 (1963).
61. *Gregory et al.* v. *Chicago,* 394 U.S. 111 (1969).
62. *Brown* v. *Louisiana,* 383 U.S. 131 (1966).
63. *Adderly* v. *Florida,* 385 U.S. 39 (1966).
64. *Gibson* v. *Legislative Investigation Commission* and cases cited therein, 372 U.S. 539 (1963).
65. *United Mine Workers* v. *Illinois State Bar Assn.,* 389 U.S. 217 (1967); *Brotherhood Trainmen* v. *Virginia,* 377 U.S. 1 (1963); *NAACP* v. *Button,* 371 U.S. 415 (1963).
66. *International Ass'n of Machinists* v. *Street,* 367 U.S. 740 (1961); *Lathrop* v. *Donohue,* 367 U.S. 820 (1961); and *Railway Clerks* v. *Allen,* 373 U.S. 113 (1963).
67. *Elfbrandt* v. *Russell,* 384 U.S. 11 (1966); *Whitehill* v. *Elkins,* 389 U.S. 55 (1967); *Keyishian* v. *Board of Regents,* 385 U.S. 589 (1967).
68. *United States* v. *Robel,* 389 U.S. 258 (1967).
69. *United Public Workers* v. *Mitchell,* 330 U.S. 75 (1947).

Amendments 2–10

70. Justice Samuel F. Miller, *The Constitution* (1893), p. 646, quoted in *The Constitution Annotated*, p. 923.
71. *Chimel* v. *California*, 395 U.S. 752 (1969).
72. *Terry* v. *Ohio*, 392 U.S. 1 (1968).
73. *Aguilar* v. *Texas*, 378 U.S. 108 (1964).
74. *See* v. *City of Seattle*, 387 U.S. 541 (1967); *Camara* v. *Municipal Court*, 387 U.S. 523 (1967).
75. *Olmstead* v. *United States*, 277 U.S. 438 (1928).
76. *Katz* v. *United States*, 389 U.S. 347 (1967).
77. *On Lee* v. *United States*, 343 U.S. 747 (1952); *Hoffa* v. *United States*, 385 U.S. 293 (1966).
78. *Giordano* v. *United States*, 394 U.S. 310 (1969).
79. 18 U.S.C. 2510–2520.
80. *Berger* v. *New York*, 388 U.S. 41 (1967).
81. *Justice White for the Court, Alderman* v. *United States*, 394 U.S. 165 (1969).
82. *Alderman* v. *United States*, 394 U.S. 165 (1969).
83. *Massiah* v. *United States*, 377 U.S. 201 (1964).
84. *Weeks* v. *United States*, 232 U.S. 383 (1914).
85. *Wolf* v. *Colorado*, 338 U.S. 25 (1949).
86. *Mapp* v. *Ohio*, 367 U.S. 643 (1961).
87. *Ker* v. *California*, 374 U.S. 23 (1963).
88. *Kinsella* v. *Singleton* and companion cases, 361 U.S. 234 (1960).
89. *Toth* v. *Quarles*, 350 U.S. 11 (1955).
90. *O'Callahan* v. *Parker*, 395 U.S. 258 (1969).
91. *North Carolina* v. *Pearce*, 395 U.S. 711 (1969).
92. *Fong Foo* v. *United States*, 369 U.S. 141 and *Downum* v. *United States*, 372 U.S. 734 (1963).
93. *North Carolina* v. *Pearce*, 395 U.S. 711 (1969).
94. *Benton* v. *Maryland* 395 U.S. 784 (1969).
95. *Bartkus* v. *Illinois*, 359 U.S. 121 (1959).
96. *Marchetti* v. *United States*, 390 U.S. 39 (1968); *Haynes* v. *United States*, 390 U.S. 85 (1968); *Leary* v. *United States* 395 U.S. 6 (1969).
97. *Albertson* v. *Subversive Activities Control Bd.*, 382 U.S. 70 (1965).
98. *Malloy* v. *Hogan*, 378 U.S. 1 (1964).
99. *Murphy* v. *Waterfront Commission*, 378 U.S. 52 (1964).
100. *Ullman* v. *United States*, 350 U.S. 422 (1956).
101. *Murphy* v. *Waterfront Commission*, 378 U.S. 52 (1964).
102. *Garrity* v. *New Jersey*, 385 U.S. 493 (1967); *Spevack* v. *Klein*, 385 U.S. 511 (1967); *Gardner* v. *Broderick*, 392 U.S. 273 (1968); *Sanitation Men* v. *Sanitation Comm.*, 392 U.S. 281 (1968).
103. For example see *Haynes* v. *Washington*, 373 U.S. 503 (1963).
104. *Miranda* v. *Arizona*, 384 U.S. 436 (1966).

105. *Griffin* v. *California*, 380 U.S. 609 (1965).
106. *Mathis* v. *United States*, 391 U.S. 1 (1968); *Orozco* v. *Texas*, 394 U.S. 324 (1969).
107. *Schmember* v. *California*, 384 U.S. 757 (1966).
108. *United States* v. *Wade*, 388 U.S. 216 (1967).
109. *Gilbert* v. *California*, 388 U.S. 263 (1967); *Davis* v. *Mississippi*, 394 U.S. 721 (1969).
110. *Davidson* v. *New Orleans*, 96 U.S. 97 (1878).
111. *Connally* v. *General Constr. Co.*, 269 U.S. 385 (1926).
112. *Tot* v. *United States*, 319 U.S. 463 (1963); *Leary* v. *United States*, 395 U.S. 6 (1969).
113. *Sniadach* v. *Family Finance Corp.*, 395 U.S. 337 (1969).
114. *In re Gault*, 387 U.S. 1(1967); *Thorpe* v. *Housing Authority*, 393 U.S. 268 (1969).
115. *Meyers* v. *Nebraska*, 262 U.S. 390 (1923).
116. *YMCA* v. *United States*, 395 U.S. 85 (1969).
117. *Griggs* v. *Allegany County*, 369 U.S. 841 (1962).
118. *Chicago, Milwaukee & St. Paul Ry.* v. *Minnesota*, 134 U.S. 418 (1890).
119. *United States* v. *Ewell*, 382 U.S. 117 (1966).
120. *Smith* v. *Hooey*, 393 U.S. 374 (1969).
121. *In re Oliver*, 33 U.S. 257 (1948).
122. *Estes* v. *Texas*, 381 U.S. 532 (1965).
123. *Sheppard* v. *Maxwell*, 384 U.S. 333 (1966).
124. *Duncan* v. *Louisiana*, 391 U.S. 145 (1968).
125. *Dyke* v. *Taylor Implement Manufacturing Co.*, 391 U.S. 216 (1968).
126. *Bloom* v. *Illinois*, 391 U.S. 194 (1968); *Frank* v. *United States*, 395 U.S. 147 (1969).
127. *Boykin* v. *Alabama*, 395 U.S. 238 (1969).
128. *Singer* v. *United States*, 380 U.S. 24 (1965).
129. *United States* v. *Jackson*, 390 U.S. 570 (1968).
130. *Fay* v. *New York*, 332 U.S. 261 (1947).
131. *Witherspoon* v. *Illinois*, 391 U.S. 510 (1968); *Boulden* v. *Holman*, 394 U.S. 478 (1969); *Pope* v. *United States*, 392 U.S. 651 (1968); and *Parker* v. *Gladden*, 385 U.S. 363 (1966).
132. *Pointer* v. *Texas*, 380 U.S. 400 (1965).
133. *Turner* v. *Louisiana*, 379 U.S. 467 (1965).
134. *Bruton* v. *United States*, 391 U.S. 123 (1968).
135. *In re Gault et al.*, 387 U.S. 1 (1967); *In re Ruffalo*, 390 U.S. 545 (1968); *Jenkins* v. *McKeithen*, 395 U.S. 411 (1969).
136. *Rosen* v. *United States*, 245 U.S. 467 (1918).
137. *Washington* v. *Texas*, 388 U.S. 14 (1967).
138. *Barber* v. *Page*, 390 U.S. 720 (1968).
139. *Johnson* v. *Zerbst*, 304 U.S. 458 (1938); *Escobedo* v. *Illinois*, 378 U.S. 478 (1964); *Swenson* v. *Bolster*, 386 U.S. 258 (1967); *United States* v. *Wade*, 388 U.S. 219 (1968); *Miranda* v. *Arizona*, 384 U.S. 436 (1966); *Mempa* v. *Ray*, 389 U.S. 128 (1967).
140. *Gideon* v. *Wainwright*, 372 U.S. 335 (1963).

141.   *Stack* v. *Boyle,* 342 U.S. 1 (1951).
142.   *Louisiana ex rel. Francis* v. *Resweber,* 329 U.S. 459 (1947).
143.   *Robinson* v. *California,* 370 U.S. 660 (1962).
144.   *Powell* v. *Texas,* 392 U.S. 514 (1968).
145.   *United Public Workers* v. *Mitchell,* 330 U.S. 75 (1947).
146.   *Griswold* v. *Connecticut,* 381 U.S. 479 (1965).
147.   Paul C. Bartholomew, "The Gitlow Doctrine Down to Date," II, *American Bar Association Journal,* August 1968, p. 787.
148.   *United States* v. *Butler,* 297 U.S. 1 (1936).

Amendments 11–25

149.   *Chisholm* v. *Georgia,* 2 Dallas 419 (1793).
150.   *Hans* v. *Louisiana,* 134 U.S. 1 (1890).
151.   *Parden* v. *Terminal Ry. Co.,* 377 U.S. 184 (1964).
152.   The Slaughter House Cases, 16 Wallace 36 (1873).
153.   *Pollock* v. *Williams,* 322 U.S. 4 (1944).
154.   The Civil Rights Cases, 109 U.S. 3 (1883).
155.   *Jones* v. *Mayer,* 392 U.S. 409 (1968).
156.   *Dred Scott* v. *Sandford,* 19 Howard 393 (1857).
157.   *Trop* v. *Dulles,* 356 U.S. 86 (1958).
158.   *Kennedy* v. *Mendoza-Martinez,* 372 U.S. 144 (1963).
159.   *Schneider* v. *Rusk,* 377 U.S. 163 (1964).
160.   *Afroyim* v. *Rush,* 387 U.S. 253 (1967).
161.   *Perez* v. *Brownell,* 356 U.S. 44 (1958).
162.   *Afroyim* v. *Rush,* 387 U.S. 253 (1967).
163.   The Slaughter House Cases, 16 Wallace 36 (1873).
164.   *Twining* v. *New Jersey,* 211 U.S. 78 (1908).
165.   *Goesaert* v. *Cleary,* 335 U.S. 464 (1948).
166.   *Shapiro* v. *Thompson,* 394 U.S. 618 (1969).
167.   *Carrington* v. *Rash,* 380 U.S. 89 (1965).
168.   *Cipriano* v. *Houma,* 395 U.S. 701 (1969).
169.   *Kramer* v. *Union Free School District,* 395 U.S. 621 (1969).
170.   *Moore* v. *Ogilvie,* 394 U.S. 814 (1969).
171.   *Williams* v. *Rhodes,* 393 U.S. 23 (1968).
172.   *McLaughlin* v. *Florida,* 379 U.S. 184 (1964).
173.   *Loving* v. *Virginia,* 388 U.S. 1 (1967).
174.   *Korematsu* v. *United States,* 323 U.S. 214 (1944).
175.   *Ex parte Endo,* 323 U.S. 283 (1944).
176.   *Plessy* v. *Ferguson,* 163 U.S. 537 (1896).
177.   *Brown* v. *Board of Education,* 347 U.S. 483 (1954).
178.   *Brown* v. *Board of Education,* 349 U.S. 294 (1955).
179.   *Mayor* v. *Dawson,* 350 U.S. 877 (1950), and *Gayle* v. *Browder,* 352 U.S. 903 (1956).
180.   *Cooper* v. *Aaron,* 358 U.S. 78 (1958).
181.   *Watson* v. *Memphis,* 373 U.S. 78 (1958).

182. *Bradley* v. *School Board,* 382 U.S. 103 (1965), and *Rogers* v. *Paul,* 382 U.S. 198 (1965).
183. *Green* v. *County School Board of New Kent County,* 391 U.S. 430 (1968).
184. *United States* v. *Montgomery County Board of Education,* 395 U.S. 225 (1969).
185. *Whitus* v. *Georgia,* 385 U.S. 545 (1967); *Coleman* v. *Alabama,* 389 U.S. 23 (1967); *Jones* v. *Georgia,* 389 U.S. 241 (1967); *Hernandez* v. *Texas,* 347 U.S. 475 (1954).
186. *Swain* v. *Alabama,* 380 U.S. 202 (1965).
187. *Hoyt* v. *Florida,* 368 U.S. 57 (1961).
188. *Griffin* v. *Illinois,* 351 U.S. 12 (1956), and *Douglas* v. *California,* 372 U.S. 353 (1963).
189. *Gray* v. *Sanders,* 372 U.S. 368 (1963).
190. *Moore* v. *Ogilvie,* 394 U.S. 814 (1969).
191. *Harper* v. *Board of Elections,* 383 U.S. 663 (1966).
192. *Carrington* v. *Rash,* 380 U.S. 89 (1965).
193. *McDonald* v. *Board of Election Commissioners of Chicago,* 394 U.S. 802 (1969).
194. *Shelly* v. *Kraemer,* 334 U.S. 1 (1948), and *Barrows* v. *Jackson,* 346 U.S. 249 (1953).
195. *Peterson* v. *Greenville* and companion cases, 373 U.S. 244 (1963).
196. *Reitman* v. *Mulkey, et al.,* 387 U.S. 369 (1967).
197. *Hunter* v. *Erickson,* 393 U.S. 385 (1968).
198. *Bolling* v. *Sharpe,* 347 U.S. 497 (1953), and *McGhee* v. *Sipes,* 334 U.S. 1 (1948).
199. *Washington* v. *Legrant,* 394 U.S. 618 (1969).
200. The Civil Rights Cases, 109 U.S. 3 (1883).
201. *United States* v. *Guest,* 383 U.S. 745 (1966).
202. 18 U.S.C. 242.
203. *Williams* v. *United States,* 341 U.S. 97 (1951), and *Monroe* v. *Pape,* 365 U.S. 167 (1961).
204. *Katzenbach* v. *Morgan,* 384 U.S. 641 (1966).
205. *United States* v. *Guest,* 383 U.S. 745 (1966); *Jones* v. *Mayer,* 392 U.S. 409 (1969); *United States* v. *Johnson,* 390 U.S. 563 (1968).
206. *Lane* v. *Wilson,* 307 U.S. 268 (1939).
207. *Smith* v. *Allwright,* 321 U.S. 649 (1944); and *Terry* v. *Adams,* 345 U.S. 461 (1953).
208. *United States* v. *Mississippi,* 380 U.S. 128 (1965); *Louisiana* v. *United States,* 380 U.S. 145 (1965).
209. *South Carolina* v. *Katzenbach,* 383 U.S. 301 (1966).
210. *Gaston County, North Carolina* v. *United States,* 395 U.S. 285 (1969).
211. *Pollock* v. *Farmers' Loan & Trust Co.,* 158 U.S. 601 (1895).
212. 3 U.S.C. 19.
213. *Dept. of Revenue* v. *James Beam Co.,* 377 U.S. 341 (1964).
214. *Harper* v. *Board of Elections,* 383 U.S. 663 (1966).
215. *Harman* v. *Forssenius,* 380 U.S. 529 (1965).

Index